"MAY CONTAIN GRAPHIC MATERIAL"

COMIC BOOKS, GRAPHIC NOVELS, AND FILM

M. Keith Booker

PRAEGER

Westport, Connecticut
London

Library of Congress Cataloging-in-Publication Data

Booker, M. Keith.
    May contain graphic material : comic books, graphic novels, and film / M. Keith Booker.
       p.   cm.
    Includes bibliographical references and index.
    ISBN 978-0-275-99386-3 (alk. paper)
    1. Comic strip characters in motion pictures.   I. Title.
  PN1995.9.C36B66   2007
  791.43′6—dc22   2007026121

British Library Cataloguing in Publication Data is available.

Library of Congress Catalog Card Number: 2007026121
ISBN-13: 978-0-275-99386-3

First published in 2007

Praeger Publishers, 88 Post Road West, Westport, CT 06881
An imprint of Greenwood Publishing Group, Inc.
www.praeger.com

Printed in the United States of America

For Skylor Booker and Benjamin Booker

Contents

A photo essay follows page 86

Introduction: From Panel to Frame

As Scott McCloud points out in *Understanding Comics* (Harper Paperbacks, 1994), the art form (sometimes known as "sequential art") that has given us comic strips, comic books, and (more recently) graphic novels is an ancient and venerable one that ultimately goes back to prehistoric cave paintings. Yet the comics, which construct narratives through a sequence of still images (panels) illuminated by dialogue and textual narration, obviously have a great deal in common with the very modern art of film. Indeed, the relationship between comics and film is so direct that Will Eisner, a leading theorist and practitioner of sequential art, declares in his book *Comics and Sequential Art* that film "is an extension of comics" (Poorhouse Press, 2006, p. 40). Given this relationship, it should come as no surprise that the film industry—always in search of stories to tell on screen—has frequently drawn upon the world of comics as a source of cinematic material. Indeed, what is at first most surprising is that film has failed to draw more extensively upon comics than it has. A quick look, however, provides an easy explanation for this phenomenon: until very recently, the technology available to filmmakers simply did not allow them the range and scope that have always been available to comic artists, whose creativity was limited only by their own imaginations. After all, it costs very little to draw an action scene (relying on readers to fill in much of the detail) that might cost millions of dollars to produce for the screen—if it can be produced at all.

With the recent advent of computer-generated imagery (CGI), more and more of the kinds of action that were once the purview of the comics are becoming available to filmmakers. This is especially the case in recent years, as continuing innovations in computer technology, digital photography, and digital editing have significantly increased the quality (and decreased the cost) of CGI. As a result, the early years of the twenty-first century have seen a veritable explosion in the production of movies based on comics, movies that are perfect for the heavy use of CGI, both because they often involve spectacular action and because it is often not necessary (or even desirable) for that action to look entirely realistic. This phenomenon has received a further boost from the growing popularity of graphic novels—essentially book-length comic books, but often with more sophisticated and adult-oriented material than that in the kinds of comics that many of us remember from our childhood reading. Thus, just as film-making technology has made it more and more feasible to bring the worlds of the comics to movie theaters, the comics themselves have begun to provide a broader and richer array of material (often not requiring extensive use of CGI) from which films might be made.

In addition, the relationship between comics and cinema has evolved to include numerous elements that go well beyond the simple adaptation of comic books or graphic novels to film. For example, many successful films not based on comics (but including some of the same material and spirit as comic books) have inspired spinoff comic books, especially in the realm of science fiction. *Star Wars* and its sequels have inspired many such comics, as have numerous other science fiction films, including the *Matrix* trilogy, which itself already has a kind of comic book feel. In addition, the world of comics has often been depicted on film, as when *Chasing Amy* (1997), directed by Kevin Smith, himself an author and fan of comic books, centers on the romantic travails of a cult comic-book artist, giving viewers an extensive view of comic-book culture. Meanwhile, Ralph Bakshi's *Cool World* (1992) centers on a cartoonist whose characters get out of control, leading to a series of crossovers between the real world and the "cool world" of the comics.

Cool World was based on an original script, but a similar crossing of boundaries between fiction and reality occurs in Henry Selick's *Monkeybone* (2001), which is based on the obscure 1997 graphic novel *Dark Town*, written by Kaja Blackley and apparently conceived specifically for adaptation to film. Here, however, the crossing of the boundary between different levels of reality has a straightforward explanation: cartoonist Stu Miley is plunged into a nightmare realm emanating from his own unconscious mind after an auto accident leaves him in a coma. Miley's experiences in this underworld make for some lively graphics, though the film ultimately descends into a rather predictable resolution as the cartoon world spills back into reality and Miley is forced to defeat his own cartoon creation (the mischievous Monkeybone) for possession of his own body and for the hand of the beautiful Dr. Julie McElroy (Bridget Fonda), Miley's would-be fiancée.

Such films were in part enabled by the growing crossover between the world of comics and the world of film that was kicking into high gear by the 1990s and that also included a heavy intermixture of video games, which also became a source for Hollywood, even as it became standard practice for virtually any successful action-oriented film to be turned into a video game, and possibly a comic as well. Indeed, with the growth of CGI in film and the increase in the quality of video game graphics, films and video games came to look more and more alike, while both were also influenced by the comics, which they influenced in turn.

This is not to say, of course, that comics had not had an impact on the film industry before the initial rise of CGI in the 1970s and 1980s, though comic-to-film adaptations (what one might call graphic cinema) had largely been relegated to the ghetto of low-budget productions intended primarily for children. For many younger filmgoers, for example, some of the most memorable movie-watching experiences of the 1930s involved the sequence of low-budget serials based on the Flash Gordon and Buck Rogers syndicated comic strips (with Buster Crabbe in the title role in both sequences). Produced in episodes of fifteen to twenty minutes in length, each serial ran for twelve to fifteen episodes that were shown weekly in theaters as a supplement to the main features in an attempt to attract young audiences. By today's standards (or even by the standards of the 1930s), the special effects of these serials were extremely crude. However, to a generation of young Americans, they offered thrilling images of other planets and other times that presented an exciting alternative to a dreary Depression-era world that was drifting toward global war.

An even more direct forerunner of modern graphic cinema involved a fifteen-part serial that ran in 1943 based on the character of the Phantom, who had begun to appear in a King Features syndicated comic strip in 1936, thus predating the debut of Superman by two years. The Phantom never quite attained the cultural prominence of Superman and Batman, but he was an important figure in the crucial superhero subgenre and has continued to appear in various formats ever since his original introduction, including the production of a major movie adaptation in 1996. Superman himself appeared in animated serials made for theaters as early as 1942 and was featured in a self-titled live-action serial in 1948, starring Kirk Alyn as the Man of Steel. Alyn returned for a second serial, *Atom Man vs. Superman*, in 1950, though he would be replaced by George Reeves in the 1951 feature *Superman and the Mole-Men*—a theatrical release of the pilot episode of the upcoming television series, *Adventures of Superman.*

Superman and the Mole-Men can thus claim to be the first theatrical film based on material from the comics, even if it was a spillover from a TV series. That series was a major success in the 1950s, especially with younger viewers, though graphic cinema made few additional inroads into theaters between that film and **Superman: The Movie**[1] in 1978. One of the rare examples of graphic cinema during this period was *Batman* (1966), also an offshoot of a television series, in this case the ultra-campy 1960s *Batman* series that featured Adam West as Batman.

Exceptions such as the low-budget Superman and Batman movies of the 1950s and 1960s only served to demonstrate the seeming lack of potential of comics as a major source of movie material. However, the advent of CGI, which was first used in the 1970s in films such as *Westworld* (1973) and *Futureworld* (1976), would eventually change everything in the world of graphic cinema. The megahit *Star Wars* (1977) was a particular milestone that further established the technical possibilities of CGI and other forms of high-tech image making, while demonstrating the box-office potential of big-budget special-effects films. The success of *Star Wars* paved the way for the making of *Superman: The Movie* as the first major Hollywood film to be based on material from the comics. While it made relatively little use of CGI, *Superman* did employ very sophisticated (and very expensive) state-of-the-art techniques, made possible largely because the huge financial success of films such as *Star Wars* suggested that the investment might be worthwhile. It was. *Superman* was a big hit, paving the way for a string of sequels. However, the Superman franchise was still regarded in Hollywood as a one-of-a-kind special case, so that Superman films remained the only major example of graphic cinema for a decade after the release of *Superman: The Movie.*

There were, of course, some examples of comic-to-film adaptations during the 1980s, but they were typically eccentric efforts that made no attempt to compete with the Superman films in the big-box-office arena. However, one such film, *Sheena* (1984) did to some extent compete with the Superman spinoff, *Supergirl*, released in the same year. Both films featured female protagonists and thus extended the coverage of superhero graphic cinema in terms of gender. However, neither film is really feminist in its orientation. In fact, *Sheena*, with television sex symbol and *Playboy* cover girl Tanya Roberts (best known for her appearances in television's *Charlie's Angels*, beginning in 1980) in the title role, comes very close to being downright sexist. *Sheena* had a strong background in the comics,

---

[1] Titles in boldface are discussed in detail in the later chapters of this volume.

where its heroine, a sort of female Tarzan, first appeared in 1937, the creation of comics' legend Will Eisner and his then-partner Jerry Iger. She appeared in several venues, including her own comic series—*Sheena, Queen of the Jungle*—which was published from 1942 to 1952 and which debuted three months before the self-titled *Wonder Woman* comic, making *Sheena* the first female protagonist with her own comic title. In the 1984 film version, Roberts prances about the screen in a scanty costume (or, at several points, no costume at all), and the feeble plot of the film seems to have been designed largely to provide an opportunity for Roberts to display her considerable physical charms. The film includes certain other visual treats as well; shot on location in Kenya (which stands in for the fictional kingdom of "Tigora"), it includes some excellent photography of African wildlife and the African landscape. Otherwise the film is just plain dumb, partly because Sheena seems a little dumb herself; attempts in the film to convey her total innocence (especially sexual) tend to make her appear a bit feeble-minded. It doesn't help that the film follows the comics in identifying Sheena as the "Queen of the Jungle," an appellation that made more sense in the comics, which were typically set in the Congo, but that is weird in the film, given that there are no jungles in Kenya and thus appear to be none in Tigora. The film was a box-office flop and drew little but disdain from critics, two facts that were also true of *Supergirl*. *Sheena* did inspire Marvel Comics to publish a spinoff comic as the *Marvel Comics Super Special #34* in June 1984, while the character of Sheena remained a factor in American popular culture into the twenty-first century, including the production of a self-titled syndicated television series (starring *Baywatch* babe Gena Lee Nolin) in 2000–2002. In all versions, Sheena remained more eye-candy than genuine hero, and it would be the late 1990s before genuinely tough, strong heroines would be common in American film, with Sigourney Weaver's Ripley of the *Alien* films (which themselves inspired a number of spinoff comics published by Dark Horse Comics) providing a notable exception.

As a film, *Sheena* was pretty much a disaster, perhaps showing what a hit-or-miss affair graphic cinema can be. Perhaps an even better illustration of this fact is Robert Altman's *Popeye* (1980), which was made by one of Hollywood's most respected directors, but which is also widely regarded as a cinematic disaster. That film brought to life one of the most beloved characters in American cartoon history, and one with a longer history than even Superman or the Phantom. The one-eyed, big-armed, spinach-eating, pipe-smoking sailor first appeared in a comic strip by E. C. Segar in 1929, then later became even more famous as the star of a long series of animated cartoons, beginning in 1933. Popeye in the 1930s emerged, along with Superman, as an animated American icon. A simple man with

staunch moral values, he is tough, loyal, determined, and always on the
side of right. He resorts to violence only when necessary, but never backs
down when threatened by the forces of evil. By 1980, Popeye also had
considerable nostalgic value, the character having become a staple of
television cartoons in the 1960s. He would seem, then, an ideal movie
hero. Unfortunately, he is more literally cartoonish than most animated
superheroes (and he is only truly super immediately after eating spinach),
which made his transfer to a live-action movie decidedly difficult. Indeed,
Popeye is generally regarded as one of the most spectacular failures in
director Altman's illustrious career. The film is a plodding one with only a
rudimentary plot, which is more interrupted than punctuated by a series
of musical numbers. The film is, however, visually interesting. For one
thing, the seaside town of Sweethaven, where all of the action takes place,
looks very much like an elaborate Disneyworld set, which may not be
surprising given that the film was coproduced by Paramount and Disney.
This set design presumably gives the film something of the flavor of a
cartoon, though it also marks the film as a postmodern artifact set in a
totally simulated environment. Robin Williams does a reasonable job as
Popeye, though his performance is a bit flat, and Shelley Duval, as Olive
Oyl, is actually funnier. All in all, the performances and the visuals are not
enough to compensate for the simplistic plot, which might have worked
in the animated shorts made for television in the 1960s, but is not really
enough to sustain a full-length theatrical film.

Popeye was followed in 1982 by another adaptation from the comics
that featured a big-name director and an A-list cast. John Huston's
Annie, like *Popeye*, is a musical, though it is a more successful one, perhaps because it was based more directly upon a successful Broadway
musical than upon the *Little Orphan Annie* comic strip that was the ultimate source of the material. Nevertheless, *Annie* is a rather lackluster
film that never quite gets off the ground. Like *Popeye*, *Annie* depends a
great deal on nostalgia appeal as it looks back to the 1930s, when the
strip was in its heyday. The film, following the stage musical, captures
many of the highlights of the comic strip, including the adoption of Annie (Aileen Quinn) by the incredibly rich and powerful capitalist Oliver
"Daddy" Warbucks (Albert Finney). The staunch Republican and free
marketer Warbucks is an arch-enemy of FDR (Edward Herrmann) and
the New Deal, as he is in the comics, but in the film the rivalry is more
friendly. Despite his gruff exterior, Warbucks is a kind soul whose positive depiction ultimately serves (in both the film and the comic strip) as
an endorsement of the ethos of American business. In the film, Warbucks
and his lieutenants save Annie from dastardly villains (as they often did in
the comics), but she never really seems in danger and all of her troubles

seem perfunctory, as if everyone in the film is just going through the motions.

Another eccentric effort of the 1980s was Wes Craven's *Swamp Thing* (1982), based on the DC comics series created by Len Wein and Bernie Wrightson. The character of Swamp Thing first appeared in 1971 and became an important and popular variation on the comic superhero, running in various sequences and produced by a series of different artists and writers, including such well-known figures as Alan Moore and Brian K. Vaughan. Basically, Swamp Thing is a superpowered humanoid mass of vegetable matter, created when scientist Alec Holland (played in the film by Ray Wise) is transmogrified in a laboratory accident. In the comic books, he battles against various forms of evil (including threats to the environment in general and to his swamp in particular). The film emphasizes his origins, his battles with the evil Dr. Anton Arcane (Louis Jourdan), and his evolving relationship with beautiful scientist Alice Cable (Adrienne Barbeau). It clearly draws upon a number of film precedents as well as the comic books, and Swamp Thing himself is particularly reminiscent of the monster in the early *Frankenstein* films. *Swamp Thing* is a competent, only slightly campy effort that has moments of genuine pathos and zany poetry. It eventually led to a sequel, *The Return of the Swamp Thing* (1989), followed by both a live-action and an animated television series in the early 1990s.

In the meantime, while there were few truly important examples of graphic cinema in the 1980s, there were important developments in CGI that would prove crucial to the ultimate ability of filmmakers to bring comics to life. Films such as *Tron* (1982) and *The Last Starfighter* (1984)—both drawing upon video-game culture, rather than comics—made important steps toward the increased use of CGI in films, while James Cameron's *The Abyss* (1989), which won the Academy Award for Special Effects, topped off the decade with some of the most convincing computer-generated images to date. Among other things, *The Abyss* was a major step forward in the generation of realistic-looking images by computer, leading ultimately to the dazzling computer-generated dinosaurs of Steven Spielberg's *Jurassic Park* (1993), a film that continued the domination of the CGI world by science fiction films, but one that also suggested new technological possibilities that would be crucial to the subsequent development of graphic cinema.

The comics themselves took a dark turn on both sides of the Atlantic in the 1980s, probably as a reaction to the cynicism spurred by the rhetoric of the Reagan and Thatcher administrations, both of which portrayed the world as a dangerous place in which good people sometimes had to do bad and violent things to survive. Tim Burton's ***Batman*** (1989) and

Batman Returns (1992) brought the *other* major comic-book superhero into the realm of major motion pictures, while also reflecting this new turn in the comics. Burton's distinctive vision of a dark, menacing Gotham City stunned audiences around the globe, showing filmgoers a harder-edged Batman filtered not just through the mainstream tradition of Batman comics, but also through the more cynical noir-inflected recent works of major comic artists such as Moore and Frank Miller. The success of *Batman* broke the Superman monopoly on big-time graphic cinema and may have seemed to open the way for a new generation of comics-inspired films. In some ways, however, Burton's vision of Batman and Gotham City was almost *too* distinctive. For one thing, it was a hard act to follow without seeming derivative. For another, it may have been too specifically cinematic, making *Batman* more a thing unto itself than a representative example of graphic cinema.

Live-action films such as *Teenage Mutant Ninja Turtles* (1990)—followed by sequels in 1991 and 1993—took graphic cinema in a very different direction that worried more about kid appeal than about convincing stories or effects. These stories feature four anthropomorphic mutant turtles who have been transformed by an encounter with radioactive waste in the New York City sewer system, giving them human intelligence and near-human size and shape. In the sewer, they meet a similarly transformed rat who happens to be an expert in the martial arts and who subsequently trains them so that they can use their ninja-like skills to battle against the forces of evil. This scenario seems pretty clearly earmarked for children. On the other hand, the films are based on the Image Comics characters created by Kevin Eastman and Peter Laird, which draw much of their energies from their fairly sophisticated parodic engagement with such sources in the comics as Marvel's *The New Mutants* (an offshoot of the *X-Men* comics, featuring teenage mutants) and Miller's version of *Daredevil*, which made heavy use of ninja-related materials. The first *Teenage Mutant Ninja Turtles* film was a hit, though the subsequent sequels declined in both quality and popularity. The franchise remained alive, however, and the Mutant Turtles returned to television in 2003. The success of that series led to the production of a computer-generated film, *TMNT*, in 2007. The use of total CGI for this film allowed the production of more spectacular action and fight sequences; it also facilitated the introduction of fantasy and science fiction motifs that go well beyond those of the original series of films.

Much of the success of the Teenage Mutant Ninja Turtles franchise has had to do with its extensive (and highly profitable) merchandising campaigns. Indeed, graphic cinema aimed at children (like children's films as a whole) has often functioned as part of multimedia marketing strategies so extensively that it is difficult to identify them as examples of graphic cinema in the strictest sense. For example, in addition to numerous toys, video games, and other items, the Mutant Turtles comics also spawned an animated television series that ran from 1987 to 1996 and that was as much a source for the film as the comics themselves. Merchandising was even more central to a film such as *Masters of the Universe* (1987), which is actually based on a series of toys produced by the Mattel company, rather than a comic, though the toys themselves were typically marketed with accompanying comic books.

If some of the parody and humor in children's films such as the *Teenage Mutant Ninja Turtles* sequence seemed to be aimed more at adult audiences, it is also the case that the early 1990s also saw several tongue-in-cheek graphic films for adults, including such efforts as *Flash Gordon* (1980), in which bad acting, a ridiculous plot, and comically cheap effects only added to the campy, nostalgic appeal. Warren Beatty's *Dick Tracy* (1990) also went for camp, though it was a much-hyped, big-budget effort with a spectacular cast of A-list actors. It also depended in a particularly overt way on audience nostalgia not only for the comic strip on which the film is based, but also for the ostensibly simpler times in which the film is set. In the film, the virtuous, courageous, and brilliant police detective Tracy (played by Beatty) encounters a rogue's gallery of villains, led by mob kingpin Big Boy Caprice (played with campy excess by Al Pacino). Tracy also wins the love of Tess Trueheart (Glenne Headly) while evading the attempted seductions of the sultry temptress Breathless Mahoney (Madonna). The banality of the film's plot is more than made up for by the its fond echoes of the visual style of the original classic comic strip, which was drawn by creator Chester Gould from 1931 to 1977. These echoes include the overall color scheme and the look of the city, but are particularly obvious in the appearances of the various villains, who are made up to resemble their warped visages in the comic strip. They thus stand in contrast to the classically handsome Tracy, making their appearances suggestive of their relative moral depravity. The film's references to the style of the comic strip make it in some ways a forerunner of a later film such as Robert Rodriquez and Miller's much darker and grittier **Sin City** (2005), though *Sin City* (partly thanks to improvements in available technology) is able to reproduce the style of its graphic-novel source much more extensively.

The Rocketeer (1991) also looks back to simpler times of moral absolutes, in this case casting its pure and virtuous hero in opposition to thoroughly evil Nazis—a group often featured as villains in the comics. *The Rocketeer* is based upon the similarly titled comic-book series by Dave Stevens; it is set in 1938 and revolves around attempts of Nazi agents to steal a rocket pack invented by Howard Hughes (Terry O'Quinn). The

Nazis hope to use rocket packs as a key tool in their plans for world domination, but their own attempts to develop such packs have failed, leading them to attempt to pilfer the American model. In the course of the complex and convoluted plot, the rocket pack falls into the hands of stunt pilot Cliff Secord (Bill Campbell), who—with the help of inventor "Peevy" Peabody (Alan Arkin)—becomes the Rocketeer of the title. Secord also manages to save the rocket pack from the Nazis and to rescue his true love, aspiring actress Jenny Blake (Jennifer Connelly), from the clutches of the dastardly Neville Sinclair (Timothy Dalton), a dashing Hollywood film star working undercover as a Nazi agent. *The Rocketeer* evokes the atmosphere of late-1930s Hollywood fairly successfully, recalling the pulp adventures of that decade, though at least one major link to the pulps of the 1930s that was present in the original comic books (which were published sporadically from 1982 to 1989, with a final issue appearing in 1995) is missing in the film. In the comic books, the rocket pack was invented by 1930s pulp hero Doc Savage, but copyright problems caused the filmmakers to drop that motif in favor of the Hughes character, possibly more recognizable to audiences in the 1990s in any case.

Richie Rich (1994) also counted on nostalgia to attract audiences. This film adaptation is based on a title character who had been featured in a number of comic-book series published by Harvey Entertainment from 1953 through the 1980s. Richie Rich, the "poor little rich boy," is the only child of the world's richest couple, and his lavish lifestyle clearly had a certain fantasy value for young audiences who could read the comics and dream of being similarly wealthy. Indeed, the various Richie Rich comics consistently served as a ringing endorsement of wealth (and of capitalism in general), presenting the Riches as benevolent rich folks who treat their employees well and have good values, treasuring family and friends more than their ostentatious wealth. The film version of *Richie Rich* has its moments, but all in all the film lacks energy and never really captures the spirit of the comics—partly because star Macaulay Culkin, at age fourteen, was beginning to lose his childish charm (and in any case seems significantly older in the film than the Richie Rich of the comics).

Richie Rich was followed by a sort of companion film in 1995 with the release of *Casper,* based on another Harvey Entertainment comic-book property, though the well-known figure of Casper the Friendly Ghost actually got his original start in cartoon shorts made for theatrical release by Paramount in the 1940s. Casper had also made numerous appearances in various animated television series over the years. Here, he becomes the first feature-film title character to be completely computer-generated (along with the film's other ghosts), but this otherwise live-action film adaptation never really captures the charm of the lovable and friendly (but often misunderstood) ghost-child who had charmed generations.

One of the most successful nostalgia-oriented graphic films of the 1990s was *The Phantom* (1996), in which Billy Zane effectively portrays the classic superhero. Set in 1938 (and thus during the early years of the comic strip on which the film is based), the film very effectively evokes the look of that time, while employing some gorgeous natural settings as well, causing renowned film critic Roger Ebert to gush that it was "one of the best-looking movies in any genre I have ever seen." The film is also great fun, accepting the pulpy premise of the comic strip with great gusto and presenting its story as the all-in-fun adventure it is supposed to be. In many ways, *The Phantom* is reminiscent of the Indiana Jones films, which were not based on comics but which had overtly sought to capture the feel of comic strips and movie serials from the 1930s. Indeed, *The Phantom* was written by Jeffrey Boam, who had also scripted the third Indiana Jones film, *Indiana Jones and the Last Crusade* (1989). *The Phantom*'s innocence and lack of pretense help to give it a 1930s feel as well, while going a long way toward making it possible for audiences to accept the plot, in which the hero (clad in purple tights, no less) emerges from his secret jungle stronghold to thwart the efforts of a criminal kingpin and a mysterious secret international brotherhood to get their hands on an apocalyptic superweapon. Zane does it all with great aplomb and with a twinkle in his eye, while at the same time staying true to the character and avoiding camp or self-parody.

The Phantom has a great deal in common with Batman in that he lacks superhuman abilities. Instead, he depends on guile, intimidation, athleticism, and marksmanship in his battles against evil, though he also gets considerable help from his trusty sidekicks, a wolf named Devil and a horse named Hero. In the course of his appearances in comic strips (and, later, in comic books) the Phantom is given a complex backstory and multigenerational history, which is also effectively evoked in the film. It turns out, for example, that the Phantom of the film is the twenty-first in a line of Phantoms who have secretly passed the role from father to son for hundreds of years, creating among the Phantom's enemies the perception that he is immortal. In addition, the Phantom is a figure of unquestioned virtue who lacks Batman's dark side and moral ambiguity. Such darker heroes had become increasingly prominent in the comics world in the 1980s (when Batman himself had become considerably darker), given the Phantom's virtue an additional nostalgic turn.

On the other hand, a whole family of works of graphic cinema, building on the success of the early Batman films, specifically focused on the dark side, creating a tradition of antiheroes in graphic cinema. Based on James

O'Barr's underground comic, Alex Proyas's **The Crow** (1994) is a stylistic tour de force in its depiction of a dark urban environment, which provides the perfect setting for its brooding, undead hero, creating what would ultimately become a cult favorite of youthful audiences, though the film's cult status was also enhanced by the publicity (and unanswered questions) surrounding the shooting death of star Brandon Lee during the filming of a scene.

1994 also saw the release of *The Shadow*, a relatively big-budget film adaptation featuring a character probably best known from the radio serials of the 1930s and 1940s (in which he was played by a variety of actors, including a two-year turn by a young Orson Welles from 1936 to 1938). Actually, though, the character originated in a pulp anthology, while he would also eventually star in his own pulp magazine, as well as a number of pulp novels, most of them written by Walter B. Gibson (under the pen name Maxwell Grant), who was also the principal author of the magazine stories. The Shadow would also go on to appear in both a comic strip and a number of comic books from the 1940s to the 1990s. He is in some ways the ultimate antihero, using the darkness that resides in his own heart to help him understand (and thus defeat) the various villains with whom he comes into conflict. Thus, the opening of the radio serials, which has become one of the best know lines from the days of radio culture: "Who knows what evil lurks in the heart of men? The Shadow knows."

The 1994 film was envisioned as the inaugural work in a Shadow movie franchise, but its lack of success derailed that plan. Alec Baldwin is okay (if uncharismatic) in the title role, and the main villain, Shiwan Khan (John Lone), the last living descendant of Genghis Khan, is suitably evil and offbeat. Even the near-racist depiction of Khan has a sort of validity, given that conniving Oriental villains were rampant in American popular culture during the vaguely 1940s setting of the film. *The Shadow* also has the appropriate 1940s look (spiced by a nostalgia-laced dose of art deco), though this look, created by director Russell Mulcahy and cinematographer Stephen H. Burum, never seems quite as convincing as it might have been, perhaps because it hovers uneasily between the look of a legitimate film noir and the look of a comic book.

As a hero, the gun-toting Shadow—with his psychic powers that render him essentially invisible to his foes—is a bit dated, and the filmmakers were not successful in updating him for a modern audience. Though a clear forerunner of Batman, the Shadow—especially as played by Baldwin—lacks charm, and it is not really clear why we should really care about his adventures. Indeed, the title character of *The Shadow* is actually less compelling than that of Sam Raimi's *Darkman* (1990), a film that was not based on an actual comic-book character but on invented character intentionally given the feel of a character from the comics. Indeed, this film was made with an invented hero precisely because its makers were unable to secure the rights to make a film about the Shadow.

Oddly enough, *Darkman* successfully captures the look and feel of comic books better than most genuine adaptations. Meanwhile, whereas the Shadow gets his powers from a Tibetan monk, Darkman (played by Liam Neeson) receives his via the more modern expedient of a science experiment gone wrong. In particular, he is a scientist whose lab is blown up by gangsters, but receives subsequent radical treatments that give him increased strength and resistance to pain. Still horribly scarred by the explosion, he develops a synthetic skin that gives him a normal appearance—but only for a limited amount of time, as the skin is unstable. As his "normal" face is essentially a mask, he can use it either to appear like his original self or to mimic the appearances of others. He remains a dark, shadowy figure, unable to live a normal life, and his unstable skin is mirrored by a rather unstable psyche. As such, he is reminiscent of figures such as the Phantom of the Opera and the Hunchback of Notre Dame, in addition to superheroes such as Batman and the Shadow. He is able, because of his newfound abilities, to get revenge against the criminals who disfigured him and to begin a career as a crimefighter—a career that would take him through two undistinguished direct-to-video sequels, *Darkman II: The Return of Durant* (1994) and *Darkman III: Die, Darkman, Die* (1996), both directed by Bradford May and featuring Arnold Vosloo in the title role.

Rachel Talalay's *Tank Girl* (1995) continued the focus on rather marginal comic-book heroes that was typical of graphic cinema, still feeling its way toward prominence, in the mid-1990s. This film has a certain satirical punch in its depiction of a postapocalyptic future world in which scant resources are dominated by a giant corporate entity known as Water and Power. However, this is a film that is really about little else but having fun. It proudly displays its origins in a British cult comic strip, periodically flashing comic book panels onto the screen and even occasionally switching from live-action to animation. The film also exuberantly embraces the anarchic punk spirit of the comic book, which helps what could have been a truly awful film to attain a certain zany energy. The pointless plot is punctuated by a number of highly entertaining moments thanks, partly to the sheer excess of Lori Petty's campy performance as the ass-kicking title character, who leads an underground guerrilla band of half-man, half-kangaroo freedom fighters into battle against Water and Power and their dastardly leader, Kesslee (Malcolm McDowell). *Tank Girl* is also notable for the appearance of a then relatively unknown Naomi Watts as Jet Girl, a mousy mechanic who, influenced by Tank Girl, becomes a formidable freedom fighter in her own right. Both Tank Girl and Jet Girl, in fact, are among the earliest examples of graphic cinema featuring genuinely strong female protagonists who are not present, in the mode of Sheena, primarily as objects for adolescent male ogling.

Barb Wire (1996) would seem to be a throwback in this regard, especially after it opens with an extended scene in which star Pamela Anderson (billed here as Pamela Anderson Lee) performs a pole dance in a tight costume, while water sprays on her in slow motion and her breasts (themselves practically icons of American popular culture) jiggle about, occasionally escaping the confines of the costume. Indeed, this scene alone pretty much undermines the film's presentation of Barb Wire as a deadly fighter against evil, and it is certainly the case that Anderson's almost cartoonishly curvaceous form remains on display throughout the film, though there is little in the way of actual nudity. In the meantime, we again get a look at a postapocalyptic world in which Anderson's Barb is a former freedom fighter who has now retreated to the "free city" of Steel Harbor to become an ostensibly cynical bar owner, looking out for number one. Meanwhile, civil war still rages in the rest of the former United States, eventually intruding into Steel Harbor itself, as Barb's former lover, Axel Hood (Temuera Morrison) shows up with his new wife, Dr. Corrina Devonshire (Victoria Rowell), a former scientist for the repressive, Nazi-like government who now carries a secret crucial to the success of the resistance. If all of this sounds familiar, it's because the plot of *Barb Wire* is based fairly directly (without acknowledgement in the credits) on that of *Casablanca*, with a few genders reversed and details changed. Luckily, however, the makers of *Barb Wire* don't get carried away with this connection (which is essentially tongue-in-cheek) and the film never makes the mistake of taking itself too seriously, even if it does get a bit away from its roots in a Dark Horse comic, looking and feeling more like a straightforward (low budget) science fiction film than a comic-book film. All in all, however, the film seems to have trouble deciding just how serious it wants to be. Apparently, neither critics nor audiences appreciated this indecision, and the film was a box-office flop, widely considered one of the worst films of the year.

Other genuinely eccentric comic book adaptations have been less successful, the most notorious case being the 1986 film based on the offbeat Marvel comic book series *Howard the Duck*. This film has a reputation as a colossal box-office failure, though it actually made a small profit when international receipts are included. Some critics also considered it one of the worst films ever made, though it has gradually gained a sort of cult following over the years, which is probably the only sort of following that would be appropriate for this particular premise. *Howard the Duck* belongs to no particular genre, but is a parody of several, especially super-hero comics and science fiction. It features a humanoid duck who has been inexplicably transported to earth from his own duck-planet, an experience that leaves him in a perpetual bad mood, though he does (in the film) help to save the earth from an invasion by malevolent aliens.

Howard the Duck is also one of the relatively few graphic films that have been primarily comedic, rather than action-oriented, though this may be one of the reasons for its own lack of success. *The Mask* (1994), loosely based on a character and concept that first appeared in several different venues in Dark Horse Comics, is one of the few exceptions to this trend. In both the comics and the film, a wooden mask turns out to have the power to transform its wearer into a big-toothed, green-faced superhero with virtually unlimited powers. In the comics, however, wearers of the mask tend to be dark, ultraviolent, and dangerous, while the film goes more for broad comedy, making the wearer of the mask (who is now also called The Mask) a comic figure whose powers largely lie in the fact that, while living in the real world, he has the versatility and resilience of a Looney Tunes cartoon character. The film stars Jim Carrey as the principal wearer of the mask, in one of the two major film roles of 1994 that made him a star (the other was in *Ace Ventura: Pet Detective*). It also features Cameron Diaz, in her first film role, as his love interest. Carrey is well cast in this comic version of the story, and the film is replete with hilarious sight gags, held together by a plot that is actually reasonably interesting. It grossed over $350 million worldwide off of a production budget of about $18 million, making it one of the biggest commercial successes of the 1990s.

The Mask helped to trigger major film careers for its two young stars and also inspired an animated television series and a sequel, *Son of the Mask* (2005). It did not, however, trigger a barrage of comic films based on comic books and graphic novels. It was not, in fact, until 1997 that another major comedy based on the comics came to the big screen. In that year, **Men in Black** was a huge hit, surpassed at the box office only by *Titanic* and *The Lost World: Jurassic Park*. This success once again proved that graphic comedies could potentially attract a large audience, a fact verified in the substantial success achieved by its sequel, **Men in Black II**, in 2002. Nevertheless, these films have remained something of a special case, and other films in this vein have tended to achieve neither critical nor commercial success, partly because, when translated from the comics to the screen, such works tend to come off as merely silly.

A classic example of this phenomenon is *Mystery Men* (1999), a super-hero spoof with a top-notch cast of comic actors in lead roles as members of a ragtag band of superheroes, including Ben Stiller, Greg Kinnear, William H. Macy, Janeane Garofalo, Hank Azaria, and Paul Reubens. The film's central supervillain, Casanova Frankenstein, is played by distinguished actor Geoffrey Rush—sporting a bizarre combination British and German accent two years after winning the Academy Award for best actor for his performance in *Shine*. In addition, one of Frankenstein's top henchmen is played by top British comedian Eddie Izzard, while his lover is played by Lena Olin. Given this cast and a $68 million budget (probably partly enabled by the success of *Men in Black*), this seemed a promising film, and it does include some pretty funny gags—perhaps the funniest of which is the presentation of Kinnear's Captain Amazing as a thoroughly commodified superhero who fights crime primarily so he can attract publicity and thus get numerous endorsement deals. He even wears patches from his sponsors, NASCAR-style, on his superhero costume. Another highlight is the depiction of the mundane day-to-day lives of the heroes, who must deal with such problems as wives and families who don't quite appreciate the superhero lifestyle. Unfortunately, such highlights are fairly few and far between, and some of the chief comic moments involve bits such as Reubens's performance as a lisping hero whose main power is the ability to emit deadly farts on command, which suggests the general level of much of the humor. In addition, the cheesy special effects (which were presumably intentionally bad, given the budget) don't add much to the humor. All in all, both the plot and the characters are uninteresting, and the film never really gets going, lacking most of the zany, surreal energy of the Dark Horse Comics series *Flaming Carrot Comics*, by Bob Burden, on which the film was loosely based. As a result, the film got mostly negative reviews and made back only about half of its production costs in worldwide box office, partly because it made less than $3 million in international receipts. However, as comic book films tend to do, it has gained a certain cult following since its release.

The 2001 film *Josie and the Pussycats*, based on a classic comic book that had also become a popular television cartoon series, is also a typical example of graphic comedy. It lacks the budget and cast of *Mystery Men*, but draws upon a better-known source. It also strives for special appeal to young audiences, while playing up the camp aspects of comic culture. The title characters are a three-girl rock band, so that the film relies heavily on the entire culture of rock music, in addition to the original comic book and cartoon, for its material. In many ways, in fact, the film draws as much on the culture of the cable music channel MTV as it does upon the original comic books. Not only does the film look essentially like a string of music videos, but it overtly acknowledges its source with frequent references to MTV.

Actually, while *Josie and Pussycats* is nominally a satire of the commodification of culture as represented by MTV, the film serves largely as a running commercial for MTV and was in fact heavily promoted on the network when it was showing in theaters. In fact, the satire of the film is really a running joke, and the film itself openly participates in precisely the kinds of commercialism that it purports to critique and that it attributes to the evil Mega Records, a recording company that laces its products with subliminal messages urging young Americans to get to their malls and spend their money on all the latest trends and fads. Yet the film itself flashes messages on the screen to the effect that *"Josie and the Pussycats* is the Best Movie Ever!"* In any case, the real message of *Josie and the Pussycats* is that America's young people are *not* being manipulated into blind consumption because they are far too smart and savvy to be so easily duped. The film thus provides assurances that actually work in the interest of the consumer culture that it purports to critique.

Josie and the Pussycats is a fairly minor film that relies on an odd combination of nostalgia for its comic-book source material and hip awareness of its contemporary pop-cultural setting. By the time it was released, however, graphic cinema was already beginning to make a turn toward bigger budgets and higher exposure, especially as Marvel began gradually to roll out film adaptations of its extensive stable of comic-book superheroes. An important step in this direction was Stephen Norrington's ***Blade*** (1998). With its half-vampire protagonist, this film brought a new edge to the notion of antiheroes in graphic cinema, though the Marvel comics' Blade character on which the film was based had actually been human. The film, however, was successful enough (with Wesley Snipes in the title role) that Blade was made half-vampire in subsequent comics. The film also inspired (to date) two sequels, *Blade II* (2002, directed by Guillermo del Toro) and *Blade: Trinity* (2004, directed by David S. Goyer, who had written the first two Blade films).

The *Blade* sequence indicates the potential of horror films based on comic books or graphic novels, though these films in fact partake of a number of genres, including action, crime, and martial arts. A basic horror film framework, supplemented by substantial contributions from other genres had also been central to *Spawn* (released in 1997, a year before *Blade*). If Blade is a superhero who fights evil despite his own decidedly dark side, *Spawn* takes the notion of the dark superhero to an extreme with its protagonist, who derives supernatural powers (many of them residing in his souped-up costume) from the forces of hell, but then turns them against evil. Michael Jai White plays Al Simmons, a professional assassin who believes he is eliminating bad guys for a U.S. government intelligence agency, only to learn that the agency itself has been hijacked by the villainous Jason Wynn (Martin Sheen) for his own purposes. Simmons is subsequently sent to a fiery death by Wynn, only eventually to be retrieved from hell by a demonic clown (played by John Leguizamo) so that he can eventually take command of Satan's armies in a planned assault on heaven. The clown, one of the personifications of a deadly demon known as the Violator, is a ludicrous figure whose presence can be amusing but who ultimately detracts from the atmosphere of the film, which is not able to rise to the level of intensity of the *Blade* films. The resurrected Simmons, still bearing the scars of his death by fire, finds that he has an array of superpowers, which he gradually discovers and begins to master. He eventually turns his powers against the clown, whom he defeats with the help of his new mentor Cogliostro (Nicol Williamson), who has been battling against the forces of hell for centuries. *Spawn* was directed by Mark A. Z. Dippé, who had essentially no directorial credentials, but who had done special visual effects work on such major films as *Terminator 2* (1991) and *Jurassic Park* (1993). And the special effects are the highlight of the film, which is otherwise a disservice to Todd McFarlane's Image Comics series, on which it is based, especially in Leguizamo's slapstick portrayal of the clown. More consistently in the spirit of the original comics was the animated television series that ran on HBO from 1997 to 1999, though the film at least captures some of the sense in which Spawn is a complex and conflicted antihero, tormented by his fate.

Spawn is not an entirely serious entry into the horror genre, though the very serious **From Hell** (2001), based on a graphic novel by Alan Moore, is a horror film of sorts that demonstrates new possibilities in the genre by combining it with historical fiction and crime fiction. Meanwhile, in addition to horror, other popular genres, such as crime fiction, have been prominent in both the comics and the cinema. Indeed, dark, noirish graphic novels have formed the basis of several recent film adaptations, including **Road to Perdition** (2002), *Sin City*, and *A History of Violence* (2005).

There have also been several film adaptations of science fiction comics, though these have probably been less prominent than the reverse: comics based on science fiction films. Indeed, perhaps the most important impact of science fiction comics on film has been the aesthetic influence of the French science fiction comic magazine *Metal Hurlant* (published in the United States in English as *Heavy Metal*) on the sf classic *Blade Runner* (1982), though there was also a direct (animated) adaptation of *Heavy Metal* to film in 1981. One of the few major examples of comic-to-film science fiction adaptations, John Bruno's *Virus* (1999), is really as much a horror film as a science fiction film, somewhat in the manner of the highly successful sequence of *Alien* films. Based on the Dark Horse comic book series by Chuck Pfarrer (and scripted by Pfarrer with Dennis Feldman), *Virus* in fact has some of the feel of the *Alien* films as a crew of humans is trapped aboard a claustrophobic ship at sea that has been taken over by a murderous alien invader that appears to regard humans as a sort of viral infestation on the ship, thus the title. *Virus* also goes for some especially horrifying scenes in which the alien entity (made of pure energy, or maybe pure information, it is able to inhabit and control various sorts of machinery) builds weird cyborg zombies, combining mechanical parts with the bodies of its human victims. Unfortunately, these concocted creatures look more ridiculous than frightening, and *Virus* is never able to attain the level of foreboding and suspense that had made the *Alien* films so special. In addition, the ending (in which the two surviving humans, played by Jamie Lee Curtis and William Baldwin, are launched from the ship out of a rocket tube, while the ship explodes behind them, killing the alien) is just plain silly. As a result, the film's negative reviews were perfectly understandable, even if the film isn't quite as bad as some reviewers seemed to feel. *Virus* was also a colossal box-office failure, making back less than half of its $75 million budget in worldwide gross receipts, an outcome that might explain Hollywood's lack of enthusiasm for further films based on science fiction comics. On the other hand, **V for Vendetta** (2006), a dark dystopian fantasy based on Moore's graphic novel, was a successful adaptation within a major science fiction subgenre, though its title character is also a superhero of sorts.

Perhaps the most interesting science fiction film so far adapted from comics is Enki Bilal's *Immortal* (2004), adapted from his own "Nikopol Trilogy" of French graphic novels. This film (which is in English) makes the somewhat confusing narrative of the graphic novels even more confusing. Add in the wooden and undeveloped characters, and it thus ultimately fails as a film. It is, however, extremely interesting in a visual sense, making extensive use of green screens to generate a detailed postapocalyptic world of the future that captures much of the visual style of Bilal's comics, while recalling a number of cinematic predecessors, of which *Blade Runner* is probably the most obvious. However, *Immortal* goes beyond the computer-generated backgrounds of the near-contemporaneous sf film *Sky Captain and the World of Tomorrow* and even subsequent CGI-heavy examples of graphic cinema such as *Sin City* (2005) and *300* (2007). In particular, most of the characters in *Immortal* are computer generated as well, an effect that for most critics was largely intrusive and disruptive, though some felt that it enhanced the overall impact of the film.

Other attempts to explore the potential of graphic cinema outside the superhero genre have had similar difficulties in attracting large audiences in the theaters. In the early twenty-first century, the action/superhero genre has been informed by a convergence of comics, film, television, and video games, and this genre certainly remains the most visible and commercially successful form of graphic cinema. Nevertheless, if graphic novels and films based upon them seem particularly well suited for the presentation of stories involving superheroes and other fantastic motifs, it is also the case that both have sometimes been used for the telling of more serious and realistic stories. A classic case is Art Spiegelman's near-legendary two-volume *Maus* sequence, which relates the experiences of his own grandfather as a Polish Jew during the holocaust in Europe. Presenting Jews as mice and Germans as cats, the story is nevertheless powerful and in no way trivializes the holocaust, though this highly successful sequence has yet to be brought to film, and such an adaptation would clearly be fraught with difficulties.

Among the most successful screen adaptations of graphic novels in the realistic vein is Terry Zwigoff's **Ghost World** (2001), based on the similarly titled graphic novel by Daniel Clowes that first appeared in his *Eightball* comic series. This film was coscripted by Clowes and Zwigoff, who also teamed up for *Art School Confidential* (2006), again based on material from *Eightball*. Perhaps the best known of all comic sequences in the realistic vein is Harvey Pekar's **American Splendor**, a comic sequence that was anthologized in two volumes in 1986 and 1987, but was republished in a single volume in 2003 along with the release of a film (directed by Shari Springer Berman and Robert Pulcini) of the same title. Here, Paul Giamatti plays Pekar in an autobiographical tale that also features numerous inserted appearances by the real Pekar.

Both *Ghost World* and *American Splendor* were small films that caused little stir at the box office but gained considerable critical respect. Together, they made it clear that graphic novels could be the basis for a wide variety of films, not just superhero blockbusters. On the other hand, such blockbusters have been one of the most important phenomena in recent American film. The increasing capabilities of CGI technology at the beginning of the twentieth century finally opened the way for the adaptation of popular comic books, especially those in the superhero subgenre, to film. After preliminary success with *Blade*, Marvel Comics led the way in this new wave of graphic cinema, beginning with Bryan Singer's big-budget adaptation of *X-Men* in 2000. *X-Men* was a huge box-office hit, roughly quadrupling its $75 million budget in worldwide gross receipts. It was also an impressive demonstration of state-of-the-art technology for adaptation of superhero comics to film, triggering a string of sequels, with each of the first two outstripping its predecessor at the box office, and a third one in the planning stages as of this writing. More importantly, *X-Men* opened the way for other Marvel superhero adaptations, including *Darkman* director Sam Raimi's 2002 film version of **Spider-Man,** a special-effects tour-de-force that cost roughly $139 million to make, but raked in an astonishing

$822 million in worldwide box-office receipts. ***Spider-Man 2*** (2004), with a mega-budget of $200 pulled in nearly another $800 million, providing a powerful demonstration of the potential of the Spider-Man franchise and of superhero movies in general. Early box-office results for ***Spider-Man 3***, released in May, 2007, were similarly spectacular. The film broke the all-time box office record for a single day on its U.S. release date of May 4, a day in which it took in well over $100 million worldwide. By the end of its first weekend in full release, it had taken in more than $380 million worldwide. If there could be any remaining doubt that graphic cinema was now big business, *Spider-Man 3*, with an announced production budget of $258 million (with rumors that it might have been as high as $300 million), was the most expensive film made to date, yet easily made back Sony's massive investment by the end of its first weekend in full release.

Other recent Marvel-based efforts have not always been quite as commercially successful as the Spider-Man franchise, though Marvel adaptations have consistently remained among the most interesting efforts in the quest to explore the possibilities of graphic cinema. Among other things, in addition to its major theatrical releases, Marvel has continued to produce minor, low-budget pieces in a somewhat experimental vein, such as the 2005 made-for-TV film *Man-Thing*. As a character, Man-Thing looks pretty much like a ripoff of the better-known Swamp Thing, though in point of fact, the Marvel character first appeared, in 1971, a month before the first appearance of the DC Comics character. And the resemblance is apparently not accidental: Swamp Thing cocreator Wein was the roommate of Man-Thing cocreator Gerry Conway at the time. In any case, Man-Thing enjoyed an extended career in various Marvel comics, but did not come to live-action adaptation until the 2005 film, a sort of low-budget B-movie effort made for broadcast on television's Sci Fi channel. The film version of *Man-Thing* is pretty dismal fare, full of clichés, bad acting, and cheesy effects. In it, an evil capitalist, Frederic Schist (Jack Thompson), dominates an entire small Louisiana town, including the surrounding swamplands, which he supposedly owns via a purchase from the Native American tribe that had held the lands for generations. The protagonist of *Man-Thing* is Sheriff Kyle Williams (Matthew Le Nevez), who has come to town from a northern city to replace the former sheriff, who has been killed. In fact, there has been a series of killings in the area, many of which (including that of the sheriff) we eventually learn were carried out by Schist himself as part of his nefarious plan to take control of the swamps, using them for his own money-making schemes and thereby destroying the fragile natural habitat. Some of the killings, however, turn out to be the work of the Man-Thing of the title, a huge, powerful, amorphous, and apparently mindless plant creature that seems dedicated to the task of defending the swamp from the destructive incursions of developers such as Schist. In the end, the Man-Thing (after only a couple of brief appearances in the film) is destroyed, but so are Schist and his plan to drill for oil in the swamps. Further, the swamplands are returned to their rightful owners after it becomes clear that Schist did not actually buy them, but simply took control of them through fraud and murder.

Marvel has also experimented with more serious, presumably higher-quality films. One of the most important follow-ups to *Spider-Man* was the 2003 film *Hulk*, featuring Marvel's green-skinned antihero. With roughly the same budget as *Spider-Man*, *Hulk* again featured state-of-the-art computer-generated special effects. However, while *Spider-Man* was clearly intended almost exclusively as high-action, youth-oriented entertainment, *Hulk* made a bid to bring superhero films into the realm of truly serious cinema. For one thing, it was helmed by the esteemed director Ang Lee, who had earlier directed such prestigious American films as the literary adaptation *Sense and Sensibility* (1995) and the highly serious psycho-social commentary *Ice Storm* (1997)—and who would go on to win an Oscar for Best Director for the 2005 film *Brokeback Mountain*. Lee had also had an impressive career in Chinese cinema, becoming known in the West for such works as *Eat Drink Man Woman* (1994). Most importantly, when slated to direct *Hulk*, Lee was coming off of his most successful Chinese film, *Crouching Tiger, Hidden Dragon* (2000), which not only brought Chinese film to the attention of mass audiences in America, but also brought martial arts films into the arena of high culture.

Lee clearly hoped to do the same for superhero films with *Hulk*, which featured such cast members as Oscar-winner Jennifer Connelly in the female lead. The Hulk had always been a complex and problematic hero, beginning with his first appearance in Marvel's *The Incredible Hulk* in 1962. Following in the tradition of Dr. Jekyll and Mr. Hyde, the Hulk is a beastlike manifestation of the dark side of Dr. Robert Bruce Banner, an otherwise mild-mannered scientist whose accidental exposure to high levels of gamma radiation has caused a condition in which he periodically transforms into the powerful green-skinned Hulk, usually when angered. The green-skinned Hulk is huge, powerful, and virtually indestructible. In most versions he is a raging, highly destructive animal, almost entirely lacking in intelligence and self-control. Banner is tormented by his inability to control the beast within him once it is released, so this basic premise carries with it a great deal of potential poignancy and psychological complexity, factors that were emphasized in the successful live-action television series *The Incredible Hulk*, which ran on CBS from 1977 to 1982, featuring Bill Bixby as Bruce Banner and Lou Ferrigno as the Hulk.

In *Hulk*, Lee emphasizes the angst suffered by Banner (Eric Bana) and by Betty Ross (Connelly), the woman who loves him. *Hulk* also contains considerably more in the way of science fiction elements than do most superhero films, though it is most distinctive among such films for the way in which it attempts to be a serious psychological drama, including the gradual revelation of the childhood traumas suffered by young Bruce when his scientist father (played in the present time of the film by Nick Nolte) attempted to kill the toddler (to prevent him from evolving into a monster) but accidentally killed the boy's mother instead. On the other hand, the film openly acknowledges its roots in the comics, including opening and closing titles and credits done in comic-book style. The film's camerawork is sometimes reminiscent of the comics as well, and its heavy use of split screens is especially effective as a sort of allusion to (though not really a recreation of) the look and feel of the comics, whose pages are divided into multiple panels. In addition, the Hulk (here entirely computer generated) is featured in a number of spectacular over-the-top action sequences, most of which involve the attempts of the U.S. military (under the command of Betty Ross's father, played by Sam Elliott) to destroy him. Both Bruce and Betty thus have difficult relationships with their fathers, and much of the film's psychological drama focuses on these vaguely Freudian struggles. The elder Banner and General Ross also have issues with each other, creating a complex emotional quadrangle of considerable promise.

Unfortunately, this psychological drama never quite becomes compelling, partly due to so-so performances from the lead actors. Indeed, part of the film's failure may be due to the fact that, as Betty Ross (the "normal" member of the emotional quadrangle), Connelly, probably the finest actor in the cast, has very little to do. In any case, the comic-book action sequences and the attempts at thoughtful science fiction and serious psychological drama do not mesh well. Further, the computer-generated *Hulk* is a bit too cartoonish, and as a result the film fails in its attempts to endow his predicament with the sort of pathos that worked so well for cinematic predecessors such as *Frankenstein* and (especially) *King Kong*. All in all, given the high expectations and extensive hype that accompanied the release of the film, *Hulk* was a disappointment. For one thing, it failed to live up to expectations at the box office, though its $245 million worldwide box-office gross was hardly a disaster. For another, while some major critics (including Roger Ebert and prominent online reviewer James Berardinelli) were reasonably enthusiastic about the film, the critical response was generally lukewarm at best. The film ends as the Hulk, having been thought killed by an atomic blast, suddenly reemerges in a remote Central American jungle, presumably paving the way for a sequel. Indeed, Berardinelli specifically hoped for a sequel in his review. It may, however, be a measure of disappointment over *Hulk* (as well as faith in the general promise of the Hulk franchise) that the Marvel followup, *The Incredible Hulk* (planned for release in 2008, under the direction of rising French star Louis Letterier, with Edward Norton in the title role) has been presented as more of a re-do than a sequel, with more emphasis on the comic-book action and less on the psychological drama.

The *other* 2003 Marvel Comics film adaptation was Mark Steven Johnson's *Daredevil* (2003), released to considerably less hype, partly because its title character was less well known than the Hulk or Spider-Man. *Daredevil* introduces film audiences to its masked hero (played by Ben Affleck), the secret alter ego of lawyer Matt Murdock, who uses acrobatics, martial arts skills, and high-tech gadgets to battle against crime. In this, he is something like Marvel's answer to Batman, and Daredevil, though a creation of Stan Lee from the 1960s, really came into his own when he received a darker makeover in the late 1970s from Frank Miller, who would do the same for Batman with the Dark Knight graphic novels. Murdock even shares with Bruce Wayne a dark childhood background. At age twelve, for example, Murdock's boxer father (played by David Keith), a reformed former thug, is murdered by gangsters whom the father has double-crossed by failing to throw a fight. At an even younger age, meanwhile, Murdock had been blinded by a toxic chemical spill as he rushed away from an alley where he spotted his then down-and-out father committing a mugging. It is, in fact, Daredevil's blindness that separates him from Batman and makes him unique as a superhero, though his other senses are superhuman, allowing him to function better than the sighted in many ways. In the film, Daredevil manages to defeat and apparently kill supervillain Bullseye (Colin Farrell), though Bullseye is able to kill Elektra Natchios (played by *Alias* star Jennifer Garner), Murdock's love interest and something of a superhero in her own right. As the film closes, however, we learn that Bullseye is alive after all, which seems to set the stage for a sequel.

The closest thing to a sequel to *Daredevil* so far, however, is Rob Bowman's *Elektra* (2005), which brings Elektra back to life, a move that was perfectly appropriate given that Elektra (who had been added to the Daredevil universe by Miller in 1981) had also been resurrected from the dead in Miller's graphic novel *Elektra Lives Again* (1991). Garner is again cast as Elektra, but here gets a starring role (slightly modified from the role she played in *Daredevil*) as a violent ninjette assassin who ultimately uses her superhuman Asian martial arts skills to battle against evil and to prevent the killing of a young girl she has been hired to assassinate. The film also supplies a number of details of Elektra's background, including her own murder as a child, after which she was revived from the dead and given supernatural martial arts training by the blind martial arts master,

Stick (Terence Stamp)—who in the *Daredevil* comics had also taught Matt Murdock how to fight. In the typical Marvel Comics mold, much of the film has to do with Elektra's coming to grips with her own background and powers and learning to use those powers in a responsible way.

Jonathan Hensleigh's *The Punisher* (2004) is another entry in the genre of films based on dark comic-book superheroes. It stars Thomas Jane as undercover G-man Frank Castle, who becomes the Marvel Comics hero of the title, dedicating himself to a violent campaign of vengeance against organized criminals—led by the wealthy and powerful Howard Saint (John Travolta) who killed his entire family. This ultraviolent film is a grim and humorless remake of Mark Goldblatt's 1989 film of the same title (which starred Dolph Lundgren as The Punisher). A sort of combination of the comics with film noir and Charles Bronson's *Death Wish*, it reveals the dark side of the comics, but is entirely lacking (despite occasional gestures in that direction) in the zaniness and campiness that one often associates with films based on comic books. As the film ends, The Punisher has completed his campaign of personal revenge (with a gruesome torture-killing of Saint) and appears to set to go forth on a more general mission of defending the weak and helpless against the strong and the evil, a career that will presumably be explored in the planned sequel.

Tim Story's *Fantastic Four* (2005) followed in the footsteps of hit film adaptations of Marvel superhero comics such as the first two *Spider-Man* films. It is based on the founding series of revived Marvel Comics, which began publication in 1961. Created by writer/editor Stan Lee and illustrator Jack Kirby, the Fantastic Four were overtly modeled on DC Comics' Justice League of America, but aimed at presenting its team of superhero protagonists in a much more human light, with many of the same problems and concerns as ordinary people. The film does somewhat the same, while placing particular emphasis on the humorous elements that were also central to the original comic books. Most of the emphasis of the film is on the origins of the group: hit by a cosmic-ray storm while on a scientific research mission in outer space, they find their DNA permanently altered to give them super powers, though it is not clear why each character receives radically different powers. Brilliant scientist Reed Richards (Ioan Gruffud), the group's leader, becomes "Mister Fantastic," with the ability to stretch and reshape his body almost limitlessly, much in the mode of "Plastic Man," who had appeared in Quality Comics from 1941 to 1956. Scientist Susan Storm (Jessica Alba) becomes the "Invisible Girl," with the power to project telekinetic force fields and to bend light, thus making herself appear invisible. As the film ends, Susan and Reed are married, and she changes her name to Susan Richards. Meanwhile, Susan's brother, the wisecracking, fun-loving Johnny Storm (Chris Evans), becomes the

"Human Torch," able to heat his body to supernova temperatures, to fly while enveloped in flame, and to control and project fire. Johnny has a great deal of fun playing pranks on the fourth member of the group, burly pilot Ben Grimm (Michael Chiklis), who is transformed into "The Thing," with superhuman strength and with a tough, super-dense body covered with orange, platelike scales. The Thing is the only one of the group who does not look fully human after his transformation, and his plight adds a certain pathos to the film, especially after his beloved wife leaves him because she is unable to cope with his monstrous appearance. Indeed, the group as a whole spends much of the film attempting to reverse the transformations that have made them superheroes, but by the end they have accepted their fate and have, in the meantime, scored their first victory over their arch-enemy from the comic books, Doctor Doom (Julian McMahon). They thus end the film essentially at the beginning of their careers as superheroes, thus setting the stage for a sequel, which became almost a certainty after the film's box-office success (with a worldwide gross of over $300 million). Indeed, June, 2007, saw the release of *Fantastic Four: Rise of the Silver Surfer*, which traces further adventures of the superhero team, while also bringing more of Marvel's extensive mythology to the screen. Also directed by Story and roughly based on the classic 1966 story arc "The Coming of Galactus" from the Fantastic Four comics, this film features the Silver Surfer (a complex and interesting sometime-hero-sometime-villain) as the principal antagonist of the Fantastic Four.

Released only one month after *Spider-Man 3* and while that film was still in theaters, *Fantastic Four: Rise of the Silver Surfer* made it clear that Marvel Entertainment was becoming a major player in the film industry, with two big-time films running in the theaters at once. The vast array of materials published in Marvel Comics over the decades had by this time inspired not only some of the most successful live-action films of all times but an array of animated adaptations as well, including several television series and a growing series of animated feature films made for television and DVD. Among the latter was *The Invincible Iron Man* (2007), a high-action straight-to-DVD animated feature that is marred by relatively crude animation and highly stereotypical depictions of Asians and Asian culture, but that nevertheless achieves a certain level of entertainment. This feature paved the way for a live-action theatrical feature based on the Iron Man character. Directed by Jon Favreau and featuring Robert Downey, Jr., in the title role, *Iron Man* is in production at the time of this writing, scheduled for a May, 2008, release. Significantly, *Iron Man* will be Marvel's first entirely self-produced feature. Marvel had previously partnered with existing studios, as in their association with Sony/Columbia Pictures for all of the *Spider-Man* films. *Iron Man* thus represents a further movement of Marvel into the film industry and provides strong evidence of the way in which the worlds of film and of the comics are gradually merging into one.

Given the success of the Marvel superhero films, it comes as no surprise that heroes from other comics publishers have made their way to the big screen in the early twenty-first century as well, though none have achieved the success of the Marvel franchises. The biggest non-Marvel superhero successes have involved the resurrection of the Superman and Batman film franchises, based on the exploits of the two brightest stars in the DC Comics universe. Christopher Nolan's *Batman Begins* (2005) and Bryan Singer's *Superman Returns* (2006) were both successful films, though they could not approach the box-office appeal of the Spider-Man franchise.

Of course, these two films had a certain built-in appeal based on the longtime popularity of their heroes alone. Other, less prominent, super-heroes have not proven such big draws, though films based on offbeat non-Marvel comic-book superheroes such as del Toro's **Hellboy** (2004) have been quite successful. Paul Hunter's *Bulletproof Monk* (2003), an action-comedy/martial arts flick based on the Image Comics comic books illustrated by Michael Avon Oeming, was not so successful. The film begins in 1943, as a nameless Tibetan monk (Chow Yun-Fat) is invested with special abilities that help him to protect the mystical Scroll of the Ulti-mate from those (especially evil Nazis) who would misuse its considerable power, which conveys the ability to rule the world. The film then cuts to sixty years later in modern-day New York, where the monk comes into a final conflict with the Nazis and meanwhile discovers the dual successors who will assume his role as protector of the scroll. These successors turn out to be a pair of hip young Americans, Kar (Seann William Scott) and Jade (Jaime King), and this film is clearly aimed at a hip young audience. Unfortunately, despite the work of a big-time Hong Kong film star such as Chow in a lead role and the presence of John Woo as one of the film's numerous producers, the film falls flat, especially in its martial arts scenes, which seem dull and uninspired in comparison to recent films such as *The Matrix* (1999) and *Crouching Tiger, Hidden Dragon* (2000), which had set a very high bar for such scenes. Audiences attuned to such films were ap-parently not impressed by *Bulletproof Monk*. Indeed, in an environment in which other comic book adaptations were scoring big at the box office, the film actually lost money. Still, it has its moments and can be fun in places, thanks largely to the incongruous pairing of the ethereal monk and the earthy Kar, a streetwise pickpocket.

One of the most unusual "superhero" comic book/graphic novel se-quences upon which a film has been based is *The League of Extraordinary Gentlemen*, a twelve-comic sequence (collected into two full-color graphic novels) written by Alan Moore and lavishly illustrated by Kevin O'Neill and originally appearing in one six-issue sequence in 1999 and 2000 and another in 2002 and 2003. Here, Moore and O'Neill present the outrageous adventures of a diverse alliance of heroes, all of whom are either characters in popular Victorian-era literature or the ancestors of characters in more modern literature. This premise opens up a wide variety of opportunities in a number of different genres, and Moore and O'Neill exploit those opportunities (in science fiction, horror, detective fiction, and spy fiction) to the fullest, from the battles of the League with the evil Fu Manchu in Volume I to their struggles against Wellsian Martian invaders in Volume II. Unfortunately, the same cannot be said for Stephen Norrington's 2003 film of the same title as the comic series, partly because the series gains a great deal of energy from its wide variety of allusions (some quite arcane) to Victoriana, while the filmmakers clearly felt they needed to limit such allusions in order to make the film more accessible to movie audiences. In fact, the film largely limits itself to Victorian characters who have been featured in well-known film adaptations, apparently assuming that film audiences are much more familiar with movies than with books. The film also eliminates much of the darkness and complexity of the graphic novels, opting instead for a lighter and campier tone that borders on silliness. The result is a mishmash that features some gorgeous special effects, but little else of interest, apart from the casting of Sean Connery as Allan Quatermain (a figure from the Victorian adventure novels of Ryder Haggard, probably best known to contemporary audiences via film adaptations such as 1985 film version of *King Solomon's Mines*, which featured Richard Chamberlain in the role of Quatermain). This casting was clever (if in an esoteric way) because the first graphic novel prominently features Campion Bond, an ancestor of James Bond, while including a number of other Bond allusions as well. The film, meanwhile, alludes to this connection at only one point, when Connery reacts with a sort of knowing wink to the audience after the League is first brought together by a mysterious personage known simply as "M" (Richard Roxburgh), which had also been the label of James Bond's handler at MI6, the British Intelligence Agency.

Francis Lawrence's *Constantine* (2005) is loosely based on the long-running comic series *Hellblazer*, from DC Comics, most recently written by Denise Mina and drawn by Leonardo Manco. The protagonist of both the comic and the film is John Constantine (played by Keanu Reeves in the film), a character who was originally created by Moore for the *Swamp Thing* comic. In the comics, Constantine is an Englishman who roams the world, interacting with supernatural forces from both heaven and hell—primarily in the pursuit of his own selfish goals. In the film,

Constantine is an American who lives in Los Angeles; he is also a much more positive figure than in the comics, primarily battling against hellish forces that intrude into the physical world—and inevitably recalling the "Neo" character made famous by Reeves in the *Matrix* films. In the course of the film, Constantine saves the world from destruction at the hands of the son of Satan, though it turns out that this Satanic plot was largely instigated by the angel Gabriel, somewhat blurring the line between the forces of good and evil and producing an air of moral ambiguity that is reminiscent of film noir. Though visually interesting, this high-action film was not highly successful, especially with fans of the comics, who generally felt that the film took too many liberties in trying to make the protagonist a more conventional film hero.

In one of the most telling signs of the marketability of films based on comics, Marcus Nispel's *Pathfinder* (2007) inspired the publication, by Dark Horse Comics, of an associated graphic novel during its own production in 2006. Then, when the film was released, the marketing of the film seemed designed to create the mistaken impression that the film was based on the graphic novel. That marketing, however, is not entirely inappropriate, as the film certainly has the look and feel of a comic-book adaptation. In somewhat the same vein, Kurt Wimmer's *Ultraviolet* (2006) is not literally based on a comic book or graphic novel, but calls attention to its comic-book style in the opening credits, which feature a series of covers from fictional "Ultraviolet" comic books. *Ultraviolet* features Milla Jovovich as Violet, a member of a race of virus-mutated humans (referred to by the humans as "vampires") who have been brutally oppressed (and almost exterminated) by a dystopian regime that uses fear of vampires to further its own totalitarian power. Jovovich had established herself as a leading female action star in films based on the *Resident Evil* video games (which were also turned into comics), and she continues that function here. *Ultraviolet* involves virtually nonstop CGI action as the sleek, scantily-clad Violet uses her considerable martial arts skills to defeat whole regiments of heavily armed human foes. The result is a film that looks and feels somewhat like a cross between a comic book and a video game. The fight scenes are reminiscent of those in Wimmer's earlier dystopian film *Equilibrium* (2002), though *Ultraviolet* lacks the thematic depth and dramatic intensity of the earlier film. It is, in fact, little more than a series of loosely connected scenes of frenetic chases and over-the-top battles.

Ultraviolet fails as a film, largely because its comic-book action and graphics are not tied together by anything resembling a compelling plot. It does, however, indicate the extent to which female action heroes had established a major presence in American film (and television) by the beginning of the twenty-first century—a tendency, incidentally, that was preceded by the presence of important female heroes in the comics, which can be said to have led the way in this regard, so much so that important female action-oriented protagonists tend to have a comic book quality, even when they are not based on characters from the comics. Thus, television series like *Xena: Warrior Princess*, *Buffy the Vampire Slayer*, and *Alias* were not based on comics, but could have been. Indeed, *Alias* has inspired a sequence of graphic novels, while *Xena* has inspired a comic series from Dynamite Entertainment, and *Buffy* has inspired an extensive range of Dark Horse comics. Similarly, film characters like Carrie-Ann Moss's Trinity of the *Matrix* films, Kate Becksinsale's Selene in the *Underworld* films, and the title character of *Æon Flux* (2005) have all had a sort of comic-book quality. The latter film, based on an animated television series that has also inspired a series of comics, was not a success, but its ability to attract Oscar-winner Charlize Theron to the title role indicates the extent to which such films had become mainstream Hollywood fare by 2005. Nevertheless, direct adaptations of comics based on female protagonists to film have yet to find major success, and such efforts as *Sheena*, *Barb Wire*, and *Elektra* pale in comparison to the potential of such films.

As of this writing, in 2007, comic books and graphic novels are still growing in importance as a source of material for film adaptation. In addition to such major box-office fare as *Spider-Man 3* and *Fantastic Four: Rise of the Silver Surfer*, the spring of 2007 saw the release of such films as Mark Steven Johnson's *Ghost Rider*, based on the Marvel Comics series of that title that ran from 1973 to 1983. A second *Ghost Rider* comic, published by Marvel between 1990 and 1998 features a different title character (who turns out to be the brother of the first Ghost Rider), but has little or no influence on the film, in which Nicholas Cage stars in the title role as Johnny Blaze, a motorcycle stunt rider who gains supernatural abilities after selling his soul to the devil, here identified as Mephistopheles (Peter Fonda). This transaction turns him into a sort of avenging demon, but his basic goodheartedness causes him to fight for good, resisting the attempts of Mephistopheles to use him as an agent of evil. And this resistance succeeds, apparently because God is on the Rider's side. As if this scenario didn't sound silly enough, when Blaze transforms into the Ghost Rider (which generally occurs only at night and only when he is in the presence of evil), he essentially bursts into flame, with his head becoming a flaming skull. His trusty bike bursts into flame as well, and both it and its rider gain extra power and resilience: he can, for example, ride straight down the side of a skyscraper without suffering injury (or vehicle damage) when he hits the ground. The Rider races about at high speeds, leaving a trail of flame and shattering pavement in his wake, battling demons and criminals, while wielding his favorite weapon, a long length of chain that can burst into flame and perform various amazing feats. Meanwhile (like many misunderstood superheroes), he must resist attempts of the police to take him down. Given this premise, *Ghost Rider* could have been much worse than it actually is, largely because the filmmakers decided to play it straight, taking the premise seriously rather than camping it up as would have been easy to do. With a budget of $110 million and a big-name star like Cage, the film actually works fairly well if one is able (a big if!) to suspend disbelief and pretend that the events being presented are actually possible. Apparently, many moviegoers were willing to grant *Ghost Rider* its premise, because the film had more than made back its production cost in the first three weeks of its release, eventually more than doubling its cost in worldwide box office.

Zack Snyder's *300*, based on the graphic novel written by Frank Miller, was the biggest box-office hit of 2007, prior to the release of *Spider-Man 3* in early May. It was also one of the most controversial films of the year. Visually interesting in a computer-generated style that clearly indicates its roots in the comics, *300* is an historical epic dealing with the Battle of Thermopylae in 480 B.C. It is also a militarist cliché-fest, soaked in blood and testosterone, glorifying violence and sacrificial death for one's "country," even though countries as we know them did not exist at the time of the events depicted in the film. Then again, like Mel Gibson's *Braveheart* (1995), this is a film that doesn't want to be confused with the facts—and isn't interested in historical accuracy. What it is interested in is the presentation of spectacularly bloody battle sequences as hordes of near-naked men impale one another on various sharp objects, demonstrating sadomasochistic tendencies that are actually more reminiscent of Gibson's *The Passion of the Christ* (2004). What makes the film even more problematic is that its subject matter (involving a historical battle in which 300 Spartan warriors led a contingent of roughly 7,000 Greek soldiers against an invading Persian army of roughly 1,000,000) offers ample opportunities for commentary on the present-day military and political situation in the Middle East. Unfortunately, the film (following the graphic novel) goes all out in its (historically inaccurate) presentation of the Spartans as paradigms of Western reason and democracy, while the Persians are presented as cruel, vicious, and entirely depraved Oriental religious fanatics. Given the tensions between the United States and Iran (the present-day counterpart of Persia) that reigned at the time of the release of the film, it was impossible for many viewers not to see the film as a paean to (American) patriotism and as a ringing endorsement of U.S. military intervention in Iran or elsewhere in the Middle East. All in all, the film reflects the very worst kinds of images and ideas that the comics have to offer, sadly verifying the otherwise inaccurate perceptions of many that the comics are nothing more than a debased medium designed to appeal to the baser instincts of teenage male readers.

Nevertheless, more thoughtful films—from *Ghost World* and *American Splendor* to *A History of Violence* and *V for Vendetta*—have demonstrated that graphic cinema need not be juvenile. Further, even films that seem designed mostly to provide excitement and light entertainment for a young audience—such as the *Spider-Man* sequences—have managed to appeal to relatively positive inclinations in their viewers. Finally, films such as the first *Batman* and the recent *Batman Returns* and *Sin City*, have proved that graphic cinema can be at the forefront of advances in cinematic art in ways that go beyond simple advances in special-effects technology of the kind that have marked many of the best superhero adaptations. With films based on comic books and graphic novels continuing to do well at the box office, the future would appear to be bright for this important category of American film.

1

The *Superman* Film Franchise

Released 1978–2006; Various Directors

ACTION COMICS, ACTION FILM: SUPERMAN COMES TO THE BIG SCREEN

If superhero comics are the heart of the comic book tradition, then Superman is surely the central figure in the tradition of superhero comics. It was only fitting, then, that Superman should be the central figure in the first major comic book-to-film adaptation, Richard Donner's *Superman: The Movie* (1978). Indeed, Superman had first come to the screen as early as 1951, in the theatrical release *Superman and the Mole-Men*, which served as a sort of trial run for the syndicated television series *The Adventures of Superman*. This extremely successful series, featuring George Reeves in the title role, became a mainstay of 1950s television and helped to solidify the status of Superman as a central icon of American popular culture. It eventually ran for a total of 104 half-hour episodes, with new episodes airing from 1952 to 1958.

Superman already had a long history even before *The Adventures of Superman*. Created by Canadian-born artist Joe Shuster and American writer Jerry Siegel in 1932 (when both were still teenagers in Cleveland, Ohio), Superman did not actually appear in print until June, 1938, in the first issue of *Action Comics*. From that point, the Man of Steel was unstoppable, becoming the centerpiece not only of a wide range of cultural products (comic books, comic strips, radio serials, live-action and animated television series, video games, and films), but of an entire American mythology. Certainly, the character of Superman has mythic dimensions that transcend the American context. He is, for example, quite clearly a figure of both Christ and Moses. Still, though he is an alien from the doomed planet Krypton, Superman was from the very beginning an avowedly American hero, from his primarily red-white-and-blue costume to his clearly pro-American ideology, embodied in his eventual famed declaration that his mission on earth was to serve as the defender of "truth, justice, and the American way."

The extensive mythology surrounding Superman's powers and background has grown and varied over the years, creating numerous complications and contradictions in his portrayal, though the central elements of his story are reasonably consistent. They also constitute one of the best-known fictional creations in American cultural history. In the best-known version of this story, Superman was born Kal-El on the distant planet Krypton, then sent to earth on an escape rocket by his father, the scientist Jor-El, on the eve of the destruction of his home planet. The small boy arrives on earth, where the weaker gravity and the radiation of the yellow sun give him extraordinary powers, including flight, super-strength, virtual indestructibility, and a variety of visual abilities (such as X-Ray vision). Taken in by Jonathan and Martha Kent, a kindly child-less couple in Smallville, Kansas, Superman is raised as a human child (named Clark Kent), only gradually discovering and developing his considerable powers. As a young adult he moves to the giant city of Metropolis (originally modeled by Shuster on his native Toronto, but later commonly seen as a stand-in for New York City). There, he maintains his secret identity as Clark Kent, working as a bespectacled, mild-mannered reporter for *The Daily Planet*, the city's leading newspaper. Meanwhile, Superman becomes a public figure, battling evil in his signature caped costume.

IT'S A BIRD, IT'S A PLANE, IT'S A FRANCHISE!: THE SUPERMAN FILMS

By the time work began on Donner's *Superman* film in the late 1970s, the vast array of materials that had already been produced surrounding the Superman character presented filmmakers with both rich resources and considerable complexities. In addition, the film was ultimately completed and released at a key time in American film history. For one thing, the huge commercial success of the first *Star Wars* film in 1977 encouraged filmmakers to go for big-budget special-effects-oriented spectaculars. For another, *Star Wars* itself was the key marker in a dramatic leap forward in special-effects technology, which made it possible to make films such as *Superman* much more effectively than could have been done earlier.

The first *Superman* film employed state-of-the-art special effects that in many ways went beyond even *Star Wars*. However, the film is not nearly as heavily dependent on special effects as many of its successors in the superhero genre, which perhaps accounts for the fact that it still holds up well nearly thirty years later, when its special effects appear primitive by contemporary standards. But the special effects of *Superman* represent only one of many aspects of the film that help it to achieve a grand, epic feel, including the spectacular opening credits and the expansive music of John Williams, which has become some of the best-known music in all of American popular culture. Even the casting of the film was epic. Though unknown Christopher Reeve was (fortuitously, as it turned out) cast as the title character, other roles were played by such recognizable Hollywood figures as Glenn Ford (as Jonathan Kent) and Gene Hackman (as bald supervillain Lex Luthor). The biggest (and most expensive) casting coup of all involved landing megastar Marlon Brando for the role of Jor-El, Superman's Kryptonian father. As related in David Michael Petrou's *The Making of Superman: The Movie* (Warner Books, 1978), director Donner achieved this epic effect only after his own epic struggle against producers Alexander and Ilya Salkind to cut the budget and to give the film a more comic, campy tone. After all, *Superman: The Movie* was an entirely new type of film with no direct predecessors, and it was not at all clear that the project would be able to attract the kinds of audiences that it ultimately did. Indeed, because of a fear that the first film would be such a bust that the second would never be released, Donner actually moved the climactic stunt that was supposed to end the second film to the first film in the hope of helping to make that first film a success. The strategy apparently worked, because *Superman* was a colossal hit. However, such moves may help account for the fact that the second film was still in a very incomplete state by the time the first film was released.

Largely as a way to save production costs, most of the footage of *Superman II* was shot by Donner during the filming of *Superman: The Movie*. By the time *Superman II* had been released in 1980, however, the Salkinds had fired Donner after an extended period of tension. On their side, the producers were concerned that Donner's filming method was too slow and too expensive. Indeed, budget overages had already led to an extended period in which work on the film had been suspended. On his side, Donner was upset that the Salkinds wanted to excise Brando's footage from the second film in order to avoid having to pay him the millions of dollars that his contract would require. Donner also felt that the Salkinds wanted the film to be too campy and that their interference was generally detracting from the film's quality. Eventually, the Salkinds replaced Donner with Richard Lester, and production was resumed. Lester reedited Donner's footage and also shot additional footage, though Hackman, in a show of solidarity with Donner, refused to return to shoot any additional scenes for Lester.

Nevertheless, *Superman II* is a fine film, still very much in the spirit of the original, even if it fails to achieve quite the same mythic feel as its predecessor. A "Donner cut" of *Superman II*, which attempts to return the film as much as possible to Donner's vision of the film, is now available on DVD. However, most critical response has suggested that Lester's version is probably preferable, though it should be pointed out that Lester did have an opportunity to shoot additional scenes and to bring his vision to fruition during production, while Donner did not. In *Superman II*, Luthor is joined by a group of supervillains from Krypton—who have the same superpowers as Superman himself, all just as Superman has decided to give up his own powers so that he can become an ordinary human and have an ordinary life with his beloved Lois Lane (Margot Kidder). He even takes Lois to the Fortress of Solitude, his secret North Pole hideout, and reveals to her the story of his origins. Predictably, however, Superman is forced to give up his own dream of personal happiness so that he can once again save the world from villainy, meanwhile conveniently giving Lois amnesia so that she will forget all that has happened in their recent time together. The film then ends with Superman's apology and pledge to the president of the United States, as he restores the American flag that had been ripped from atop the White House during the recent reign of villainy: "Sorry I've been gone so long. I won't let you down again."

Superman III (1983) was also directed by Lester, but it nevertheless marked a distinctive change in the *Superman* film sequence. The campy, comic elements that had been present in the films from the beginning here came to the fore, making this film essentially a parody of itself. Strangely enough, Luthor (the principal comic character from the first two films) is absent here. Superman's nemesis in this film is evil corporate magnate Ross Webster (Robert Vaughn), while the most important comic elements are provided by the presence of Richard Pryor as computer whiz Gus Gorman. As is usually the case with Superman stories, supervillain Webster must try to get the Man of Steel out of the way so that he can pursue his nefarious schemes unimpeded. In this case, he does so first by employing Gorman to help him manufacture some synthetic Kryptonite; Gorman gets one ingredient wrong (substituting tobacco tar for an unidentified element), so the synthetic Kryptonite doesn't kill Superman. Instead, it splits him into twins, one evil and one good, somewhat in the way a transporter malfunction in the classic *Star Trek* episode "The Enemy Within" (1966) created an evil Kirk to oppose the good original. The good Superman emerged triumphant, but then finds himself even more threatened by an evil supercomputer that Gorman develops for Webster. Superman wins out again, with assists from the basically good-hearted Gorman and from the buxom Lorelei Ambrosia (Pamela Stephenson), Webster's supposedly airheaded mistress (who is a secret intellectual heavyweight). As the film ends, Webster has been brought to justice, while Superman helps Gorman and Ambrosia go straight.

The Superman franchise expanded in 1984 to include the ill-fated *Supergirl*, executive produced by Ilya Salkind and starring Helen Slater as Superman's young female counterpart. *Supergirl* featured such stellar cast members as Faye Dunaway, Peter O'Toole, and Mia Farrow, but drew mostly negative reviews and failed at the box office. *Superman IV: The Quest for Peace* (1987) then continued the decline of the franchise. It deals with the theme of nuclear disarmament, and there is additional satirical potential in its treatment of the attempts of lowbrow media mogul David Warfield (Sam Wanamaker) to take over the *Daily Planet* and turn it into a profitable (but tawdry) tabloid. The film was even directed by Sidney J. Furie, with solid credentials as a maker of films such as the Vietnam war drama *The Boys in Company C* (1978). One might thus have expected the fourth installment in the *Superman* film sequence to return to a higher level of seriousness. However, this film—produced not by the Salkinds but by the low-budget kitsch-meisters at Golan-Globus Productions (who cut the film's budget in half just before filming began)—was so silly (and so awful) that it brought the once-mighty film franchise to a halt for nearly twenty years. Most of the original cast returned for *Superman IV* (Reeve is better than ever in his moments as the bumbling Clark, though he is beginning to seem a bit tired as Superman), but the actors, whatever their chemistry together, were unable to salvage the film from its ridiculous plot and cheesy look. Here, Superman (concluding that he is by now a true earthling) decides to rid the earth of nuclear weapons, despite the earlier direction from Jor-El that he should not interfere in the planet's history. Luthor (with Hackman returning in the role) counters by producing a nuclear-powered supervillain to battle Superman for supremacy on the planet. Nuclear Man, of course, is defeated, while Luthor is returned to prison—though Superman himself learns a bit of humility and realizes that he cannot force the people of earth to become peaceful before they choose to do so on their own.

Superman III was not a good film, but it made a tidy profit at the box office. *Superman IV* failed both critically and commercially, suggesting that the franchise had run its course. As a result, no Superman films appeared in the 1990s, during which time the popularity of the Superman comics was in decline as well; younger, hipper superheroes seemed to have greater appeal for comic-book readers of the decade. Nevertheless, Superman remained one of the most recognizable figures in American popular culture, maintaining a presence in several animated television series, including *Superman: The Animated Series*, which ran from 1996 to 2000 and took Superman animation to a new level of sophistication. Moreover, even in the wake of the *Superman IV* fiasco, the Superman figure returned to live-action television in 1988 in *Superboy*, created by Ilya and Alexander Salkind and focusing on Clark Kent's college years at Shuster College in Siegelville, Florida. This moderately successful series ran for four seasons in syndication. Meanwhile, its 1992 demise was followed by an even more successful series, *Lois & Clark: The New Adventures of Superman*, which ran for four seasons on the ABC network, beginning in 1993. The Superman saga then moved into the twenty-first century with the introduction of *Smallville* on the WB network in 2001 (still running as of this writing on the CW network, successor to the WB). Focusing on Clark Kent's teen years in Smallville, this series (clearly influenced by its WB predecessor, *Buffy the Vampire Slayer*, with a dash of *The X-Files* thrown in for good measure) continued the emphasis on personal relationships that began in *Lois & Clark* while tracking young Clark's gradual realization of his super powers, complicated by the normal problems of teenagers growing into adulthood. *Smallville* also updates the Superman story, stipulating that the toddler Kal-El arrived on earth only in 1989, making the action of the series contemporaneous with the first-run broadcasts.

Attempts to return Superman to the big screen were rumored throughout the 1990s, including one proposed version to be directed by *Batman* director Tim Burton, featuring Nicholas Cage as Superman. These efforts came to naught, but Superman returned to theaters in *Superman Returns* (2006), helmed by *X-Men* director Bryan Singer and featuring obscure television actor Brandon Routh in the title role. Released by Warner Brothers with considerable hype, this film grossed over $200 million in domestic box office receipts alone, though it may have cost as much as $270 million to produce, making it a relatively moderate (counting international receipts, DVD sales, and so on) commercial success, while reviews of the film were lukewarm at best. Nevertheless, the film is interesting, particularly as a companion piece to the original *Superman: The Movie*. It is worthwhile, then, to consider the two of them in greater detail.

THE MAN OF STEEL THEN AND NOW: *SUPERMAN* AND *SUPERMAN RETURNS*

Superman: The Movie is informed by a refreshing (and intentional) innocence that seems well in keeping with the status of the title character as an idealized figure of uncompromising virtue, in addition to his various physical superpowers. Despite the presence of a number of comic, even campy elements, the film is intensely respectful of Superman's cultural legacy. It neither challenges nor extends the inherited mythology of Superman as a cultural icon of all-American virtue. Instead, it takes that mythology seriously, attempting to convey the spirit of that mythology in film. *Superman: The Movie* is in many ways the ultimate Hollywood entertainment film. Much in the mode of *Star Wars*, it is Hollywood moviemaking (and mythmaking) on a grand scale, nostalgically looking back to the cultural past of film (and of Superman), while forging ahead on the cutting edge of filmmaking technology. A big project in more ways than one, *Superman* was filmed over a period of nineteen months and employed more than one thousand crew members, ultimately running through the largest production budget in the history of film to that time.

Superman is, to an extent, a formulaic superhero film, but it should be remembered that, at the time it was made, it was a highly original film that created the formula followed by so many successors. As the first major theatrical film based on a comic-book superhero, *Superman* broke new ground—and did so so successfully that it remains a standard against which superhero films are judged thirty years later. For example, despite the fact that the Superman story is so well known, the film spends a significant amount of its running time on the story of the title character's origins, including an extended sequence on the doomed planet Krypton, followed by a fairly quick account of the childhood and youth of Clark Kent in the all-American town of Smallville. Subsequent superhero films have typically followed suit, focusing in their initial segments on the origins of their central figures.

On the other hand, while *Superman* was an unprecedented film in many ways, it is also a film that quite consciously draws upon a number of important predecessors and traditions in American film, some of them definitely bordering on cliché. The link to *Star Wars* is particularly obvious, including the fact that John Barry, the production designer for *Superman*, had also been the production designer for *Star Wars*. Both of these films also feature the music of John Williams, which is as instrumental as Barry's designs to the overall impact of the films. But *Superman* also draws upon a number of more general precedents in American film, participating in so many genres and American cultural myths that it becomes a sort of summation of American cultural history from the 1930s to the 1970s. As the film moves from Krypton to Smallville, for example, it enters the realm of the prototypical American small town, a key locus of American myth. However, while any number of works of American culture (long dominated, after all, by urban production) have treated the myth of the American small town skeptically and ironically, *Superman* (in keeping with its general air of cheerful innocence) here plays it straight, embracing the small-town milieu of Smallville with Norman Rockwell enthusiasm. Growing up in Smallville, with its population of hard-working, right-thinking, and straight-shooting ordinary folks is clearly key to the development of Clark Kent into the righteous defender of truth, justice, and the American way that we see in the remainder of the film, after he moves to Metropolis to assume his role as protector of humanity. Metropolis, meanwhile, is certainly a more dangerous and complicated place than Smallville had been, but it is hardly an urban nightmare and its greater moral complexity produces more comedy than tragedy.

Superman even draws on precedents in film comedy. Superman himself is certainly a larger-than-life figure, but Luthor and his cartoonish minions (effectively played by Ned Beatty and Valerie Perrine) are definitely comic-book characters that add comic elements. Meanwhile, Reeve plays Superman as modest and unassuming, making it much easier for audiences to warm up to him. Superman is especially humanized (and made more likeable and accessible) through his relationship with Lois Lane, which forms a sort of screwball romantic comedy subplot that is quite central to the entire film. Superman is further brought down to earth through Reeve's hilarious portrayal of the bumbling Kent, a performance that Reeve claimed to have modeled on Cary Grant's appearances in a variety of romantic comedies.

Superman is also humanized when Luthor zaps him with the requisite chunk of Kryptonite, a plot device with a long and honorable history of creating difficulties for Superman, who otherwise seems almost too invincible for the creation of any sort of real suspense. Here, Superman does at one point seem in serious danger from the Kryptonite, but is then rescued by Eve Teschmacher (Perrine), Luthor's presumably evil mistress, whose basic good-heartedness kicks in when she sees Superman helpless and on the verge of death. This scene is only one of many unapologetically sentimental clichés that are employed in the film (such as the scene in which Superman rescues a kitten stuck in a tree), enhancing its air of innocence and wonder and thus actually becoming strengths, rather than weaknesses.

In the film's central action sequence, Superman saves millions of people on both coasts of the United States as he defeats Luthor's schemes to wreak havoc (and make personal profit) by hijacking deadly missiles and launching them in both directions. This segment provides the film's most important actions sequences and most impressive special effects. However, in the course of saving millions, Superman is so busy that he fails to save Lois, who is killed in a landslide in the midst of all the action. Superman is at his most human as the film reaches its peak emotional moment when he realizes in agony that he has failed to save the one person who now means the most to him. The power of this scene is further enhanced by the way it echoes the earlier moment in the film when young Clark Kent, despite his powers, experienced the frustration of not being able to save his father from death by a heart attack.

This time, however, Superman refuses to accept failure. In a key stunt cannibalized by Donner from the original planned ending of *Superman II*, Superman goes into orbit and flies around and around the earth against its direction of rotation so rapidly that he somehow (the physics of the effect are never explained, and probably couldn't be) makes time go backward, turning back the clock to a time before Lois's fatal accident. He then swoops back down to earth and saves Lois before that accident can occur, then makes the rest of the world safe by scooping up Luthor and his sidekick Otis (Beatty) and depositing them in a high-security prison, where they can await trial for their recent misdeeds. The warden need not thank him, Superman selflessly explains, because "We're all part of the same team." In a sequence that would be used to close *Superman II–IV* as well, Superman then flies back into orbit, cruising through the peacefulness of space and emphasizing his role as guardian of the planet—while also possibly recharging his batteries with sunlight. Reeve flashes his winning grin directly into the camera, then flies away, reassuring us that he will be there when needed.

Thus, after all the dangers and difficulties he has recently experienced, Superman wraps up the film's central dilemmas quickly, easily, and perhaps all too neatly. The ease with which Superman solves seemingly insurmountable problems is, of course, part of his charm, part of his fantasy value. And the ease with which the film's plot dilemmas are resolved is part of the charm of the film as a work of pure entertainment that looks back to simpler and presumably more innocent times in American history. *Star Wars* is again here the closest analogue to *Superman*. Both films, for example, have strong roots in both myth and classical Hollywood film. They feature simple, black-and-white, good-vs.-evil plots of a kind once popular in Hollywood film, but their quasi-allegorical characters tend to have superhuman capabilities, thus providing links with myth. Both *Star Wars* and *Superman* are unabashed works of popular culture, intended primarily for entertainment, and achieving that goal both through impressive special effects and an unpretentious celebration of the kind of simple, straightforward oppositions that had given the pulp fictions of the 1930s their innocent appeal. The films thus combine technological sophistication with moral simplicity, making them paradigmatic expressions of key American national myths.

The simple, innocent morality of these films helped them to appeal to children, but it also had a great appeal for adult audiences in the United

States in the late 1970s. After the trying times of Vietnam and Watergate, American audiences were eager for the kind of reassurance provided by simple verities and uncomplicated expressions of the ultimate power of good to defeat evil. This same hunger on the part of American audiences led fairly soon after the release of *Star Wars* and *Superman* to the election of Ronald Reagan to the U.S. presidency, and the Reagan message—with its call for a return to traditional values, its presentation of international politics as a simple opposition between good and evil, and its belief in the fundamental value of free enterprise—appealed to very much the same sort of desires as did these films.

Among other things, the numerous links between *Superman* and *Star Wars* point to the extent to which *Superman* is, in fact, a story of bene-volent alien invasion and thus a work of science fiction. Indeed, the opening sequence on Krypton is pure science fiction, emphasizing that Krypton is an alien planet with an alien culture and (crystal-based) technology. This sequence also reminds us that Jor-El is a scientist, who not only sends his son Kal-El to earth in a homemade spaceship, but also supplies the infant with information-storage crystals containing the accumulated knowledge of dozens of advanced civilizations from the "twenty-eight known galaxies." However, Kal-El is enjoined from interfering in the history of earth, which might explain the fact that this advanced knowledge is not really utilized in the subsequent plot of the film to the extent that it might have been. After all, sharing such knowledge with the people of earth would represent a definite and powerful intervention in their history.

The failure to explore this advanced alien knowledge in any substan-tive way may make *Superman* weak as a work of science fiction, but Superman is clearly a figure of fantasy and myth more than science fiction. *Superman Returns*, released nearly thirty years after the original *Super-man*, definitely takes Superman in darker and more realistic directions (though not nearly to the extent that *Batman Begins* had done with DC Comics' *other* superhero in 2005), presumably updating the story for a more jaded generation of filmgoers. Among other things, it includes far more in the way of realistic violence, as in one gut-wrenching sequence in which Luthor and his minions (the latter now more sinister than com-ical) brutally beat a Kryptonite-weakened Superman, nearly killing him. *Superman Returns* is also more self-conscious than its predecessors, less able comfortably to proclaim Superman an all-American hero. Here, Su-perman returns to earth after a futile five-year round-trip in space to seek remnants of the civilization of Krypton, thus echoing the long absence of the Superman character from the big screen. This return, declares *Daily Planet* editor Perry White (Frank Langella), is big news, just as Warner Brothers did everything possible to hype the resurrection of the Superman film franchise. White exhorts his staff to concentrate their efforts on covering every aspect of the story of Superman's return, but his instructions are suggestive of the inability of this new film to achieve the mythic innocence of the original *Superman: The Movie*. Rather than declare that Superman is important because he embodies everything American, White simply urges his staff to try to find out whether Superman still stands for "truth, justice, all that stuff."

This replacement of "the American Way" by "all that stuff" suggests a definite cynicism, but the skepticism embodied here seems directed not at Superman but at the American way, which the film seems unwilling to equate with truth and justice in the post-9/11 world of the United States as international bully. As a result, a comparison of these two films provides a fascinating glimpse at the evolution of American film—and American culture as a whole—in the decades between the two films. On the other hand, it is also the case that dropping "the American way" from the list of items to be defended by Superman actually dates back to the beginning of the *Lois & Clark* television series in 1993, in which Superman pointedly tells Lois Lane in an early meeting that he is on earth to defend "truth and justice." In addition, *Superman Returns* is not so much a rejection of the Superman tradition as a self-conscious extension of it. The film quite openly acknowledges its predecessors, to the extent that it is in many ways a sort of nostalgia film designed to appeal not only to a new audience of Superman fans but to fans of the original films as well. Indeed, the film looks back to the past in a number of ways. In addition to its direct references to the original films, the overall design of the film (in terms of sets and costumes) has a nostalgic feel as well. Though the film seems set in a world contemporary to that of its release, it combines styles of clothing and architecture from a variety of decades dating back at least to the 1930s (as in the art deco style of the *Daily Planet* building), making it impossible to place the film exactly in time, just as Metropolis (however associated it might be with New York) is never really located geographically. As I discuss in my book *Postmodern Hollywood* (Praeger, 2007), this lack of historical and geographical specificity is typical of postmodern film, though in this case it can also be attributed to a conscious attempt to achieve a sort of mythic timelessness, as well as to include a specific acknowledgement of the nearly seven decades of Superman as an American cultural icon.

Superman Returns particularly seeks to return to the epic magnitude of *Superman: The Movie*, lost in the gradual descent into farce of the first three sequels. Both films are self-consciously *big*—and both were, at the time they were produced, among the most expensive films ever made. Indeed, almost all of the elements that *Superman Returns* borrows directly from the original seem intended to produce a sense of grandeur. For example, it reproduces the grand style of the original film's opening credits and reuses much of John Williams's original epic music, including the well-known title theme. Singer even brought back a deceased Marlon Brando (using a combination of computer-generated images and footage from the original film) to play the role of Jor-El, much as Kerry Conran's *Sky Captain and the World of Tomorrow* (2004) had used computer magic to bring back legendary (but long dead) British actor Laurence Olivier to play a brief (but key) role.

Superman Returns is a stunningly beautiful film whose state-of-the-art special effects easily eclipse those of the original. Shot entirely in high-definition video, the film is a landmark in the movement from conventional film to video as the medium of choice for moviemakers, especially those who wish to employ extensive digital effects. Whatever else it might be, *Superman Returns* is a masterpiece of filmmaking technology. For example, one of the key technical problems of the original film was the production of believable flying sequences—the film was even marketed with the tagline "You will believe a man can fly." That result was achieved only with considerable suspension of disbelief on the part of audiences, though the film was special enough that most viewers were happy to go along. Meanwhile, the flying sequences themselves were produced mechanically, with an array of wires and harnesses that literally (and sometimes painfully) hoisted Reeve into the air. Singer had access to better and more elaborate flying rigs, as well as more advanced cameras and the latest in digital image generation, which reduced Routh's physical discomfort and led to the production of far more believable flying sequences than in the original. The same can be said for all of the action sequences, which are truly spectacular in *Superman Returns*. Even the settings, as in the presentation of Metropolis (or even the Kent farm in Smallville), look far better than those in *Superman: The Movie*.

All of this said, while *Superman Returns* is an exciting, state-of-the-art action flick, it lacks the genuine magic of the original *Superman*, perhaps because it is so technically accomplished that it becomes more a work of engineering than of art. Most of all, though, *Superman Returns* simply fails to escape the shadow of the original film, especially in the way that Routh's competent (but uninspired) performance fails to dislodge the memory of Reeve's Superman—partly because Routh, rather than trying to make the part his own, at times almost seems to be imitating Reeve, especially vocally. This imitation is often dead-on, but that fact only serves continually to remind the audience that Routh is *not* Reeve. Similarly, twenty-three-year-old Kate Bosworth seems far too young and beautiful to be Lois Lane, who should, in this film, presumably be at least five years older than in the original *Superman* film but instead looks at least ten years younger than Margot Kidder's original Lois.

Surprisingly, the only cast member of *Superman Returns* who does seem to measure up to the original is Kevin Spacey, who in some ways had the biggest shoes to fill. But Spacey, himself an Oscar winner, after all, steps in more than adequately for Gene Hackman as Lex Luthor. Indeed, the casting of Spacey is itself almost an allusion to the earlier films, continuing the tradition of placing a distinguished actor in the role. Meanwhile, Spacey's performance, somewhat like that of Routh, seems designed almost as an homage to his predecessor, and Spacey at times even looks a lot like Hackman. But Spacey's Luthor is darker and more interesting than Hackman's, while maintaining the over-the-top zaniness that made Luthor so much fun in the earlier films. Indie queen Parker Posey is great fun as Hackman's mistress as well, capturing some of the flavor of Perrine's earlier performance, but coming off as a bit spunkier and more willing to cross swords with Luthor.

Superman Returns does go beyond the original *Superman* films in its science fictional exploration of the potential offered by the advanced, crystal-based technology of Krypton. Indeed, while the first half of the film focuses on the stir caused by Superman's return to earth, the second half focuses on Luthor's scheme to hijack Kryptonian technology from the Fortress of Solitude and use it to construct an entirely new (Kryptonite-laced) continent off the east coast of the United States, causing a rise in ocean levels that will leave much of the inhabited world underwater, killing billions. Thus, if Luthor's missile-based plot of *Superman* reflected some of the key anxieties of the cold war years, his plot in *Superman Returns* is also very much of its time, as global warming threatens to bring about catastrophic rises in ocean levels through the melting of the polar ice caps.

Meanwhile, it is almost impossible to ignore the parallels between the role of America in the world of the early twenty-first century (including milituarist interventionism and irresponsible U.S. environmental policies that contribute to global warming) and Luthor's lack of concern for the consequences to others of his self-serving actions (and his haughty decla-ration that no one dare challenge him because of his access to superior military technology). Thus, the film's earlier refusal to continue the tradi-tion of characterizing Superman as a defender of the American way is here enhanced by the way it comes very close to identifying *Luthor* as the real representative of official American ideology, even though the film seems to go out of its way to suggest that the United States would bear the brunt of the catastrophic effects caused by Luthor's new continent. In any case, this film does seem to cast Superman more in the role of a global hero (among other things, it includes media coverage of his heroic feats around the world, not just in America) than an American one.

Even if it does involve advanced alien technology, Luthor's plot (and Superman's subsequent foiling of it) is still pretty weak as science fiction (and full of logical inconsistencies), though it is certainly no more cartoonish and unbelievable than the Luthor plot of *Superman: The Movie*. If anything, there is more drama this time around, as Superman's easy victory in the first film is replaced by an extremely close call in which he nearly dies after being beaten, then stabbed by Luthor with a Kryptonite shiv, after which he topples into the ocean and nearly drowns. Even after he defeats Luthor, summoning every last ounce of strength to hoist Luthor's new continent into space and send it hurtling away from earth, a spent Superman plummets helplessly back to earth and crashes to the ground, then spends an extended stay in a hospital on the brink of death. Superman thus comes off in this film as decidedly more vulnerable, potentially boosting the human interest element of the film. *Superman Returns* also goes well beyond its predecessors in exploring that element through the portrayal of the personal relationships of its characters, which are generally here more fully fleshed out than in the earlier films.

Superman includes a number of sentimental elements, such as the depiction of an aging Martha Kent (played by distinguished film actress Eva Marie Saint) as she waits anxiously, but necessarily anonymously, outside the hospital in which a critically ill Superman lies near death. Her face tells it all as she agonizes over the plight of her adopted son, unable to share her pain with anyone, lest his secret identity be revealed. As with *Superman: The Movie*, much of the emotional element of *Superman* involves the romantic relationship between Superman and Lois Lane, here made significantly more complex by the fact that when Superman returns after a five-year absence, Lois is engaged to be married to journalist Richard White (James Marsden), the nephew of Perry White. Richard is a good man, and Lois seems committed to him, though there is never much doubt in the film that Superman is her true love. All of this is further complicated because Richard and Lois apparently have a young son, Jason (Tristan Lake Leabu), to whom they are both much devoted. During the course of the film, it becomes clear to the audience, however, that Superman is the actual biological father of Jason, who is beginning to demonstrate superpowers (as when he hurls a piano across a room, crushing a villain who menaces his mother). Lois, though, following in the tradition of Jonathan and Martha Kent, has urged the boy to keep his powers a secret, apparently even from Richard.

Richard does not appear to know the boy's true parentage, though he seems to have his suspicions. Still, the film clearly implies that he loves the boy and that with Richard, Lois and Jason have a chance for a normal, happy family life that would never be possible with Superman as husband and father. Superman knows this, too, and the film gains a certain poignancy from his realization that he can never be fully human and must in many ways remain a lonely outsider, unable to experience the normal joys of human life. In one scene, we see Superman perform the morally dubious act of using his superhearing to eavesdrop on Richard and Lois, discussing her earlier encounter with Superman. Lois tells Richard that she never loved Superman, and we see the pain in the face of the Man of Steel as he hears her declaration. We know she's lying (it seems that no one is free of sin in this film), but Superman seems to believe her, or at least to recognize her assertion as a sign that she now prefers to maintain her relationship with Richard, rather than return to Superman. In this sense, the Superman of this film begins to take on some of the existential angst usually associated with a character such as Batman, though Superman's loneliness here remains less dark and more sentimental than Batman's. This sentimentality peaks as Superman, realizing that Jason is his son, visits the sleeping boy and delivers a fatherly soliloquy that echoes the earlier message recorded for him by his own father, Jor-El, in whose footsteps Kal-El now seems fated to follow as a father who can only help and guide his son from a distance.

The presence of Superman's son adds a highly intriguing element that is never quite fully explored in this film, though it does offer interesting possibilities for a potential sequel—which Singer has already signed to direct. As it stands, though, the Jason subplot in *Superman Returns* is a disappointment; it feels a bit tacked-on and never quite gets beyond the level of sentimental cliché, even if the film seems to want to suggest that the Jason story is the film's emotional center (signaled by the way the boy repeatedly plays Hoagy Carmichael's "Heart and Soul" as he practices at the piano). Meanwhile, the failure fully to exploit this aspect of the film is indicative of the shortcomings of the film as a whole. Despite all of the extra human interest elements, *Superman Returns* is ultimately a rather ordinary effects-driven summer blockbuster action film. It is a spectacular film, but one that lacks heart and certainly fails to capture the magic of the original *Superman* movie. The difference between *Superman* and *Superman Returns* can perhaps be summed up in the closing sequence, in which Superman, as in the previous four films, flies into orbit and looks directly into the camera before going off to patrol the planet from space. Here, though, Routh fails to reproduce Reeve's trademark grin, instead settling for a slight hint of a smirk (or perhaps grimace) as he flies by the camera, thus emphasizing in a single moment the darker and heavier tone of *Superman Returns*, while also providing one last reminder that Routh, however well he looks and sounds the part, lacks the charisma that had made Reeve such a success in the role. Still, the lack of magic that plagues *Superman Returns* is as much a matter of the film's context as of any fault in the film itself. With the aid of Singer's digital prestidigitation, it is a simple matter for audiences of *Superman Returns* to believe that a man can fly. In the world of 2006, however, it is more difficult for either filmmakers or filmgoers to imagine simple moral absolutes that he might fly to defend.

2

The *Batman* Film Franchise

Released 1989–2005; Various Directors

BATMAN: SUPERHERO WITH A DARK SIDE

With the Superman film franchise on the ropes with the disaster that was *Superman IV* in 1987, it might have appeared that superhero films had seen their best days, at least for some time to come. Nothing could have been further from the truth. The tremendous success of the film version of *Batman* in 1989, directed by Tim Burton and featuring the unlikely (but highly effective) casting of Michael Keaton in the title role, made it clear that superhero films were alive and well, even if they had come a long way from the original introduction of *Superman: The Movie* in 1978. Indeed, it would be hard to imagine two films being more different than the noirish, dystopian *Batman* and the cheerfully optimistic *Superman*. Then again, Batman and Superman had represented opposite ends of the superhero spectrum since their introduction in the late 1930s.

In collaboration with artist Bill Finger, writer Bob Kane created the character of Batman (originally the Bat-man) in 1939 for the comics division of National Publications (later known as DC Comics) in direct response to the tremendous success of the Superman character for the same company beginning a year earlier. Batman and Superman were thus linked from the very beginning and are nearly contemporaneous. The two have been the leading characters in the DC Comics universe ever since their creation in the 1930s and, especially in the popular imagination (as opposed to die-hard comics' fans), they remain the two best-known superhero figures in American culture.

Batman, on the other hand, is not a superhero in the strictest sense. He is highly intelligent, extremely strong and athletic, and very well trained in the martial arts. His everyday alter ego is billionaire Bruce Wayne, whose wealth gives Batman access to the resources needed to develop the wide array of high-tech devices that he uses to supplement his own abilities as a crime fighter. All of these attributes combine to make Batman a formidable figure, though no one of his abilities is genuinely superhuman. Instead, it is the combination of his various capabilities (along with his courage and dogged determination as a crime fighter) that makes Batman special.

Because he lacks actual superpowers, Batman has always been a much more human figure than Superman. He has also (as emphasized by his dark costume, including a mask, and by his choice of a bat as his emblem) always had a decidedly dark side that sets him distinctly apart from the ever-virtuous Superman. Indeed, Batman is frequently referred to as The Dark Knight, an appellation made especially prominent beginning with Frank Miller's decidedly dark graphic novel *Batman: The Dark Knight Returns* (1986), which features an aging, cynical, and particularly vicious caped crusader. Miller's work was a clear influence on the original *Batman* film, as was Alan Moore's similarly dark *Batman: The Killing Joke* (1988), especially in its impact on the depiction of the Joker in the film.

The most obvious model for the original Batman was the masked hero Zorro, who had been a popular figure in pulp magazines since 1919 and had sprung to particular prominence in 1920 with the success of the silent film *The Mask of Zorro*, with Douglas Fairbanks in the title role. As a crusader against injustice, Zorro wears a black costume with mask and cape. He can also be rather cruel in his dealings with evildoers, while his secret identity is that of an independently wealthy nobleman, anticipating Batman's wealthy and powerful alter ego. But Kane also had darker predecessors in mind when he created Batman, including The Shadow, Dracula, and the murderous title character of the 1926 silent horror film *The Bat*.

With such forerunners, it was little wonder that Batman himself had a dark streak, emphasized in the pulp style of his early stories in *Detective Comics* and explained by the backstory that was supplied for the character. In particular, Batman fights crime because of the brutal murder of his parents in his childhood. This horrific event, which the boy Bruce Wayne personally witnessed, has haunted Wayne ever since, leading him eventually to dedicate himself to bringing criminals to justice, though it is often a violent, vigilante sort of justice of which many in more polite society might disapprove. Batman's persona and costume are specifically designed to strike fear in the hearts of even the most hardened criminals, making him a rather menacing figure. But this menace goes beyond mere style. Unlike

Superman, who tends to use as little physical violence and inflict as little physical harm on his adversaries as possible, Batman can be extremely ruthless, ultraviolent, and even murderous.

Of course, as with Superman, there have been numerous variations, additions, and subtractions to the Batman mythology over the nearly seven decades of his career as an American cultural icon. This evolution adds up to a complex cultural history, made even more so by the complexity and moral ambiguity of Batman himself. There is, for example, an entire library of fan-oriented "guides" to Batman, of which some of the best and most informative are Les Daniels' *Batman: The Complete History* (Chronicle Books, 1999) and Scott Beatty's *Batman: The Ultimate Guide to the Dark Knight* (DK Publishing, 2005). In addition, Chip Kidd's *Batman Collected* (Watson-Guptill Publications, 2001) chronicles the wide array of Batman merchandise that has been marketed over the years.

Given the complexity of the Batman story and the centrality of Batman as a figure in American popular culture, it is not surprising that Batman and his associated mythology have received a substantial amount of attention from academic critics, drawn by the ongoing prominence of this darkest and most violent of superheroes. Volumes such as *The Many Lives of the Batman: Critical Approaches to a Superhero and His Media*, edited by Roberta E. Pearson and William Uricchio (Routledge, 1991), and Will Brooker's *Batman Unmasked: Analyzing a Cultural Icon* (Continuum Books, 2000) have added substantial new insights to our understanding of Batman as a cultural icon, as well as uncovering otherwise forgotten aspects of Batman's long cultural history. For example, Brooker notes that while several *Detective Comics* covers of the World War II years reflected patriotic, prowar concerns, the actual contents of Batman stories during this period seemed largely unconcerned with the war, maintaining their focus on Batman's "parochial" battles with usual foes such as the Penguin and the Joker. For Brooker, this phenomenon illustrates the extent to which Gotham City functions in the Batman comics as a sort of world unto itself, though it also suggests the way in which Batman was always far less of an icon of Americanism than Superman has been.

Like Superman, though, Batman has appeared in a panoply of comics and other media, some differing greatly from others in their characterization of Batman. For example, one of the best known images of Batman comes from the campy *Batman* television series that ran on ABC from 1966 to 1968, with Adam West in the title role. An associated low-budget theatrical film (now available on video as *Batman: The Movie*) that was essentially an extended episode of the series was also released in 1966. The farcical *Batman* series, a signature work of American popular culture in the 1960s, was a huge hit upon its initial broadcasts in early 1966, but its contrived situations, over-the-top acting, and farcically cartoonish presentation quickly grew old with audiences. They also took Batman in new directions that were dramatically different from his heritage in dark, brooding crime drama, while making it difficult for audiences who knew Batman primarily through this series ever to take the character seriously again.

All of that changed with the release of Burton's *Batman* in 1989. Though featuring Keaton, an actor known for his own over-the-top comic performances in such films as Burton's then-recent *Beetlejuice* (1988), this film, clearly influenced by Miller's Dark Knight take on Batman, takes the character seriously indeed. Keaton may not have quite the right look for Batman, but his understated performance gives just the right hint of the darkness and torment that underlie the character of Batman, a suggestion that is perfectly reinforced by the design of the film's Gotham City as a dark, dystopian hotbed of crime and corruption, visually influenced by the noirish future city of *Blade Runner* (1982), but going beyond anything previously seen on film as a visual representation of urban decadence. The film was a smash hit, both critically and commercially. It more than made back its $35 million budget during its first weekend of release and went on to take in more than $250 million in domestic box office. Critics, meanwhile, raved over the film's stunning visuals, though some (including the influential Roger Ebert) complained that the movie was a triumph of style over substance.

In any case, Burton's original Batman film returned the Dark Knight to a central place in the American popular consciousness, and it was no surprise that this original film was followed by a string of sequels. Batman also became even more prominent in the comic-book culture of the 1990s and was a central figure in a number of animated television programs of that decade, of which *Batman: The Animated Series* (1992–1995) was perhaps the most notable and the one that attempted to portray Batman in a spirit most akin to that of the Burton film.

BRIGHT LIGHTS, DARK KNIGHTS: BATMAN GOES TO THE MOVIES

With its groundbreaking visual style, *Batman* was a definite gamble. The gamble paid off. Not only was *Batman* the top-grossing film of 1989, but it subsequently did especially well in video sales. Like *Superman* before it, *Batman* also became the first in a series of films. Indeed, *Batman* is a film clearly designed from the beginning to become the foundation of a franchise, perhaps because it was made by Warner Brothers, who had already had considerable success with the Superman franchise. It is no accident that the first *Batman* film ends as the bat-signal is installed in

Gotham City so that Batman can be called when the city needs his help in future crises, that is, future films.

1992 saw the release of the first sequel, *Batman Returns*, again directed by Burton and again featuring Keaton in the title role. With a much bigger production budget ($80 million), Burton was able to produce even more in the way of dark, disturbing visuals, but the style of the second film is still essentially that of the first, though perhaps a bit more cartoonish. This similarity may account for the fact that it had somewhat less of an impact on audiences (and did somewhat less well at the box office, though it was still a major hit, with over $160 million in domestic box office receipts). Here, Danny DeVito stars as the main villain of the piece, the dwarfish, deformed Penguin. The Penguin has a genius with gadgets that rivals Batman's own, but he has lived his entire life in the sewers of Gotham City after having been abandoned by his parents in his infancy due to his deformities and vicious disposition. Desperate for acceptance and validation, the Penguin attempts to get himself elected the mayor of Gotham City, with the support of sinister business tycoon Max Shreck (Christopher Walken). Penguin's plan is, of course, foiled by Batman, whose intervention leads to the villain's death.

Named for the legendary German actor who played a vampire so well in the silent classic *Nosferatu* (1922) that many suspected him of being a vampire himself, Shreck is described as Gotham's leading citizen, and the fact that he turns out to be every bit as evil as the Penguin makes a vague gesture toward criticism of capitalism as a form of legalized crime. But this film is about atmosphere, not social criticism. That atmosphere, meanwhile, is significantly enhanced by the performance of Michelle Pfeiffer as Catwoman, a complex blend of heroine and villain who is both an ally and a foe of Batman, while her alter ego, Shreck's formerly frumpy assistant Selina Kyle, becomes Bruce Wayne's love interest in the film.

The Catwoman character (a longtime staple of the Batman legacy) is clearly presented as a sort of female version of Batman, who himself tells her, "We're the same. Split right down the center." She is apparently killed eight times in *Batman Returns,* but (as a cat) still has one life left. The character was interesting enough eventually to return in her own spinoff film, 2004's *Catwoman,* with Halle Berry in the title role. The film was a bust, partly because it made Catwoman less dark and more virtuous than she had been in *Batman Returns.* In the meantime, the Batman sequence itself, beginning with *Batman Forever* (1995), had turned away from the darkness of the first two films, in which Batman's personal darkness threatened to make him an unattractive figure, virtually indistinguishable from the criminals he so despised. However, retracing the arc of the Superman film sequence, the lightening of tone in *Batman Forever* turned out to be merely a step in a decline toward campiness and silliness, which would eventually result in the all-out self-parody of the next sequel, *Batman & Robin* (1997). *Batman Forever* also marked a shift in director from Burton, a leading postmodernist image-maker, to the more commercially oriented Joel Schumacher, though Burton still served as a producer. The casting also took a significant turn. Nicole Kidman appears here as criminal psychologist Dr. Chase Meridian, continuing the trend of featuring one of Hollywood's top female leads as Batman's love interest. The casting of the peripatetic Jim Carrey as the Riddler and top actor Tommy Lee Jones as Two-Face continued the trend of major stars as the villains, potentially overshadowing Batman himself. The cast of characters is expanded in *Batman Forever* to include Batman's young sidekick Robin (Chris O'Donnell), but the real change is that Batman here is played by Val Kilmer, in a change of casting that probably could never have been done with the Superman films. This change was presumably made possible by the fact that Batman's appearance is determined primarily by his costume and mask, making the casting change less distracting to audiences, though it is also the case that Keaton never made the role of Batman his own in the way that Christopher Reeve *was* both Superman and Clark Kent.

Kilmer isn't awful as Batman, but he is surrounded by a cartoonish environment that consistently defeats his attempt to play Batman straight, in the manner of Keaton. Kilmer is also defeated by truly bad dialogue and by the campy performances of the rest of the cast. Even Kidman's Meridian is cartoonish, and her supposedly snappy exchanges with Batman—presumably meant to recall the witty dialogue in such noir films as *Double Indemnity* (1944)—come off more like parodies of film noir dialogue. Meanwhile, the two main villains dominate the film even more than the Joker and the Penguin had dominated the first two films, with Jones surprisingly delivering a performance that is almost as over-the-top as that of the hyperactive, rubber-faced Carrey. Though *Batman Forever* contains better action sequences than its predecessors, the remainder of the film represents a significant decline from the first two Batman films as well, especially in the way Schumacher responded to criticism that the first two films had been too dark to be suitable for children by virtually eliminating the elements of gritty noir drama that had made the first two films special. Gotham itself is visually more garish and cartoonish, while even the camera movements are exaggerated, giving the film a more cartoonish look (almost reminiscent of the 1960s television series), especially in the frequent shots of shocked villains contorting their faces into the lens as Batman foils their various schemes.

Schumacher returned to direct *Batman & Robin* and O'Donnell returned as Robin, here playing an expanded role. Otherwise, however, the casting took some bizarre turns, the strangest of which was the deployment of Arnold Schwarzenegger, then still a major action star, in a campy turn as the film's chief villain, Mr. Freeze. Meanwhile, George Clooney, then still very early in what would eventually become a distinguished and successful career as a film actor, was (mis)cast in the role of Batman. Clooney said in later interviews that he played Batman as gay, which might actually have been interesting, given the long legacy of questions about the sexuality of the character, whose fetishistic costume would certainly fit right in in a gay leather bar. Clooney's portrayal, though, comes off simply as wooden and awkward, making Batman seem almost like a crime-fighting robot.

The fourth Batman film followed in the footsteps of *Superman IV* by nearly killing off the franchise in which it participated. However, while the later *Superman Returns* was not really able to restore the Superman franchise to its former glory, the 2005 Batman comeback film, *Batman Begins*, was by many accounts the finest of all the Batman films. A story of the origins of Batman as a superhero, the film draws upon a range of Batman comics, perhaps most centrally Frank Miller's graphic novel *Batman: Year One* (first published in single issue form in 1986–1987), Jeph Loeb's *Batman: The Long Halloween* (single issue publication 1996–1997), and the 1989 single-issue comic by Dennis O'Neil and Dick Giordano, *Batman: The Man Who Falls.* Helmed by young British director Christopher Nolan and featuring Christian Bale in the title role, *Batman Begins* certainly comes the closest of any of the Batman films to capturing the psychological complexity that makes Batman unique among superheroes. It also captures, but in a grittier way, the noir-like atmosphere of Burton's two *Batman* films, probably thanks partly to the contributions of screenwriter David S. Goyer, who cowrote the script with Nolan and who had earlier scripted such films as *Dark City* (1998) and all three of the *Blade* films. It also helped that Bale may be the first Batman who was actually ideal for the role. In addition, Nolan was perfectly suited to recapture some of the dark visual flair of Burton's Batman films, while adding his own distinctive touches, aided by a vast $150 million budget. The film was successful enough (drawing rave reviews and grossing nearly $400 million in worldwide box office) that both Nolan and Bale have been signed to make still another sequel, tentatively entitled *The Dark Knight* and slated for release in 2008. Together, the first *Batman* and the recent *Batman Begins* demonstrate the potential of Batman as a movie hero.

BATMAN AND *BATMAN BEGINS*

Before *Batman*, Tim Burton had directed only two feature films, *Pee-wee's Big Adventure* (1985) and *Beetlejuice* (1988). These two highly interesting films established Burton, a former Disney animator, as a director with a distinctive visual flair. Both are farcical comedies, though they both contain hints of darkness. In addition, Burton's earlier work for Disney, including the shorts *Vincent* (1982) and *Frankenweenie* (1984), had shown a definite unDisneylike dark streak. It was with *Batman* that Burton's dark side and his flair for the visual truly came together, partly because of the subject matter and partly because of the simple fact that, for the first time, Burton had a substantial budget with which to realize his cinematic vision.

In *Batman*, that vision is dazzling, perfectly enhanced by Danny Elfman's score, just as rousing and majestic as John Williams's score for *Superman*, but decidedly darker and more ominous—with just an occasional nod and wink to the film's more cartoonish elements. *Batman* is, however, typical of all of Burton's films in that the visual elements dominate the film, leaving it weak on plot. Indeed, as I have noted in my book *Postmodern Hollywood* (Praeger, 2007), Burton's films sometimes come off almost like slide shows, as a series of dazzling images only loosely tied together by plot. And it is certainly at the level of plot that both of Burton's Batman films are at their weakest, which could be a serious problem given their participation in the superhero genre, a form generally strong on plot.

Batman, however, is more interested in capturing the look and feel of its menacing Gotham City, which here might just as easily have been named Gothic City. The film narrates the first appearance of Batman in the city amid a fresh wave of crime that has brought the already crime-ridden city to the brink of total anarchy. It does not, however, explain in any detail the origins of Batman, simply stipulating that billionaire Bruce Wayne, long tormented by the death of his parents and aided by his faithful butler, Alfred (Michael Gough), has decided to don the garb of the caped crusader to intervene in the crime wave. In the meantime, the situation is made even worse when mobster Jack Napier (Jack Nicholson) is deformed into a permanent exaggerated grin in an accident in which Batman is involved and which was caused by the attempts of his own boss, criminal kingpin Carl Grissom (Jack Palance) to do him in because Napier is having an affair with the aging Grissom's beautiful young wife Alicia (Jerry Hall).

The bitter Napier, obviously unhinged, embarks on a spree of bizarre crimes as The Joker, beginning with the revenge killing of Grissom. He is also determined to wreak revenge on Batman, especially after Batman intervenes in his attempt to abduct prominent photojournalist Vicki Vale (Kim Basinger), with whom Napier has become enamored and who is also the new love interest of Bruce Wayne. Here, Keaton plays Wayne as suave and sophisticated, but thoughtful and decidedly quieter and more reserved than some depictions of Wayne (as a noisy playboy swinger) have been. Wayne, especially in his courtship of Vale, even has an aw-shucks side that suggests he is really just a regular guy, despite all his wealth.

Eventually, the Joker does manage to abduct Vale, though with Batman (who has meanwhile deduced that it was a young Napier who had killed his parents years earlier) in hot pursuit. In the ensuing action sequence, Batman predictably catches up, defeats a series of the Joker's minions, then polishes off the Joker, who is sent plummeting to his death as he falls while attempting a daring escape by helicopter. Batman is helpless to prevent the fall (and barely manages to save himself and Vale from a similar fate), but it is nevertheless a key marker of the difference between Batman and Superman that Batman's opponents often die, while Superman virtually never kills. As the film ends, Batman has announced his ongoing availability to help fight crime in Gotham City. Meanwhile, Vale heads off for a rendezvous with Wayne, riding in Wayne's limo with Alfred at the wheel—and possibly suspecting that Wayne might secretly be Batman.

This seemingly happy ending does not, however, obscure the film's overall dark tone. In this sense, *Batman* is a very typical Burton film, one that might, at first glance, appear to be an entertainment for children, but one containing dark and disturbing elements of a kind hardly suited for younger viewers. This is true even of the elements of the film that seem most cartoonish, particularly in Nicholson's spectacular over-the-top performance as the Joker. Nicholson's performance is hilarious, but in a deranged way that suggests deep psychological disturbance, making the Joker terrifying even beyond the way that clowns are often frightening to children.

In addition, when compared with the understated performance of Keaton, Nicholson's performance establishes a tendency that would continue over the next three Batman films of having Batman play it straight, in a mode of gritty, noirish realism, while the villains are overtly cartoonish, preposterous, and exaggerated. As a result, the confrontations between Batman and the villains become confrontations between different cultural spheres, making *Batman* and its immediate sequels a strange generic mix of film noir and campy cartoon, with the balance of the mix gradually shifting to the cartoonish side as the sequence proceeds—at least until the advent of *Batman Begins*, which reverses the trend and for the first time plays the Batman story entirely straight, treating both the hero and the villains in the noir mode, flavored in this case by a hint of Asian martial arts pictures.

The unusual mixture of film noir with cartoon, combining genres with jarringly different tones, is absolutely crucial to the overall texture of the Batman films. Of course, many postmodern films have gotten considerable mileage out of such generic combinations, with the comics-inflected mixture of film noir and science fiction in *Blade Runner* being a particularly successful example—and one that is especially relevant to *Batman*. However, the combination of noir and cartoon is a particularly uneasy one that many critics have rejected, feeling that film noir (with its cynical tone and rejection of the notion of heroism) and superhero cartoons (with their typically optimistic vision of virtuous heroes saving the day) are simply too different comfortably to reside in the same film. That difficulty may account for the positive critical reception of *Batman Begins*, in which the cartoon element is almost entirely absent. On the other hand, all of the Batman films—like the entire history of Batman as a cultural phenomenon—actually draw upon a number of genres. For example, Batman's reliance on high-tech gadgetry has always brought an element of science fiction into his various representations, with science fiction becoming an especially strong element in Batman stories beginning in the late 1950s, at a time when science fiction itself had moved to the forefront of the American cultural imagination. In addition, especially after the popular success of the James Bond films (beginning with *Dr. No* in 1962), Batman's gadgets tend to evoke memories of the cold war espionage drama. It is certainly the case that the aging scientist Lucius Fox (Morgan Freeman), who supplies Bruce Wayne with the high-tech devices he needs in order to become Batman in *Batman Begins*, plays much the same role for Batman as had the figure of Q for James Bond.

Fox is only one of several new elements that inject new energies and motifs into the Batman film series in *Batman Begins*. Most obvious here is the contribution of British director Christopher Nolan, even younger (he was thirty-five when the film was released) and less experienced than the then relatively unknown Burton had been when chosen to helm *Batman*. Still Nolan's credentials were strong. Both *Memento* (2000) and *Insomnia* (2002) were powerful films, strong on gritty noir atmosphere but also effectively narrated in highly inventive and unconventional ways. By the time Nolan followed *Batman Begins* with *The Prestige* in 2006, he had established himself as a leading postmodernist filmmaker, with particular technical strengths as an image-maker, just as Burton would eventually do.

As far as new aspects in the film itself are concerned, the most obvious are the martial arts elements, which begin as a bitter and tormented Bruce Wayne travels to Asia in search of enlightenment, only to wind up in a squalid prison camp, fighting with the other prisoners. Soon afterward, he is rescued from the prison by the mysterious Henri Ducard (Liam Neeson, to an extent building on his credentials as a dark, shadowy figure from 1990's *Darkman*). He then travels to the hidden mountaintop training camp (in an unidentified Tibet-like location) of the League of Shadows, a thousands-of-years-old top-secret organization of ninja-like agents, headed by Ducard and the suitably inscrutable Ra's Al Ghul (Ken Watanabe). At the camp, Wayne not only receives advanced martial arts training, but learns mental discipline as well. In particular, he learns to conquer and even embrace his deepest fears, which in his case involve a deep-seated horror of bats, rooted in a childhood experience in which he fell into an abandoned well and was attacked by a swarm of the winged rodents. The other aspects of the genesis of the Batman character as presented in the film are compelling as well, and additional interest is generated by new takes on such well-known characters as the butler Alfred (played by Michael Caine as younger and tougher than the elderly gent to whom we are accustomed) and Police Commissioner Gordon (here played by Gary Oldman as a young and upcoming police sergeant, one of the very few honest cops on Gotham's corrupt police force). The Bond-like tradition of featuring a Batman babe in a central role is here continued through the portrayal of idealistic assistant district attorney Rachel Dawes (Katie Holmes), whose own dedication to fighting crime makes her potentially the most interesting female lead in a Batman film since Pfeiffer's Catwoman, though the youthful (and even more youthful-looking) Holmes is probably miscast in the part.

Such familiar elements help to make *Batman Begins* attractive to fans of the earlier Batman films and of Batman in general. As a whole, however, *Batman Begins* is an effective drama that stands very much on its own and that clearly sees itself more as the beginning of a new Batman film sequence than as a continuation of the old one. The title of the film thus has a double meaning: not only does the film narrate Bruce Wayne's initial invention of his Batman persona, but it seems to see itself as a sort of reboot of the entire Batman legacy. Nolan's visual presentation of Gotham City is less striking than Burton's more expressionistic vision, if only because it has Burton's films as a predecessor. Nolan's city also shows the influence of *Blade Runner*: though grim, dirty, and decaying, the city is also slightly futuristic, featuring such elements as prominent monorails moving high above the city's streets. All in all, though, Nolan's Gotham City is decidedly more realistic than Burton's, in keeping with the generally realistic texture of the film.

Gotham is still a troubled city, though, riddled with crime and corruption—so much so that Ra's Al Ghul and the League of Shadows have determined that the city must be destroyed (somewhat in the mode of the Biblical Sodom and Gomorrha) in order to cleanse the world of its moral contamination. While still training with the league, Wayne learns of this plan to wipe Gotham from the face of the earth and is even asked to help lead the assault. In response, he battles the entire garrison of ninjas and destroys the camp, killing the man identified as Ra's Al Ghul. He almost kills Ducard as well, but saves him in return for his own earlier rescue from prison. Later, however, we learn that Wayne killed an impostor and that Ducard is the real Ra's Al Ghul, as he resurfaces in Gotham City and nearly completes its destruction, only to be foiled (in a spectacular action sequence) by Batman, working with the help of Gordon.

Ra's Al Ghul is in fact a villain from the comics, having first appeared as Batman's foe in *Batman* 232 (June 1971). Still, he is a departure from the kind of supervillain generally associated with the comics, having reportedly been created specifically as a Bond-style villain in response to the popularity of the James Bond films and novels. Ra's Al Ghul is certainly outside the range of typical film noir villains, adding an almost supernatural element that is lacking in the film's other villains, though his powers are not as clearly supernatural here as they are in the comics. In the film, he is much grittier and more believable than the outrageous villains of the earlier Batman films. He is also a much more complex figure than his predecessors in that he seeks neither revenge nor personal gain. He is not even evil in the usual sense, but seems genuinely to believe that he is doing a good thing for the world by attempting to destroy Gotham City. He is not a man without morals, but simply a man with his own unconventional system of morals and with the resolve to do whatever is necessary to impose his system on the world. In some ways, the film's most frightening villain, however, is Dr. Jonathan Crane (Cillian Murphy), who is again not immoral, but simply amoral. A psychiatrist (working, partly unwittingly, for Ra's Al Ghul), Crane has developed a powerful drug that induces immediate violent panic and horror, making its victims imagine that their deepest and most dreaded nightmares are coming true. Crane is a bit over the top, but not cartoonish in the mode of the earlier Batman villains. He is genuinely creepy, adding significantly to the film's dark atmosphere, but as a soulless scientist and physician who cares nothing about his patients but only about pursuing his own interests, Crane is a believable modern nightmare.

Ra's Al Ghul plans to destroy Gotham by dosing the entire population with Crane's drug, causing the citizens to tear the city (and each other) apart in their subsequent panic. This plan doesn't really make sense, partly because it leaves no room for help to come to the city from the outside, though this aspect of the film is perfectly consistent with the long legacy of treating Gotham as a sort of microcosmic world unto itself. In any case, the threatened destruction of Gotham adds considerable suspense to the film, while the depiction of the city's decay gains considerable interest in *Batman Begins* because of its greater emphasis (relative to the

Burton films) on the plight of the city's impoverished, forgotten, and largely homeless underclass as the true victims of the city's decline. This emphasis, consistent with the film's quest for realism, also introduces an element of social criticism into *Batman Begins*. This criticism is further enhanced by the film's depiction of the flipside of this poverty—the city's wealthy and powerful—as decadent and corrupt. For one thing, the powerful and well-connected crime lord Carmine Falcone (Tom Wilkinson) moves easily among the upper echelons of Gotham society, suggesting that his own criminal inclinations are perfectly compatible with the attitudes of the city's most "respectable" citizens. For another, a major element of the plot of the film involves the machinations of the evil capitalist Richard Earle (Rutger Hauer), who, along with his sinister associates, has seized control of Wayne Enterprises during Bruce's seven-year absence while training in Asia. Earle is the prototypical heartless capitalist, interested only in turning a profit, even if he must take the company in directions (such as weapons development) completely incompatible with the virtuous vision of the Wayne family in originally building the company. The film clearly implies that the poverty of so many in Gotham is largely due to the greed of unscrupulous operators such as Earle and Falcone (clearly depicted here as birds of a feather), who have diverted a significant share of the city's resources for their own selfish and socially irresponsible purposes.

As Wayne returns to Gotham City from Asia, Earle is in the process of taking Wayne Enterprises public in a maneuver that will take the company out of Wayne family control and make Earle himself fabulously wealthy. When Wayne asks about the plan, Earle (regarding Wayne as an ignorant and irresponsible playboy) condescendingly explains that it is "complicated." Earle, in fact, clearly has contempt for the entire Wayne family, including Bruce's father, who devoted himself to helping others through working as a physician, preferring to let others run the Wayne company business. That decision might have been a bad one, given that it has paved the way for an unscrupulous operator such as Earle to gain the helm of the company. Bruce Wayne cannily turns the tables, however, aided by Earle's underestimation of him. Wayne sets up a complex structure of dummy financial institutions that allows him secretly to buy up most of the company's stock in the initial public offering. Back in control of the company, he fires the stunned Earle and makes the virtuous Fox (a former top executive of Wayne Enterprises who has recently been fired by Earle) the new CEO, a role he had long played in the comics.

Earle's "crimes" are made even more sinister by the fact that he has apparently done nothing illegal, as opposed to Batman, who repeatedly breaks the law. Here, the system itself is rotten, and there is little correlation between legality and virtue. Meanwhile, the economic nature of

Earle's misdeeds suggests the element of economic injustice that underlies the capitalist system of Gotham, where so many suffer in such deep poverty, while others revel in ostentatious wealth. Meanwhile, Earle's machinations echo the discovery in the film that the League of Shadows had tried once before, decades earlier, to destroy Gotham through economic manipulations that plunged the city into a deep depression—again suggesting that the city is a world of its own, with its own independent economy.

It was during this depression that Bruce Wayne's parents had been killed by a mugger driven to desperation by his own poverty. Subsequently, it was the city's shocked reaction to their deaths that galvanized the population into positive action to end the depression, only to have the city later sink even further into corruption and malaise. The resultant parallels between the history of Gotham City and the history of the United States (which survived its own depression in the 1930s only to find itself in a seeming moral crisis by the early twenty-first century) are inescapable, if not pursued in detail within the film.

In the course of *Batman Begins*, Wayne Manor is burned to the ground, destroyed by the League of Shadows. But, as the film ends, Wayne vows to rebuild the mansion exactly as it was before—except with a few changes to give better access to the newly established batcave. He and Gordon, now promoted to lieutenant, set up the bat-signal, echoing the end of Burton's *Batman* and paving the wave for a potential string of future adventures (i.e., sequels). Indeed, there is plenty of work left for Batman to do, and Gotham's problems have hardly been solved as the film ends. Ra's Al Ghul has been killed (apparently) in a spectacular monorail crash, but Crane is still at large, along with half the inmates of an insane asylum he had earlier emptied. Gotham remains a grim, threatening place for which Batman is the appropriate hero. By the end of the film, Dawes has learned that Bruce Wayne, a man she once loved, is Batman. But she realizes that her Bruce Wayne no longer exists. The Wayne she now sees is merely a mask, while Batman is his true identity—and must remain so as long as the world is the dark place it is. She hopes, however, that someday the world can be changed so that Batman is no longer needed and her Wayne can return. Given the film's apparent desire to establish parallels between the history of Gotham and the history of the United States, the element of social criticism in this ending—which stipulates that Gotham is in the throes of a moral crisis exacerbated by a crisis in leadership—is quite clear.

In the meantime, the first sequel is even directly previewed as the film ends: Gordon reveals to Batman that a new supercriminal, the Joker, is now threatening Gotham. Indeed, the Joker will be featured in *The Dark Knight*, played by Heath Ledger in a bit of unlikely casting that adds interest to the already intriguing question of how an inherently cartoonish villain such as the Joker can function in the grim universe of this new Batman sequence. After all, the character of the Joker is the crux of the difference between *Batman* and *Batman Begins*. Nicholson's highly entertaining (if rather disturbing) portrayal of the Joker introduces an element of campy comedy that, whatever its dark side, would be entirely out of place in the latter film. In addition, the key action sequences of *Batman* revolve around the Joker's crimes and Batman's attempts to thwart them, which make them come off more as parodies of action sequences. *Batman Begins*, on the other hand, is just as strong on atmosphere as is Burton's film, but its more realistic tone allows it comfortably to include some extremely effective action sequences, including one of the most spectacular chase scenes ever filmed, as a fleet of police cars vainly pursues the new high-tech Batmobile (now much more technologically believable than in the original films) through the streets of Gotham.

Ultimately, the differences between *Batman* and *Batman Begins* are testimony to the complexity of Batman and the comics universe in which he resides, both of which allow for a wide range of possible characterizations. The differences between the films can also be taken as a commentary on American film history in the intervening sixteen years, including a trend toward better and more expensive special effects, as well as a shift to greater darkness in the typical tone of American films. But film history is largely a reflection of the broader history of the world at large, and the differences between *Batman* and *Batman Begins* also indicate changes in American culture between 1989 and 2005. The doubleness of *Batman* was perfect for a conflicted post-Reagan America still governed, at the time of the release of the first *Batman* film, by Reagan's hand-picked successor but growing skeptical about both the Reagan economic plan and the movie-derived, cliché-ridden rhetoric of Reaganite patriotism. On the other hand, *Batman Begins*, despite the central role played by its British director and numerous British cast members, seems perfect for the more cynical, but more fearful post-9/11 and post-Iraq invasion America of 2005.

3

The Crow
Released 1994; Director Alex Proyas

UNDERGROUND COMICS COME TO HOLLYWOOD—OR NORTH CAROLINA

Superman and Batman, the longtime mainstream stars of DC Comics, dominated the field of films based on comics from the late 1970s well into the 1990s. One of the first films to break this dominance was 1994's *The Crow*, whose vision of urban darkness was clearly influenced by the Gotham City of the first two Batman films, but which in many ways was a radical departure from the tradition of Superman and Batman big-budget blockbusters. For one thing, the film was based not on well-known cultural icons, but on the hero of an original underground comic book series by James O'Barr (published in 1989). For another, it was a relatively low-budget (roughly $15 million) film made by independent studio Carolco Pictures (whose studios, where *The Crow* was made, were located in North Carolina, rather than Hollywood, for budgetary reasons). It thus lacked the major studio backing of the Warner Brothers' Batman and Superman films, though Carolco had produced a few major hits, most notably James Cameron's *Terminator 2: Judgment Day* (1991). Still, despite the low budget for the film and the lack of name recognition for the comic-book character on which it was based, *The Crow* was a hit, grossing nearly $100 million worldwide. Part of this success no doubt arose from the publicity surrounding the fact that the film's star, Brandon Lee (son of martial arts film legend Bruce Lee), was accidentally shot and killed during the filming of a scene for the film. The film was thus completed and distributed after the death of its star, adding irony to fact that the events of the film itself take place after the death of the protagonist, who must rise from the dead in order to pursue his mission. But *The Crow* also features an extremely effective combination of subject matter, visual style, and music that made the film a success in its own right, especially with young adult audiences, with whom it became a cult favorite. Indeed, *The Crow* proved popular enough that it became the founding film in its own movie franchise, though the three sequels (each with a different star and director) have failed to approach the aesthetic or financial success of the original. *The Crow* also came to television in the one-season series *The Crow: Stairway to Heaven*, which ran during 1998 and 1999 in Canada and was subsequently aired on the Sci Fi Channel in the United States.

O'Barr's original comics (eventually published and now back in print as a single volume graphic novel) derived their darkness from O'Barr's own attempts to deal with the sense of loss and despair that resulted from the death of his girlfriend in an accident caused by a drunk driver. In an attempt to cope with his feelings, O'Barr subsequently joined the Marines and was stationed in Germany, where he illustrated military manuals and began (in 1981) early work on the development of what would become *The Crow* comic-book series. It was not until 1989 that the comic would finally be published, but it was then a major success in the underground comics world, becoming the top-selling black-and-white independent comic of all time. O'Barr's own suffering and quest for catharsis inform every page of *The Crow*, a poetic and emotionally powerful work that captures, both thematically and stylistically, a sense of darkness and existential angst that have made it a favorite of the Goth subculture, but that have also appealed to a broader spectrum of youthful readers—the same group that made the film adaptation such a success.

BACK FROM THE DEAD: REVENGE AS CATHARSIS IN *THE CROW*

The Crow begins with a panoramic nighttime shot of a dark and decaying city, illuminated by numerous fires that redden the sky. The film's opening thus closely echoes that of Ridley Scott's *Blade Runner* (1982), establishing that film as a crucial predecessor, especially in the look of its decaying city, shown almost exclusively at night in the rain. On-screen text in *The Crow* tells us that it is Devil's Night (October 30), and we eventually learn that arson is an annual Devil's Night tradition in this city, which is never named. However, the "celebration" of Devil's Night is normally associated with the real-world city of Detroit, where annual outbursts of arson and other acts of vandalism by hooligans date back at least to the

1930s and became a prominent tradition in the 1970s. They were still a tradition in 1994 when the film was released, having been supplemented by ordinary businessmen and other citizens destroying their own property so they could blame the destruction on Devil's Night thugs and collect the insurance. Partly because of negative attention brought to the phenomenon by *The Crow* on its release in 1994, the destruction associated with Devil's Night would lead to the official organization, beginning in 1995, of curfews and "Angel's Night" programs, in which neighborhood patrols walk the streets of Detroit in an attempt to quell the violence and destruction of "Devil's Night." In any case, the very name of the "holiday," combined with its proximity to Halloween, adds an air of the demonic and the supernatural, helping to establish an appropriate atmosphere for the events to follow.

Meanwhile, the premise of the film is also established early on in voiceover narration that informs us that some cultures believe that crows escorted the souls of the recently deceased to the land of the dead and that sometimes these crows bring the dead souls back to the land of the living to right certain egregious wrongs that make it impossible for the souls to rest in the afterlife. Crows do, in fact, figure in many world mythologies, often as figures of evil or death: it may be no accident that the collective noun for a group of crows is a "murder." On the other hand, crows are sometimes associated with death in positive ways and are indeed associated with transitions into the afterlife, though neither the comic nor the film is particularly interested in an accurate portrayal of any particular mythology involving crows.

The action of the film commences with a cut to a wrecked loft where police are investigating a recent gruesome crime. They are led by one Sergeant Albrecht (Ernie Hudson) who seems to be one of the few honest cops on the force—a fact that may be responsible for his recent demotion. Albrecht (who is a minor, incidental character in the comic) will ultimately become an ally of the Crow, much as a young Jim Gordon would later aid Batman in *Batman Begins* (2005). It turns out that the loft had been the home of protagonist Eric Draven (played by Lee) and his beautiful fiancée, Shelly Webster (Sofia Shinas), who have been viciously attacked by a gang of thugs. Draven lies dead in the street below, while Shelly, brutally beaten and raped, clings to life before being taken to the hospital (where she dies after thirty hours of agony, with Albrecht at her side). Meanwhile, the scene gains poignancy from the fact that Draven and Shelly were scheduled to be married the very next day, while Shelly leaves behind a young street urchin, Sarah (Rochelle Davis), whom she had been taking care of.

The film, having established this background, jumps forward by one year, to the next Devil's Night, when a crow with supernatural powers visits Draven's grave and brings him temporarily back to life so that he can seek revenge against those who killed him and Shelly, thus allowing their souls to rest at last. Indeed, the basic plot of *The Crow* is a simple revenge fantasy as Draven systematically seeks out and kills his own killers—though it is clear that he seeks revenge not for his own death, but for the killing of Shelly and of the beautiful love they shared. These killings also bring about his own emotional catharsis, making it possible for his soul to rest at last. This basic premise allows for considerable action and provides a sort of justification for the ultraviolent nature of that action. However, the basic revenge plot of the film serves merely as a scaffolding on which to hang the film's powerful urban visual imagery, post-punk alternative rock soundtrack, and strange atmospheric combination of bleakness and beauty, despair, and hope.

In addition, the plot is enhanced by the fact that the resurrected Draven has been endowed with a number of superhuman powers. For example, he has the strength of ten men and is virtually indestructible. He can leap from rooftops without injury; knives and bullets can wound him, but the wounds magically heal within seconds, providing some interesting visual effects. He also seems to be able to come and go undetected, almost ghostlike. Finally, he has psychic powers as well; he can read the minds of others, absorbing their memories and experiences, and he can later pass those memories and experiences on to others. The Crow thus participates, though in a highly unusual way, in the superhero genre, even if the mainstream superhero he resembles most is Batman, who lacks the Crow's supernatural abilities. For example, the Crow is a dark and tormented figure who seems to come out only at night. He is also an imposing figure whose appearance seems designed to strike fear into the hearts of the villains he pursues. He dresses all in black and sports a wild mane of dark hair that frames a face done in eerie black-and-white clown-like makeup. Further, at the scene of each of his killings, he leaves a calling card, inscribing his crow-shaped insignia (generally either in fire or in blood) as a message to the other criminals on his list. This insignia is again reminiscent of Batman's bat-shaped emblem, though this sort of marking goes back at least to Batman's central forerunner, Zorro.

The Crow's program of revenge takes on an additional dimension in the way it conforms to the notion of *contrapasso*, or "counter-suffering," by which the souls in hell in Dante's *Inferno* receive punishments that are specifically designed to correspond to the sins they committed while alive. Here, Draven kills each of the four thugs who killed him and Shelly in a manner that echoes their own roles in the crime and their general criminal inclinations. Thus, Tin Tin (Laurence Mason), an expert in killing with knives, is killed with his own weapons, made into a sort of human pin-cushion. Draven next kills the drug-loving Funboy (Michael Massee) with multiple injections of morphine, after first rescuing Sarah's mother Darla (Anna Thomson) from Funboy's clutches, cleansing her of drugs and sending her back to begin caring properly for her neglected daughter. The next thug, T-Bird (David Patrick Kelly), is an arson specialist who is sent to a fiery death when Draven straps a bomb between the villain's legs, setting it to explode as T-Bird's car goes off a pier. Finally, the last thug, Skank (Angel David), who had earlier thrown Draven from a window in the loft, is killed by being thrown from a window, following a spectacular action sequence in which the Crow interrupts a board meeting in which the crime lord Top Dollar (Michael Wincott) is exhorting his minions to go out and create spectacular explosions that will overcome the banal event that he sees Devil's Night (which he supposedly invented) as becoming.

Wincott, incidentally, is a highlight of the film. His Top Dollar is brilliantly menacing, endowed with a strong air of perversion, taking his greatest joys from the pains of others. Top Dollar is very much a comic-book character, even though his role is greatly expanded in the film from that in the original comic books, so that his portrayal is mostly original to the film. Dressing in vaguely nineteenth-century garb, he is a lover of exotic swords, of which he has a large collection and which he loves to use to skewer his victims. Yet he is also (within the context of the world of the film) quite believable in the unlikely role of a criminal kingpin who is more interested in creating chaos and mayhem for sheer sport than for turning a profit. The air of decadence that surrounds Top Dollar is greatly enhanced through his relationship with his sinister half-sister Myca (Bai Ling). This relationship is clearly sexual, though in a seemingly twisted way. In one scene, for example, they have just had sex with another woman, with whom they apparently got so rough that they "broke her." Viewing the dead body, Myca grabs her knife and begins to cut out the eyes—which she and Top Dollar later burn, inhaling the smoke and apparently getting high from it.

Such bizarre scenes help to establish the strong *good vs. evil* opposition that informs the film, thus ensuring that audiences will not be put off by the Crow's violence in meting out retribution. The film comes dangerously close to a combination of racism and sexism in its stereotypical portrayal of the Asian woman Myca as an emblem of Oriental perversion. However, Myca is apparently only half Asian (she and the Caucasian Top Dollar supposedly have the same father), and she is certainly no more evil or perverse than her brother—or any number of other characters in the film. Ultimately, Myca and Top Dollar also meet appropriate fates: the eye fetishist Myca falls to her death after her eyes are pecked out by the magical crow, while Top Dollar falls from a rooftop and is impaled on a spike, just as he had impaled so many others on his sword.

Such colorful villains (Jon Polito's turn as a sleazy pawnbroker in league with the thugs is another highlight) help to make *The Crow* far more interesting than it might have been, spicing the film with a zaniness that nicely complements the dark look of the city, helping to create a comic-book atmosphere that makes the overall effect much less dark and depressing than it might have been. Ultimately, though, the title character is very much the heart of the film, providing in one figure a sort of microcosm of the film as a whole. Not only is Lee's Eric Draven central to the action of the film, but he embodies the dark look of the film with his clothing, hair, and makeup. As a rock musician, he echoes the film's soundtrack, and even contributes to the soundtrack as he plays his guitar (though the actual playing was done by Lee's guitar teacher, not Lee himself) while sitting on lonely rooftops at night.

Draven/The Crow is very much a comic-book character, one-dimensional and constructed to play a specific role in the plot. Not only does he have impossible superhuman powers, but he has very little real depth to his character. Though he is not quite as brutally violent in the film as he is in the O'Barr comics, he is, in fact, not fully human, and the film clearly suggests that only those aspects of his character needed for his quest of vengeance have been brought back from the grave. He is thus single-mindedly driven by this quest vengeance and, while he experiences a great deal of emotional anguish along the way, that anguish does not include doubt about the rectitude of his mission. He still has a gentle side, especially in his memories of Shelly and his dealings with young Sarah, but he feels no inclinations toward mercy as he systematically executes his victims. Presumably, audiences are meant to feel no such inclinations, either. *The Crow* is a film constructed mostly from stark black-and-white colors, both visually and morally, and in that sense the film as a whole is perfectly in tune with the portrayal of its protagonist.

When slated to direct *The Crow*, the Egyptian-born Australian Alex Proyas had only one credit as the director of a feature film (an obscure—but visually interesting—Australian science fiction film entitled *Spirits of the Air, Gremlins of the Clouds*, released in 1989). He did, however, have significant experience as a director of music videos, an experience that served him well in the making of *The Crow*, in which music plays such an integral role, just as the music of such performers as the Joy Division, Iggy Pop, and the Cure had provided inspiration for O'Barr's original comic. The Cure joins hard-rocking bands such as Pantera, Nine Inch Nails, and Rage Against the Machine in the powerful soundtrack, which perfectly matches the film's furious, nonstop, comic-book action. The musical motif is enhanced by the fact that Draven is himself a rock musician by trade, with the attendant implication that he has the soul of an artist, adding extra dimensions to his character. Ultimately, though, *The Crow* is more striking for the way it looks than the way it sounds. The film's dark, rain-drenched urban landscape, however much it might owe to such predecessors as *Blade Runner* and *Batman* (1989), is a masterpiece of visual style that exercised considerable influence on subsequent films in its own right. Indeed, in *The Crow* Proyas and cinematographer Dariusz Wolski captured the look and feel of comic-book noir in a way no film ever had—or would, until the advent of *Sin City* in 2005. One of the most important films to carry this vision forward was Proyas's own science fiction film *Dark City* (1998), a box-office bust (also filmed by Wolski) that has won critical acclaim and a devoted cult following. It remains, in fact, Proyas's most important film to date, though he also helmed the commercially successful big-budget special-effects extravaganza *I, Robot* in 2004.

The Crow is significantly less polished than *Dark City*, but the roughness of the film is very much in keeping with the brutal violence of its plot and the urban squalor of its setting. The city of O'Barr's comics was identified as Detroit, and the film contains vague hints that its city can be associated with Detroit as well, thus evoking memories of the *Robocop* films that were set quite explicitly in that troubled city. Indeed, *Robocop* (1987) resembles *The Crow* much more than is immediately obvious. After all, *Robocop* is essentially the story of a man who is brutally attacked and essentially killed, then essentially brought back to life (this time through technology, not magic), subsequently seeking revenge against his own killers. However, the city of *The Crow* is never explicitly identified as Detroit, allowing it to take on almost allegorical (or even mythic) dimensions as a stand-in for decaying cities everywhere. Much of the cityscape is computer generated, giving Proyas and his crew considerable flexibility in designing the city, which in some ways looks very much like a generalized decaying American city of the very near future and in others resembles a Gothic European city of the nineteenth century.

This combination of settings from different continents and different centuries gives the film a very postmodern flavor. The film is clearly postmodern in other ways as well, perhaps most obviously in the way the resurrected Draven gradually recovers his memories through jolting flashes of images from the past, giving the film a fragmented, quick-cut quality reminiscent of music videos, which is typical of postmodern film in that this kind of editing echoes the fragmented and confusing nature of everyday existence in the postmodern world. In the case of *The Crow*, of course, this stylistic echo of music videos is entirely appropriate, given Proyas's background and given the central atmospheric importance of the film's soundtrack. *The Crow* is also postmodern in its generic hybridity;

rather than confine itself to the conventions of any one genre, it is a crime film, a love story, a superhero film, and a horror movie, all rolled into one. As such, it draws upon a number of predecessors in different genres and forms. In addition to O'Barr's comics and to other comic-book predecessors (such as Batman), *The Crow* draws upon a number of important generic forebears in film and literature, including film noir, the European Gothic tradition (including horror films), and cyberpunk science fiction.

One of the film's screenwriters, John Shirley, had established himself as a leading cyberpunk novelist via the publication of such works as *City Come-a-Walkin* and the *Eclipse* trilogy, works with a hard edge that foreground the punk aspect of cyberpunk. Given the darkness of his work, it is not surprising that Shirley would ultimately produce considerable work in the horror genre as well. The tone of Shirley's work was perfect for *The Crow*, and the fact that he himself had been a punk rock musician for a time was no doubt excellent preparation as well. Thus, while the film contains none of the high-tech implants and computer-generated virtual-reality worlds that are typically associated with cyberpunk, it does retain much of the feel of cyberpunk in its ability to maintain its cool energies amid the urban blight in which its characters find themselves, a blight that is typical of cyberpunk, as in the urban "Sprawl," a vast slum featured in William Gibson's Matrix trilogy, perhaps the central work in the entire phenomenon of cyberpunk. *The Crow* is also, like cyberpunk, set in a very near future (the film's makers have stated that they saw it as occurring "five minutes into the future.") Finally, the magical crow here has an almost cybernetic quality in the way it serves as an auxiliary source of data for Draven as he goes about his mission of vengeance.

The thematic focus on crime and revenge in *The Crow* is more typical of film noir than of cyberpunk. Then again, there are many points of contact between cyberpunk and film noir, as can perhaps best be seen in the cyberpunk novels of K. W. Jeter (including one entitled *Noir*, published in 1998), which draw overtly on the noir tradition. In film, the intersection of science fiction and film noir can be seen most obviously in *Blade Runner* (to which Jeter has written two novelistic sequels), which served as a central aesthetic inspiration for the entire cyberpunk movement and whose distinctive visual presentation of an urban future was specifically modeled on the visual style of the classic films noirs of the 1940s and early 1950s. Except for a few extra Gothic twists, the dark, dismal urban setting of *The Crow* certainly resembles the typical film noir setting, down to its presentation in virtual black-and-white. The city is painted almost entirely in blacks, browns, and grays, accented by oranges, yellows, and (especially) reds from the numerous Devil's Night fires that punctuate the landscape. Flashes of red also tend to be used to punctuate moments of violence.

The main characters tend to dress in black-and-white as well, and the title character's makeup means that even his face is in black-and-white. In particular, there are virtually no blues or greens in the film's color palette, which enhances the grimness of the visuals, while also setting them apart from reality and giving them a sort of other-worldly quality. This color scheme also adds to the way in which the film's cityscape (again recalling *Blade Runner* and cyberpunk) is almost entirely manmade, with virtually nothing surviving from nature, which has presumably been destroyed by the sprawl of corruption and pollution produced by the city and its inhabitants.

The thematic focus on crime and revenge in *The Crow* is also reminiscent of film noir, even if the characters in the film are somewhat exaggerated versions of the kinds of villains and problematic heroes one finds in film noir. This exaggeration can perhaps be attributed to the comic-book roots of the film, but it could equally well be attributed to the film's contacts with the European Gothic tradition. The influence of the Gothic tradition on the look of *The Crow* is considerable. In addition, the motif of rising from the dead is quite central to the Gothic tradition, which features such crucial posthumous figures as Frankenstein (assembled from body parts harvested from cadavers) and Dracula (who literally rises from his grave each evening to go about his work). Indeed, both Frankenstein and Dracula can be regarded as crucial predecessors to the figure of the Crow. In the O'Barr comics, several of the Crow's adversaries refer to him as "the vampire"; that overt identification is missing from the film, but there are numerous similarities between the Crow and the figure of the vampire. As signaled by the name of the protagonist, Edgar Allan Poe's raven is an obvious Gothic predecessor as well. Ravens are, after all, a type of crow, and the actual birds used in the making the film were in fact ravens. Draven even recites lines from Poe's "The Raven" during his confrontation with Polito's spectacularly slimy pawnbroker. Perhaps more importantly, the Gothic genre as a whole provides thematic and atmospheric background to the film's presentation of a dark city (almost every scene is set at night) riddled by corruption, but also shot through with supernatural energies.

Of course (especially in the case of Frankenstein), the Gothic tradition overlaps significantly with European Romanticism, and *The Crow* includes a number of Romantic elements. The soulful Eric Draven, a black-clad tormented outsider who has no real place in the land of the living, is clearly a sort of Byronic hero, and much of the film's unique texture has to do with its ability to suggest the Romantic elements of his quest for vengeance, which is clearly designed not so much to avenge his own death, or even Shelly's, but to seek retribution for the way the thugs destroyed the special beauty of Eric and Shelly's mutual love. At the same time, his ability to seek this retribution suggests that love is stronger than evil—or even death. In addition, the influence of the European Gothic tradition on *The Crow* is filtered through that more recent Gothic offshoot, the horror film, including those featuring classic Gothic characters such as Frankenstein and Dracula. In particular, the distinctive, atmospheric visual style of *The Crow* shows the clear influence of the horror films produced by Hammer Films, especially during their heyday in the late 1950s, when films such as *The Curse of Frankenstein* (1957) and *Dracula* (1958) breathed new life into the two central monsters of the Gothic tradition and brought world-wide attention to the low-budget British studio. Each of these films would ultimately trigger numerous sequels, while helping to establish Hammer's horror films, campy and schlocky though they might have been, as masterpieces of a particular visual style that effectively evoked an atmosphere of horror.

The Crow creates some of that same atmosphere while transplanting it to a more modern, even futuristic setting. Yet the overall atmosphere of *The Crow* is far more complex than that of the Hammer films, partly because it draws upon so many different genres and traditions, and partly because of its odd mix of darkness, violence, death, love, and beauty. This unique mixture is surely part of the secret of the ongoing success of *The Crow* as a cult favorite, a phenomenon that has led to the production of a string of sequels. Unfortunately, none of these sequels has been able to recapture the rich complexity of the atmosphere of *The Crow*.

THE CROW DESCENDS: THE SEQUELS FALL FLAT

It might have seemed that Lee's death would bring the franchise to an end, but the success of the initial film triggered the relatively quick production of a followup, *The Crow: City of Angels*, directed by Tim Pope and released in 1996. Here, rather than have a different actor play Eric Draven, the action shifts to Los Angeles, where another, entirely different, murdered individual is brought back from the dead. Actually, though specifically set ten years or so later than the original *Crow*, this film is almost more a remake than a sequel, as it attempts to recreate, one by one, the elements that had made the first film a success. Still set in a dark, crime-riddled urban environment, *The Crow: City of Angels* again features a magical crow, which this time brings one Ashe Corven (Vincent Perez) back from the dead to take revenge on a gang of thugs who killed him and a loved one. The plot then basically consists of his arc of revenge against the thugs, culminating in the defeat and death of the crime lord who ruled them. This time, however, the murdered loved one is the murdered man's young son, which adds an additional sentimental element to the film. The main element that is added in this film is a potential romantic interest for the suggestively named Corven (he rises from the ashes, as it were, while crows belong to the genus *Corvus*). Further, this love interest is the same Sarah who had appeared in the first film, now all grown up (and played by Mia Kirshner). This added element potentially creates a conflict for Corven, who might thus be tempted to try to remain among the living rather than return to the dead with his son. However, the film does not really emphasize this conflict, which is in any case resolved when Sarah is killed by the crime lord, Judah Earl (Richard Brooks), allowing her to join Corven and his son in the afterlife.

Despite the presence of so many of the same elements, *The Crow: City of Angels* fails to recapture the magic of the original *Crow*. For one thing, while Pope might have seemed the perfect director for the sequel due to his experience directing music videos for Goth-rock groups such as The Cure, he lacks Proyas's visual flair, and the sequel's overall look (especially in its presentation of the nighttime city) is not nearly as striking or effective as in the original. In addition, the gang of thugs in this second film entirely lacks the zany energy of the thugs in the first film, just as their leader, even though he is himself now endowed with supernatural powers, is never able to project anything like the sense of menace that accompanies Wincott's Top Dollar. More importantly, Perez's competent performance in the central role lacks the charisma of Lee's performance, which in fact seems all the more impressive in comparison. All in all, however, the biggest problem with the second film may simply be that it attempts to recreate the first film all too closely, so that we've seen it all before, done more stylishly by a better director with a substantially better cast.

That being the case, one might have expected the third Crow film to be even less effective. On the other hand, with rising star Kirsten Dunst in a leading role and veteran film actors such as Fred Ward and William Atherton on hand as well, Bharat Nalluri's *The Crow: Salvation* (2000) did seem to have a bit more promising cast than its immediate predecessor. This film also varies the plot at least a bit. This time a young woman is murdered, and her boyfriend, Alex Corvis (Eric Mabius), is framed and then executed for the crime. A magical crow then predictably resurrects the executed Corvis, who subsequently bands with his girlfriend's sister, Erin Randall (Dunst), to wreak revenge on the killers. In this case, however, the killers are a group of rogue cops, headed by a powerful police captain (Ward). Ultimately, however, none of the characters in this film are convincing or even enjoyable, and it completely fails to achieve the atmospheric effects of the original *Crow*.

The fourth Crow film (like the fourth Superman and Batman films) is bad enough that it has probably killed off the franchise for the foreseeable future. *The Crow: Wicked Prayer* (2005) features former child actor (of *Terminator 2* fame) Edward Furlong as the Crow. Unfortunately, Furlong in Crow makeup looks more like a drag queen than a terrifying avenger. His main antagonist isn't very scary, either. David Boreanaz plays the role of a gang leader determined to become the antichrist and bring about the Apocalypse, recalling Boreanaz's role as a soulful vampire in the *Buffy the Vampire Slayer* and *Angel* TV series. But Boreanaz is completely unconvincing here as a potential world-ending demon, perhaps because the plot is just plain silly. As a whole, the film is pretty much a mess, lacking in almost all of the elements that made the first Crow movie special. For one thing, the setting moves to the rural Southwest, which allows the film to tap into the importance of crows to Native American mythology, though in point of fact crows are typically negative figures in that mythology, where they are typically depicted as malevolent tricksters. In any case, this shift in setting loses the urban edge that was so crucial to the original film. This shift creates an entirely different look, accompanied by an attendant shift in the soundtrack away from the hard rock of the earlier films. The overall result is a film that looks and feels much lighter and less menacing than the original; the multigeneric plot of the original is here replaced by almost pure horror story, but the horror-story plot is hackneyed, unfrightening, and basically ridiculous. In fact, *The Crow: Wicked Prayer* is a film that can't even take itself seriously, occasionally veering into self-parody, but even its apparent efforts at self-parody fall flat.

If nothing else, the collective sequels to *The Crow*, which include so many elements of the original, but which completely fail to recapture the magic of that film, demonstrate just how difficult it is to articulate what makes a good film. Certainly, each individual element of *The Crow* is better than the corresponding element in any of the sequels, from the performances of the actors, to the cinematography and soundtrack, to the screenplay and the overall vision of the director. The first Crow film also does a much better job of capturing the combination of Romanticism and brutality that inform the original comics. But *The Crow* is also a perfect example of a film that is greater than the sum of its parts, and much of its success comes, not from the excellence of any one aspect, but from the way the different aspects of the film mesh so well together, whether it be the way the soundtrack reinforces the cinematography or the way the portrayal of the villains perfectly offsets the portrayal of the hero.

4

Men in Black and *Men in Black II*

Released 1997 and 2002; Director Barry Sonnenfeld

PUTTING THE COMIC BACK IN COMICS: CONSPIRACY AS FARCE

When Barry Sonnenfeld's *Men in Black* was released in 1997, the strongest trend in graphic cinema of the past decade had been toward darker and darker depictions of troubled superheroes in morally ambiguous situations. But, if films such as the first two Batman movies, *Darkman*, *The Crow*, and *The Shadow* seemed to be taking graphic cinema in this darker direction through most of the 1990s, Barry Sonnenfeld's *Men in Black* took a turn toward farcical comedy. The film was based on the similarly titled comic books by Lowell Cunningham, which themselves grew out of UFO conspiracy theorists' suspicions that government-employed agents (or at least someone claiming to be government agents), dressed in black, were systematically attempting to squelch all evidence of the presence of alien invaders on planet earth. The film, however, took a much more humorous tone than had Cunningham's comic books. As such, the film was also a sort of spoof of alien-invasion narratives in general, narratives that had reached a new prominence in the film world with the success of Roland Emmerich's *Independence Day* a year earlier. As a spoof of alien-invasion films, *Men in Black* had an excellent pedigree. For one thing, it costarred Will Smith, who had also been one of the stars of *Independence Day*. It was also executive produced by Steven Spielberg and made primarily by Spielberg's Amblin Entertainment production company, which had been responsible for two of the best and most successful alien invasion films of all time, *Close Encounters of the Third Kind* (1977) and *E.T. the Extraterrestrial* (1982).

Both *Men in Black* and its sequel, *Men in Black II* (2002), openly engage in a parodic dialogue with the tradition of alien-invasion narratives. For example, in one hilarious moment in *Men in Black II*, Agent J (Smith) watches a television program that purports to shed light on various secret conspiracies (including the government's Men in Black program). Noting the shoddy special effects that are used to illustrate the narrative, J quips that this feeble effort "looks like Spielberg's work," poking fun at the products of Amblin Entertainment—and thus at the *Men in Black* films themselves. Indeed, one of the most important sources of humor in both *Men in Black* films is their cheerful lack of self-seriousness and willingness to poke fun at their own premises. In this, the films have a great deal in common with their most recent predecessor, Tim Burton's *Mars Attacks!* (1996), another alien-invasion spoof that specifically refers back to the low-budget science fiction films of the 1950s, including such films as the hilarious 1959 alien-invasion/zombie flick *Plan 9 from Outer Space*, directed by the notorious Ed Wood, who himself had been the subject of Burton's offbeat 1995 biopic, *Ed Wood*. However, the most direct predecessors of the *Men in Black* films, in tone and spirit, are probably the *Ghost Busters* films of the 1980s, which are similarly farcical (featuring ghosts as antagonists instead of alien invaders), while including a number of effective action sequences that complement and enhance the comedy. In addition, rather than look back to the sf films of the 1950s, the *Men in Black* films significantly update their parodic frame of reference by spoofing the big-budget science fiction films of the 1990s, referring more to such works as *Independence Day* than to the campy productions of earlier decades. This is especially obvious in its use of state-of-the-art special effects—as opposed to the intentionally crude special effects of *Mars Attacks!* That the effects of the *Men in Black* films are used largely for the production of sight gags demonstrates the comic potential of CGI, while at the same time serving as a potential parodic commentary on the reliance of contemporary science fiction films on special-effects technology.

TECHNOLOGY, UFOLOGY, AND THE MOVIES

In addition to their parody of contemporary science fiction films, the *Men in Black* films gain energy from their engagement with contemporary interest in conspiracy theories, in this sense building directly upon the success of such recent works as the contemporary alien-invasion/conspiracy television series *The X-Files*. However, the notion of sinister government agents (or even aliens posing as government agents) dressed in black and acting as part of a conspiracy to suppress evidence of the existence of UFOs goes back to the 1950s. Meanwhile, the comic potential of the men in black conspiracy theory had been displayed in *The X-Files* itself in the classic 1996 episode "Jose Chung's *From Outer Space*" (April 12, 1996), which parodied that program's own characteristic concerns with the mythology of UFO conspiracy. There, wrestler (and, later, governor of Minnesota) Jesse Ventura and *Jeopardy* game-show host Alex Trebek do a hilarious turn as two men in black, charged with suppressing precisely the kind of evidence of alien invasion that the show's protagonists, FBI agents Mulder and Scully, are seeking to uncover.

Men in Black, following Cunningham's comics, gives the notion of men in black a new twist by making the title characters the good guys, protecting earth from alien invasions, though they also suppress evidence of such invasions, on the grounds that they are so common that earth's population would be too terrified to continue their lives if they knew about them. The $90 million film, however, is anything but terrifying, even if its central plot involves an alien plan to destroy the earth. The film's numerous sight gags and broad, often slapstick, humor proved a big hit with worldwide movie audiences, who attended the film to the tune of nearly $700 million in box office. This number rivaled (though not quite matched) the success of *Independence Day* and made *Men in Black* (at the time) one of the ten top grossing films of all time. Not surprisingly, this success eventually triggered a mega-budget sequel. *Men in Black II* (2002) featured the same stars and director as the first film, and indeed captured much of the same comic spirit of the original. With a considerably larger budget (roughly $140 million), the second film has even better special effects than *Men in Black*, but otherwise does little that the original hadn't already done. It was still a substantial success at the box office, however, pulling in over $400 million in worldwide gross receipts.

Men in Black begins with an extended sequence that follows a dragonfly as it flies along a highway, accompanied by eerie music that suggests that the bug might be an alien—a notion that is reinforced by one shot in which it flies across the moon as background, echoing a famous shot from Spielberg's *E.T.* Only seconds after this shot, an on-screen credit reminds us that Spielberg is the executive producer of *Men in Black*, reinforcing the connection. Soon afterward, however, the bug reveals itself to be an ordinary terrestrial insect as it splatters (after several near misses) on the windshield of a panel truck. The driver of the truck curses the bug in annoyance at the soiling of his windshield, indicating the cavalier way in which humans are willing to slaughter insects, which are considered so far beneath humans as to be unworthy of compassion. This then sets the stage for the arrival of a powerful alien invader who is essentially a giant alien insect—with the twist that the invader regards humans as beneath contempt and unworthy of compassion, partly because of their own brutal treatment of earthly insects, whom the invader regards as relatives.

Meanwhile, the truck on which the bug splatters is carrying a load of incoming illegal aliens from Mexico—though one of the new arrivals is, in fact, an extraterrestrial in disguise. This opening sequence thus suggests parallels between existing U.S. immigration issues and the issues of extraterrestrial alien invasion that are the principal material of the film. But *Men in Black* is hardly interested in using its alien-invasion premise for the purposes of serious commentary on immigration questions, or anything else. Instead, as this opening sequence already indicates, *Men in Black* is playful, ironic, and allusive, engaging in dialogue with a variety of issues and a range of earlier texts, but all in fun, all for the purpose of creating comic entertainment, even if such engagement occasionally offers opportunities for viewers who wish to think seriously about the potential implications of this dialogue.

This use of an alien Bug as the film's principal antagonist taps into a long science fiction tradition, in which aliens are often buglike—especially if we are not meant to sympathize with them. For example, another of the top-grossing films of 1997 was Paul Verhoeven's *Starship Troopers*, which features swarming hordes of alien "bugs" engaged in combat with heavily armed human troops. Based on Robert A. Heinlein's 1959 novel of the same title, *Starship Troopers* is a special-effects-driven gorefest featuring the spectacular destruction of large numbers of the insectile aliens by their human foes. Though apparently meant at least partly as a satire of Heinlein's militaristic vision, *Starship Troopers* ultimately became a spectacle of violence in its own right, and succeeded largely on those terms, though its roughly $129 million in worldwide box office paled in comparison to the success of *Men in Black* or its sequel.

In *Starship Troopers* and other works featuring alien bugs (such as Orson Scott Card's well known 1985 sf novel *Ender's Game*) alien bugs usually appear as swarms of interchangeable units driven by a single group mind. *Men in Black*, however, deviates from this tendency by featuring a single invading Bug. This Bug arrives on earth, crashing its flying saucer on a remote farm where the farmer, Edgar (Vincent D'Onofrio) has just been shown verbally abusing his wife. The film thus casts the farmer in an unsympathetic light, helping to ensure that the comedy will not be impeded by Edgar's subsequent experience, in which the alien Bug kills him and hijacks his body so that it can use it as a disguise, in the tradition of such sf classics as *Invasion of the Body Snatchers* (1956). Unfortunately, the alien does not seem to understand human physiology very well, and so apparently does not realize that the disguise is not very good. The hijacked "Edgar" looks much more like a zombie from one of the "Living Dead" movies than a regular human farmer, and his ridiculous appearance becomes one of the running jokes of the film. Meanwhile, the Bug subsequently kills an exterminator, then ironically uses the man's Zap 'Em Exterminators truck to drive to New York in pursuit of its mission on earth.

That mission involves the pursuit of a tiny pocket galaxy that resides inside a marble-like sphere and that the Bug has reason to believe is currently on earth. Indeed, the galaxy is currently in the possession of a member of the royal family of the planet Arquil, who happens to be hiding out on earth—and who has hidden the galaxy inside an ornament attached to the collar of his pet cat. The galaxy is tremendously valuable as a source of "subatomic energy," so the Arquillians are willing to do anything to protect the ornament, just as the Bug is willing to do anything to acquire it, leaving the earth caught in the middle of this conflict between powerful, advanced alien species, either of which is willing to sacrifice the earth and all of its inhabitants in order to advance its own agenda. Indeed, through much of the film an Arquillian battle cruiser hovers in orbit over earth, preparing to destroy the entire planet in order to prevent the pocket galaxy from falling into the hands of the Bugs.

Earth, meanwhile, is defended by the top-secret Men in Black organization, headed by the hilariously deadpan Chief Zed (Rip Torn) and featuring a collection of black-suited human agents, as well as a panoply of comic aliens who work with and for them. Indeed, it turns out that the earth is teeming with aliens, most of whom are harmless and who are here with official permission, the main restrictions being that they must register with the Men in Black and keep their presence a secret from the population at large. One of the most common ways they do so is by disguising themselves as humans, and another of the running jokes of the two films is that numerous prominent humans (such as Michael Jackson, Martha Stewart, and Elvis Presley—who didn't die but merely returned to his home planet) are among these disguised aliens. When aliens get out of line, the Men in Black step in, defending the earth with an arsenal of high-tech weaponry, much of it obtained from alien sources.

We are introduced to the Men in Black organization and their elaborate secret New York headquarters (located under the ventilator building of the Brooklyn-Battery Tunnel) early in the film as Agent K (Tommy Lee Jones), the group's top operative, recruits and trains New York police officer James Edwards (later, Agent J) to be his new partner. K also makes clear the ultrasecret nature of the entire operation, pointing out to Edwards that once he joins the organization, he will drop off the net and officially cease to be, all records of his existence having been expunged. He can tell no one outside the organization about his work, or even have any life outside the organization. Indeed, the Men in Black seem to devote a large portion of their resources precisely to concealing all evidence of their own existence—as well as all evidence of the presence of aliens on earth. Of course, given that the earth is teeming with aliens, humans will occasionally observe them despite the best efforts of the Men in Black, who respond by erasing the memories of these observations with hand-held devices known as "neuralizers," providing another of the film's many running gags.

Eventually, Agents J and K, aided by sexy (and possibly kinky) medical examiner Dr. Laurel Weaver (Linda Fiorentino), manage to rescue the miniature galaxy, saving the earth from being caught in the crossfire of an interstellar war. They also destroy the Bug (that has shed its human disguise and taken on its true, insectile form) in a spectacular slapstick battle at the site of the 1964 New York World's Fair that tops off the entire film. Along the way, J and K encounter an array of humorous aliens from whom they seek information, including Frank, an alien disguised as a talking pug. Perhaps the funniest of their alien informers is sleazy pawnshop owner Jack Jeebs (Tony Shalhoub), who happens to stock an array of advanced alien weaponry. He also has the ability to regenerate his head after it has been blown off, presenting the opportunity for one of the film's most hilarious sight gags as the tiny new (computer-generated) head pops out of Jeebs's neck and gradually inflates to full size.

K, as it turns out, knows Jeebs (and his regeneration capabilities) well from past encounters, though an unknowing J is shocked when K rather nonchalantly blows off Jeebs's head when the alien resists interrogation. In fact, K, after thirty-five years as a Man in Black, is intimately acquainted with most of the aliens he and J encounter in the course of the film. Indeed, a central element of the film involves the extent to which even the most bizarre alien encounters are absolutely routine, at least for the initiated like K. In particular, the film gains considerable comic energy from the contrast between K's casual nonreactions and J's expressions of extreme discomfort and astonishment as they encounter one bizarre phenomenon after another. This contrast is part of the larger dynamic between Smith and Jones, who become a classic on-screen duo, with the low-key, deadpan Jones serving as the straight man and Smith as the hyperkinetic, over-the-top slapstick comedian. And the combination works well: not only is Smith much funnier beside the poker-faced Jones, but Jones himself is hilarious precisely because his lack of reaction stands in such sharp contrast to the overreactions of Smith.

At the end of *Men in Black*, Agent K retires from the organization to return to the wife he left thirty-five years earlier in order to join the group. J, having received his baptism under fire, becomes K's replacement, while Weaver, excited by the action she has observed, becomes J's new partner, Agent L. Meanwhile, in one last ironic turn, we discover that our own galaxy parallels the pocket galaxy featured in the film in that it actually resides inside a marble that is being played with by a giant alien, along with a collection of other pocket galaxies—with the potential implication that this alien's galaxy in turn resides inside a marble within a still larger galaxy. This final twist, which reveals that the universe is not at all what our best scientific knowledge had thought it to be, reinforces a central point of the film: that ordinary individuals know very little about the way the world works but are willing nevertheless to assume that it works according to principles understood by experts, even if the knowledge of those experts is well beyond the kin of common people. By disputing the scientific understanding of the nature of the universe, the film further implies that these experts don't know what they're doing, either.

This aspect of the film is another way in which *Men in Black* is very much a work of the 1990s. Popular culture, even comedy (and sometimes especially comedy), often responds to the characteristic fears and anxieties of the society in which it is produced. Thus, the alien invasion films of the 1950s reflected the concerns of a cold war America that felt itself embattled and surrounded by threatening enemies, both in the Soviet bloc and in the Third World. By the 1990s, America had no such enemies that were truly perceived as threatening. Instead, Americans were more concerned that the world around them was driven by complex forces beyond their understanding. They were convinced that the true power in the world lay in secret networks and elaborate conspiracies (perhaps even involving their own government), a perception that was central to the success of *The X-Files*, with its convoluted government-sponsored plots and its group of alien invaders who were as confusing as they were threatening. In this sense, *The X-Files* is a sort of serious version (though it had its own self-parodic moments, as with the "Jose Chung" episode) of *Men in Black*. The latter also draws very directly upon the anxieties of the period, even as it pokes fun at them. Partly because it is intended to be a mere entertainment—but in a way that is characteristic of postmodern culture—*Men in Black* seems uncomfortable with any kind of direct social commentary, preferring to approach contemporary anxieties through the stress-relieving mode of comedy.

If *Men in Black* is uninterested in a serious commentary on our contemporary fascination with the possibility that giant conspiracies were afoot in our world, it also avoids any kind of specific political commentary.

In particular, it avoids any potential political controversy over the secrecy of the Men in Black organization by suggesting that the group is entirely autonomous, outside of any direct governmental control and unaligned with any particular political perspective. Further, the film stipulates that this secrecy is well motivated and that J's initial doubts about the rectitude of this practice are misguided, while K's more experienced judgment about the necessity of secrecy is to be trusted. Indeed, as opposed to the tradition that Men in Black are themselves sinister and possibly aligned with alien forces, the film implies that the very existence of the Men in Black organization is reassuring amid the uncertainties of the postmodern world: if complex, clandestine networks constitute the most important threat to the lives of individuals in the 1990s, then it is surely a good thing that a benign secret organization is working to defend and protect those lives. In addition, *Men in Black* has an almost nostalgic quality in the way it looks back to the presumed verities of earlier times. In particular, in its opposition between the entirely virtuous Men in Black and the entirely evil invading Bug, the film suggests that however complex our postmodern world might be, the texture of life can still sometimes be reduced to the simple good vs. evil oppositions that were so central to public perceptions of global politics during the cold war.

The texture of American fear and anxiety changed dramatically on September 11, 2001, when it became clear that the direct sorts of attacks so feared in the 1950s were still a very real possibility, even in a world where the United States was the only superpower. This event to some extent restored the American consciousness to a cold war mindset, with "terrorists" now playing the role that had formerly been played by communists. Indeed, much of the old rhetoric of the cold war was unpacked, dusted off, and applied directly to official descriptions of terrorists as vile antagonists bent on destroying the American way of life, if only out of sheer jealousy and resentment that life in America was so wonderful. Still, even the overt violence of 9/11 had a postmodern quality: it was the result not of an assault by a rival nation state but of a carefully crafted plot on the part of a worldwide network of secret conspirators. Among other things, the bombings clearly cast a shadow over *Men in Black II*, which was in production at the time of the attacks. For one thing, as a film that tried to make light comedy out of an alien attack on New York City, the sequel clearly had to tread very carefully lest its comedy be perceived as offensive to the memories of those who suffered and died in the 9/11 attacks. Those attacks had at least one very direct and specific impact on *Men in Black II* as well. The film's climactic scene was to have occurred at New York's World Trade Center, thus following the first film in choosing an easily identifiable setting with symbolic resonances for the big final battle. Those resonances, of course, were very different after 9/11, so this setting was dropped in favor of a final climactic explosion over the Statue of Liberty, thus still ending the action at the site of a well-known landmark, but one that was not directly related to the attacks of the previous September.

BEEN THERE, DONE THAT: *MEN IN BLACK II*

Men in Black was a hard act to follow, which may account for the fact that it took five years for the sequel to appear, despite the huge success of the original. In the meantime, Smith, despite the disastrous *Wild Wild West* (1999), had solidified his credentials as a major movie star with his Oscar-nominated performance in the title role in the biopic *Ali* (2001). *Men in Black II* was thus set for Smith, as J, to take the lead role in the film. On the other hand, the role of Agent J had to be substantially modified in the second film. The comic success of *Men in Black* crucially depends upon the responses of the neophyte Agent J to the various shocking revelations he encounters as he first learns of the Men in Black organization and is then thrown into his crucial, world-saving first mission with no experience and little training. A cocky, streetwise cop who believes he has seen it all, J is forced, in the course of the film, to come to grips with the extent to which his knowledge of what really goes in the world is so limited, suddenly becoming a naïf in the new world to which he has been introduced. But this source of humor was not available to the sequel, which takes place five years later than the original, with J now a relatively experienced agent.

Some initial comic energy is gained in *Men in Black II* from J's attempts to deal with the well-meaning, but inept efforts of his new partner, Agent T (Patrick Warburton), apparently one in a series of failed partners after the departure of Agent L to return to work in the morgue. Soon afterward, however, an impending crisis requires that Agent K be reactivated, retrieved from his very ordinary civilian life as Kevin Brown, a rural postmaster. Brown seems relatively content, though he has become estranged from his wife, and much of the humor of the early parts of the film derives from his skepticism about the notion of once again becoming a Man in Black. Meanwhile, his reactivation results in a sort of reversal of the relationship between J and K in the first film, with J now serving as a mentor to K, who (having been neuralized upon retirement) initially remembers nothing of his former career as a Man in Black.

After a few comic moments, K returns to his old, world-weary self, with J again playing the role of his wisecracking partner. However, without the comic energies derived from J's lack of experience in the first film, the two central characters are never quite as funny in the second film as they had been in the first. Meanwhile, Rosario Dawson is fine as Laura Vasquez, a pizza waitress who becomes involved in their efforts, though she is again not as funny as Fiorentino had been in the first film. With the good guys clearly producing less comedy in the sequel than they had in the original, *Men in Black II* attempts to compensate by making their antagonist funnier. To a certain extent, this attempt succeeds, and Lara Flynn Boyle's turn as Serleena, the film's beautiful but deadly alien invader, is a comic gem. Johnny Knoxville's performance as Scrad/Charlie, Serleena's two-headed (but incredibly stupid) lackey, also adds comedy, while Shalhoub returns as Jeebs and is still funny, though his regrowing head is not quite as hilarious when you've seen it before. Frank the pug returns as well, and his expanded role (he serves as J's partner after T and before the return of K) produces some of the comic highlights of the film.

Still, even with all of these elements in place, *Men in Black II* feels flat and uninspired relative to the first film, though "relative" is definitely the key word here. For one thing, *Men in Black* was one of the most successful comedies ever (in terms of generating both laughs and profits), so it provides an extremely high standard for comparison. In addition, the success of *Men in Black* came largely from the fact that it was such a refreshing film, not quite like anything audiences had seen before. On the other hand, *Men in Black II*, as a direct sequel, was almost exactly like something audiences had seen before. Indeed, *Men in Black II* falls prey to the same shortcoming that dooms so many sequels to mediocrity: it tries to recreate the original film more than extend it, but (given that we already have the original film) there's really no need to do so. Had *Men in Black* never been made and had *Men in Black II* been the initial film in the sequence, it would have probably been a far better and funnier film—even if every frame were exactly the same as it is now. As it is, though, with the first *Men in Black* already in place, the sequel seems flat, recycled, and (most of all) pointless. Indeed, much of the humor of the sequel references specific moments from the first film and thus only works if one remembers the appropriate scene from the original.

It doesn't help that the plot of *Men in Black II* is a bit confusing. This plot involves the efforts of Serleena to recover the mysterious "Light of Zartha," though we're not sure what that is or why she wants it until the film is nearly over. Still, *Men in Black II* does have moments in which it can be highly entertaining, beginning with the opening pretitle sequence featuring Peter Graves as the host of a low-budget television reality show, thus reprising the role that Graves had also played in director Sonnenfeld's *Addams Family Values* (1993). The show, "Mysteries in History," is vaguely reminiscent of the long-running real-world series "Unsolved Mysteries," hosted by Robert Stack; like that show it features dramatic reenactments of mysteries from the past. In this particular episode, Graves focuses on widespread rumors that a "quasi-government agency known as the Men in Black" secretly operates to protect earth from alien invaders. He then reports on one particular story involving this agency, illustrated by hilariously cheesy special effects. This story involves reports that in 1978, aliens from the planet Zartha brought the Light of Zartha (still unidentified), a powerful cosmic force that, in the wrong hands (such as those of Serleena), could lead to the annihilation of Zartha. In the reenactment, the beautiful Zarthon princess, Lauranna (played in the reenactment by Paige Brooks), turns the Light over to the Men in Black, asking them to hide it from Serleena—depicted in the reenactment as a (cheaply constructed) many-tentacled monster. According to Graves's narration, the Men in Black are unwilling to intervene, lest the earth itself be threatened. They thus decline Lauranna's request, but nevertheless delay Serleena long enough that the Zarthons are able to escape with the Light, though Serleena eventually sets out after them, vowing to destroy any planet that gets in the way of her quest.

This story, of course, sets the stage for the plot of *Men in Black II* itself, which involves Serleena's return to earth after she realizes that the Light has actually been here all along and that the Men in Black only made it appear that it had left earth. As the opening titles roll, an alien ship flies through space, eventually crashing to earth in a New York park. A metallic (and possibly menacing) tripod, vaguely reminiscent of those in H. G. Wells's *The War of the Worlds* (1898) and its classic 1953 film adaptation, arises from the crash site. Then, in one of the film's numerous sight gags, the tripod turns out to be tiny, as we see when a dog approaches it and towers over it. A diminutive alien creature, seemingly half worm and half plant, descends from the tripod, frightens the dog away with a vicious snarl, then crawls along the ground until it encounters a magazine lying in the dirt. Flipping through the magazine, it encounters a two-page ad for Victoria's Secret featuring a beautiful lingerie model (Boyle). The alien worm (Serleena) then transforms, taking on Boyle's appearance. Standing in the park in underwear, she is immediately accosted by a mugger, who puts a knife to her throat and tells her she tastes good. He then drags her behind a bush. We hear signs of a struggle, and Serleena emerges with a bloated belly, having eaten the mugger, who turns out to taste good in his own right. Realizing that her appearance no longer matches that of the model in the ad, Serleena goes back behind the bush to throw up and regain her girlish figure—in what can be taken as a commentary on one of the strategies used by models in general to stay so thin.

This first scene sets the tone for the rest of the film, in which Serleena's beautiful exterior masks the murderous malevolence with which she pursues her quest to find the Light, while J retrieves K from the post office (where most of the other employees, unbeknownst to him, are aliens) to aid in the effort to stop her from getting the Light, even though they have no idea what it is. Along the way, J meets and becomes romantically interested in Vasquez, so much so that he declines to neuralize her after she witnesses one of Serleena's murders—and even after he has revealed to her that Serleena is an alien and that he is a member of a top-secret group charged with stopping such invaders.

Soon afterward, Serleena attacks and takes control of the Men in Black headquarters, before K can be deneuralized using the high-tech equipment there. He subsequently has to be treated with a jerry-rigged unit being held by Jeebs in his basement, which leaves him with a very spotty memory of his past work as a Man in Black. The work of J and K is further complicated by the fact that Serleena releases a rogue's gallery of alien prisoners from Men in Black headquarters to serve as her henchmen. J and K manage to fight through these aliens fairly easily, though Serleena herself is considerably more formidable, especially as J and K don't really know what she's after.

In the course of their search for the Light, J and K are led to a locker in Grand Central Station that contains a tiny pocket world (echoing the marble-galaxies of *Men in Black*) whose tiny inhabitants worship K as the "light giver" because he had earlier left them his illuminated watch. A clue in the locker leads them to view the episode of "Mysteries of History" that opened the film, jogging K's memories of the real events of 1978, in which he had been centrally involved, including a romantic entanglement with Princess Lauranna—in direct violation of the rules of the Men in Black and his own better judgment. However, we do not realize until the film is nearly over that Vasquez herself is the Light, the daughter of Lauranna and destined leader of the planet Zartha, who must return to her people to prevent their conquest by Serleena. She is also probably the daughter of K, though that fact is never quite verified in the film.

In the final analysis, J and K destroy Serleena in a final rooftop battle, blowing her up in a final spectacular display of fireworks over the Statue of Liberty, perfectly rhyming with the fact that the film opened on the July 4 weekend in 2002. Meanwhile, in another key gag, the statue's torch turns out to contain a huge neuralizer that zaps the memories of the throngs who witnessed the final explosion. Saved from Serleena, Vasquez flies away to her home world, both she and J saddened that they cannot be together—though the film at least attempts to make it clear that the real relationship at the heart of *Men in Black II* is not that between J and Laura, but that between J and K. Finally, in an echo of the ending of the first film, we learn that our world, like that of the tiny aliens we observed earlier in grand Central, exists inside a locker in a much larger universe—and so on. Thus, even the film's final (presumably clever) twist is a mere recycling of the final twist in the first film, which pretty much sums up the trouble with the sequel, which seems to have no real message beyond the messages that were already embedded in the original.

As a result, though even the sequel was a big moneymaker, there seems to be little impetus toward making still another sequel. Nevertheless, the films remain a well-known part of the American popular culture of their time. Further, in addition to the two theatrical films, the Men in Black premise inspired an animated children's television series that ran on the Kids' WB network from 1997 to 2001, thus roughly spanning the period between the two films. The series essentially picks up where the first film leaves off and again features Agents J, K, and L, voiced by Keith Diamond, Gregg Berger, and Jennifer Lien, respectively. The first film also spawned two successful soundtrack albums, while the title song also appeared on Smith's double-platinum rap album *Big Willie Style*. The films and the television series also inspired a series of video games on various platforms, as well as the "Men in Black: Alien Attack" ride at the Universal Studios Orlando theme park. The Men in Black film franchise and the marketing surrounding it have thus come to constitute one of the most successful and recognizable products of American popular culture in recent years.

5

The *Blade* Trilogy

Released 1998–2004; Various Directors

MARVEL GOES FOR BLOOD: THE *BLADE* FRANCHISE

With the rise of the Comic Book Code in the 1950s, comics in America took a turn away from lurid sensationalism—but also toward banality and mediocrity. By the 1970s (partly as a result of the emancipatory political movements of the 1960s), this repressive veil was beginning to lift, and the comics were able to pursue darker and more violent themes. Among other things, this development allowed classic comic-book heroes (such as Superman and Batman) to begin to move in darker directions. It also allowed the comics to explore whole new genres, such as horror and crime fiction, in a much more effective way, returning to the vein that had originally been explored in such publications as EC Comics' *Tales from the Crypt* in the early 1950s.

The horror mode in the comics had relatively little initial impact on the world of film, even though horror films themselves were entering a particularly rich period in the 1970s. That would change in a big way in 1998 with the release of Stephen Norrington's *Blade*, a box-office hit that was also a major critical success, suggesting rich possibilities for the exploration of comic-book horror in film. The title character of *Blade*, a superhuman vampire hunter, was a relatively minor figure in the world of comics, suggesting that graphic cinema need not limit itself to well-known (and thus immediately marketable) characters from the comics. Part of the success of *Blade* could no doubt be attributed to its timing, in that the film was released amid an upsurge of interest in vampire tales, perhaps because they function so well as allegories about AIDS and other forms of bodily "contamination" that were central fears of the 1990s. In 1992, for example, superstar director Francis Ford Coppola brought the classic Dracula story back to the big screen, this time featuring a big-name cast, superb cinematography, and a budget well beyond anything previously available to vampire films. *Bram Stoker's Dracula* was a solid box-office success, while garnering a number of positive reviews. It also gave a sort of credibility to the vampire film, while attempting (in more ways than just through the title) a return to a more faithful representation of the original novel upon which the entire Dracula cultural phenomenon has been based. Soon afterward, Neil Jordan's *Interview with the Vampire*, based on the vampire stories of Anne Rice, was a big hit in 1994, while also pulling vampire films even more into the Hollywood mainstream with its A-list cast, including such headliners as Tom Cruise and Brad Pitt. By 1997, meanwhile, the series *Buffy the Vampire Slayer* (itself based on a 1992 film written by series creator Joss Whedon) had come to television, beginning a seven-year run that would make it one of the most respected pop hits in TV history.

Vampire slayer though he may be, the deadly, black-suited, gun-toting Blade is no Buffy. Nor is he a well-known figure from vampire lore, as was the case with both Coppola's and Jordan's main vampire figures. *Blade*, in fact, arose to Hollywood success from quite obscure origins. In 1973, writer Marv Wolfman and artist Gene Colan created a character called "Blade" as a supporting character in the ongoing Marvel comic *Tomb of Dracula*. Blade went on to have an extensive and varied career in various Marvel comics (battling Dracula and various other vampires), though he never became a major figure in the Marvel universe, a fact that may have been something of an advantage to the filmmakers. Blade's obscurity made it possible for them to take greater liberties with the character because he was not as well known as other Marvel figures, such as Spider-Man, with whom Blade even teamed to fight evil in one issue of the *Spider-Man* comic. For example, the film's Blade is an American from Chicago, while the Blade of the comics is British.

The film's Blade is, in fact, based very loosely on its predecessors in the comics, though the success of the film and its sequels has actually led Marvel to make certain modifications to make the character in the comics more like the one in the films. Moreover, Blade has become a more prominent figure in the Marvel world, returning to star in his own self-titled comic, written by Marc Guggenheim and drawn by Howard Chaykin, beginning in September, 2006. The films also inspired a short-lived (but positively reviewed) television series that ran for a short stint on Spike TV from

June to September, 2006, with Kirk "Sticky" Jones in the title role. Blade has also been featured in video games, but the three films remain the most prominent venue for the character in recent popular culture. *Blade* grossed roughly $130 million worldwide, which was sufficient to trigger the making of two sequels. *Blade II*, a visual tour de force helmed by rising superstar image-maker Guillermo del Toro, grossed $150 million, while *Blade: Trinity* (2004) took in a somewhat disappointing $130 million worldwide. However, by the standards of early-twenty-first-century blockbusters, the *Blade* films were relatively inexpensive to make, and all were profitable. Moreover, the success of the first *Blade* film ushered in a sort of Golden Age of films based on Marvel comics; *Blade* was quickly followed by film adaptations featuring better-known Marvel characters, beginning with the highly successful *X-Men* (2000) and continuing with the megahit *Spider-Man* (2002).

BLADE: BIRTH OF A HERO

Blade begins with a quick exposition of the origin of its central character, as we observe Blade's birth (stipulated to occur in 1967, though the comic-book character was born in 1929). There is no explanation at the time of what we are seeing, but it will eventually become clear. An African American woman is simply wheeled into a hospital, bleeding profusely from the neck, apparently "bitten by some kind of an animal." She goes into labor, and her baby is delivered by C-section as she slips toward death. The film then cuts to its opening title sequence, with fast-motion frames showing people rushing about the streets of Chicago as night falls, leading to the first present-day scene of the film, in which an ultracool and sexy-looking young woman named Racquel (played by Traci Lords) drives with a man she has apparently just met to what appears to be a hip dance club, though they ominously walk through a meat-packing plant on the way into the club.

Inside the incredibly crowded club, a throng of dancers gyrates to hard-driving techno-dance music in low ambient light accented by flashing strobes. Suddenly, as the dancers move more toward a frenzy, the overhead sprinkler system begins to shower them with blood. It quickly becomes clear that most of the revelers are vampires and that Racquel has brought the newcomer for them to feed on. Terrified, he attempts to crawl to safety, but seems doomed until he looks up to find himself at the feet of Blade (Wesley Snipes), clad in black leather, and looking even scarier and more formidable than the vampires. In the somewhat unlikely sequence that follows, he shoots up the club, using hollow-point bullets laced with garlic that cause the vampires he shoots (including Racquel) to explode and disintegrate in spectacular fashion.

This high-action scene sets the tone for the remainder of the film, which really has more the feel of an action film than a traditional vampire film. What really makes the *Blade* films special, of course, is their ability to mix the horror and action genres so effectively, with just the right hint of comic-book elements to remind us that, however much an antihero he might be, Blade is among other things a participant in the tradition of comic-book superheroes. In addition, the action in the club scene, with its vampires dancing to contemporary music, is indicative of the self-consciously cool nature of the films, which obviously want to appeal to young audiences and to stave off any possible perception that vampire films might be old-fashioned, despite their lengthy pedigree. For example, all of the *Blade* films forgo the Gothic look that is typical of the vampire genre, aiming instead for more of an urban film noir look. However, the films are also overtly contemporary, replacing the vaguely nostalgic feel of many neo-noir films with a soundtrack and cinematography that very clearly place them around the beginning of the twenty-first century. This is not to say that *Blade* and its sequels strive for gritty realism. There are numerous examples of extreme camera angles, fast-motion sequences, and intrusive lighting that help to create a look that meshes with the supernatural subject matter of the film, while the crucial fight sequences are definitely over-the-top, highly choreographed, and almost more like dance than combat, even if they can be extremely violent and bloody.

Crucial to the up-to-date feel of the *Blade* films is their title character, whose dark sunglasses and flowing black leather coat may reflect a sensitivity to sunlight due to his half-vampire nature, but whose overall appearance also suggests a very contemporary coolness. Except for his light-sensitivity (that still allows him to go out in sunlight), Blade lacks the vulnerabilities of vampires, but has their strength and resilience. He is thus a sort of supervampire, though one who fights, luckily, on the side of humans, partly in a quest for revenge for the death of his mother. Snipes plays the character in a very low key, talking softly and carrying a big blade. When he does talk, he uses very contemporary lingo. He also talks tough, his near whisper clearly veiling bitterness and seething anger, not only at the vampires he is slaying, but at his own fate in life. He has the tragic edge of many of the great superheroes, especially Batman, though he goes well beyond Batman in the way he seems to be carrying the weight of the world on his broad, strong shoulders. After all, he is fated by the facts of his birth not only to wage a battle against evil, but to wage a battle against an evil the existence of which is unknown to the vast majority of the population, who live out their routine, sugar-coated lives entirely

unaware of the incredible violence and evil that lurk just beneath the surface of their seemingly tranquil society. Blade also differs from figures
such as Batman in that his battle against evil is financed not by his own
independent wealth but by his own career as a thief. After all, in the dark
world in which he lives, a few routine thefts pale in comparison to the
incredibly evil he must fight. Finally, Blade has an extra tragic edge from
the fact that he is constant danger of "turning," of becoming a vampire
itself, his transformation being delayed only by a serum to which he is
developing an increasing resistance.

Blade's mentor and advisor is Abraham Whistler (Kris Kristofferson), himself an aging former vampire hunter who has dedicated himself
to killing vampires ever since a vampire killed his wife and two young
daughters years earlier. Whistler discovered the young Blade when the
latter was thirteen years old and has groomed him to be his successor
ever since. Whistler is a character in the tradition of the aging gunfighter,
still formidable, but past his prime and ready to hand the reins over to
his younger protégé. From his long experience, Whistler is an expert on
vampires and their culture. He is thus a sort of Van Helsing figure (and, indeed, the first name of the vampire expert from Bram Stoker's 1895 novel
Dracula was Abraham) though one who is again updated to the contemporary world. He spends much of his time in a high-tech workshop, crafting
weapons for Blade to use, while also working to find more effective ways
to prevent Blade from being overcome by his natural bloodlust and going
vampire.

Of course, any successful superhero film requires good supervillains,
and the *Blade* franchise comes with a built-in stock of them in its vision of
a shadowy underworld peopled by superhuman vampire villains. Again,
however, these are not your father's vampires. For one thing, the vampires of the film are not the romantic, even tragic figures often seen in
vampire films. Instead, they are mostly sleazy thugs, sometimes comically
so, as with the lackey Quinn (Donal Logue). In addition, we see a range
of vampire "types," in the film, including one, the bloated androgynous
vampire librarian Pearl, who is a Jabba the Hut lookalike. Finally, while
these vampires are as bloodthirsty as any ever seen on film, they also suck
the blood of human society metaphorically, running a variety of capitalist
enterprises and exerting tremendous financial power and influence on
the world at large. At least in the city of the film, for example, we are
told that they "own" the police, who generally do their bidding rather than
attempting to stop them. In return, vampires keep a low profile and limit
their operations to a level that can go undetected. However, the principal
villain of *Blade*, the vampire Deacon Frost (Stephen Dorff) is so up-to-date
that even this corporate world of vampirism as big business is old fashioned

by his standards. Dorff, constantly employing laptop computers and other high-tech devices, is young, hip, and deliciously evil as Frost—so much so that he won the year's MTV Movie Award (a measure of contemporaneity in the movies if there ever was one) for best villain. Impatient with the willingness of the three-piece-suited corporate rulers of the vampire world to limit their operations and thus stay beneath the radar of human society, Frost wants to go for dominion over the entire planet. He thus concocts a plan to resurrect the vampire god La Magra, taking the power of the god into himself to give him the ability to conquer the world.

This plan and Blade's attempt to stop it provide the central plotline of the film, gaining resonance from the fact that the resurrection of La Magra requires a liberal dose of the blood of a Daywalker (a vampire able to go out in sunlight), such as Blade. This supernatural plot may be the film's greatest weakness, though it does contribute to the film's effort to create a sort of alternative vampire mythology of its own, often by adding new, up-to-date elements. For example, in the course of the film, Karen Jensen (N'Bushe Wright), a beautiful young pathologist who has been bitten by Quinn and is thus on the verge of becoming a vampire herself, discovers that the chemical EDTA (described in the film as an "anticoagulant," though it is typically used for other things) is explosively destructive to vampires, thus adding a modern scientific element to the arsenal of vampire hunters, just as the film also stipulates that some traditional antivampire weapons, such as crosses, actually have no effectiveness whatsoever.

Blade's final confrontation with Frost gains poignancy from the fact that Blade's dead mother has arisen as a vampire herself (as the victims of vampires are wont to do). In fact, she is now working as an agent of Frost. She thus helps to lure Blade into Frost's clutches, allowing him to capture and bleed Blade as part of a complex ritual that also involves the sacrifice of the twelve members of the Shadow Council of the House of Erebus (a sort of Board of Directors of corporate vampirism). As a result of this ritual, Frost takes on the powers of each member of the Shadow Council, which combine with the blood of the Daywalker to allow him to become the vampire god La Magra, and thus presumably to conquer the world in a vampire apocalypse. He also gains immunity to conventional antivampire weapons, such as garlic and silver. What Frost does not count on is the fact that Jensen manages to rescue Blade and restore him to health by allowing him to drink her blood. Blade then manages to destroy Frost/La Magra with a heavy dose of EDTA. He then declines Jensen's offer to cure him of vampirism and thus make him entirely human because he wants to retain his superhuman abilities so that he can continue to combat vampires wherever he finds them. The film thus ends with a final scene set in Moscow, as Blade pursues his vampire hunt in the Russian capital, emphasizing the global nature of his battle against vampires.

BLADE II: DOING THINGS IN STYLE

Blade is a distinctive film with a look and feel of its own, and its vampire-film-as-action-film premise breaks genuinely new ground in American cinema. Given this distinction—and given its commercial success—the film was almost certain to become the founding work in a franchise. At the same time, it is such a distinctive film that any sequels would seem to be in danger of repeating the fate of sequels such as *Men in Black II* by failing to add anything really new or distinctive of their own. However, in the hands of director Guillermo del Toro, who had already established himself as a master of high-style horror in such films as *Cronos* (1993) and *Mimic* (1997), going beyond *Blade* was no problem at all for *Blade II*. *Blade II* is, in fact, a visual masterpiece, a tour de force of blood and guts that takes violence and gore into the realm of (computer enhanced) high art, while taking additional inspiration from pop-cultural sources such as Japanese animé. It also never loses touch with its comic-book roots, thanks partly to the work of Mike Mignola, creator of the *Hellboy* comics, as a visual consultant. *Blade II* is much scarier (and yet much funnier) than *Blade*, a film whose shadow it easily escapes.

If there is a conventional "sequel" problem with *Blade II*, it lies in the fact that the title character, still played by Snipes, is still pretty much the same as he had been in *Blade* (though with perhaps a bit less existential angst), therefore adding very little that is truly new. In fact, the main addition in terms of Blade himself is simply visual and fairly minor. Blade's long, flowing black coat now has a bright red lining that meshes perfectly not only with the bloodiness of the film but with its overall visual flair, giving him a more dashing look. Otherwise, we learn very little about the character that we didn't already know. Indeed, Blade himself is much less prominent as a central figure in the sequel than he had been in the original, becoming merely the leader of an ensemble force of vampire hunters, rather than a lone warrior. Moreover, the characters in general almost become secondary to the unique look of the film, which manages to combine over-the-top comic-book action with an atmosphere of genuine horror in a way that actually works and seems neither campy nor inappropriate. If the first *Blade* was both an action movie and a horror movie, the emphasis was definitely on the former. *Blade II* reverses this emphasis, adding significantly more horror elements, in terms of both plot and atmosphere, with a substantial Gothicism added to the film noir look of the first film.

At the same time, *Blade II* includes a great deal of playfulness, including a long list of references to comic books other than those in which Blade had appeared and verbal and visual allusions to classic films such as *The Godfather* and *Apocalypse Now*.

Most of the action of the film takes place in Prague (where, in fact, most of the film was shot), a much more conventionally Gothic setting than the city of the first film. In addition, in a twist that takes the film into genuinely new plot territory, most of the other members of the vampire-hunting team led by Blade (also known as the Bloodpack) are themselves vampires, members of an elite vampire strike force, a sort of vampire Dirty Dozen. Originally trained by the ancient vampire lord Damaskinos (Thomas Kretschmann) to fight Blade himself, they have now been called into action to fight side-by-side with Blade against a group of new mutant vampires, known as "Reapers," who have recently arisen from a single mutant forebear, Jared Nomak (Luke Goss). The Reapers feed on both vampires and humans, turning their victims into Reapers at such a rate that they threaten to quickly spread across the face of the entire planet. These Reapers, horrible, hairless, pale, blue-veined creatures somewhat in the tradition of Nosferatu, are the visual center of the film, setting the tone for a bloodfest that includes even more action than the first film, despite being much more of a horror film than the original *Blade* had been. The Reapers are also invulnerable to garlic and silver; they can be killed by a stake through the heart, but their hearts are encased in a nearly impenetrable cage of bone. Thus, in most cases, sunlight is the only weapon that works against them. In an added twist of horror, the mouths of the Reapers blossom outward to reveal horrifying, writhing blood-sucking workings within, somewhat in the way the mouth of the creature in the *Alien* films opens wide to allow the extension of an even more terrible mouth from within.

Surprisingly, Whistler, seemingly killed in the first film, is resurrected early in the film as Blade rescues him from a facility in which the vampires have been keeping the old man in storage, milking him of blood (a fact that is comically emphasized by the fact that the factory is labeled the "Moo-Cow" milk factory. Blade manages not only to revive Whistler, but to restore his humanity. The two then join forces with Blade's new human sidekick, Scud (Norman Reedus), though there are tensions between Scud and Whistler from the very beginning. These tensions turn out to arise from Whistler's sharp instincts, because Scud (who wears a tee shirt that alludes to the *Hellboy* comic throughout the film) is actually a "familiar," a human working in league with the vampires. Then again, through most of the film, Blade himself is working with the vampires in their assault on the Reapers. The vampire strike-force itself includes some interesting and compelling characters, and one of the ways *Blade II* succeeds in going beyond *Blade* (or any previous vampire film) involves its depiction of vampires as distinct individuals with their own identities, predilections, and concerns, rather than simply a mindless horde of interchangeable predators.

Damaskinos himself is an extremely interesting figure, a highly Gothic, old-style vampire who is dramatically different from figures such as the first *Blade* film's Deacon Frost (though he still spends a lot of time in very modern activities such as consulting his lawyer and watching television). Probably the most interesting character among the vampires is the burly and powerful Reinhardt (played by Ron Perlman, who would soon play the title role in del Toro's 2004 film adaptation of *Hellboy*). The surly Reinhardt is resentful of Blade's presence in the group, yet he has (thanks to Perlman's performance) a kind of rough charm. The female lead of the film is also one of the vampires, the beautiful Nyssa (Leonor Varela), first introduced to us as she arrives at Blade's workshop headquarters along with her compatriot Asad (Danny Jon-Jules), dressed in ninja-like garb, apparently bent on attacking the headquarters. After a flurry of martial arts action (triggered when Whistler opens fire on them, assuming they are hostile), they are finally able to deliver their message of conciliation from Damaskinos, who wants to join forces with Blade to battle the Reapers.

Blade ultimately agrees, though he and the Bloodpack (especially Reinhardt) never quite trust each other, creating tensions that add significant plot possibilities. Actually, the main plot is highly predictable, as Blade defeats the Reapers, personally killing Nomak, after a series of spectacular action-fight sequences. However, these sequences are extremely stylish, partly because they occur in a series of perfectly chosen settings, beginning with another vampire dance club, in a kind of echo of the beginning of the first film. This setting helps to motivate the loud music and fast pace of the ultraviolent, over-the-top fight scenes, which include a significant amount of collateral damage to the ordinary vampires who happen to be dancing in the club when the attack begins. The fighting then moves to other sites, including a very Gothic abandoned church (a Los Angeles church was actually used for the shooting of this sequence) and a very Old World-looking Prague sewer. The general thrust of the plot is also accented by a number of twists and turns. For example, in addition to the revelation of Scud's treachery, we eventually learn that Nyssa is the daughter of Damaskinos. More importantly, we learn that Nomak did not become a Reaper via an accidental mutation, but was in fact created by Damaskinos as part of a sinister project to create a new and deadlier strain of vampires. Damaskinos, of course, betrays Blade along the way, nearly torturing him to death before he is rescued by Whistler, enabling Blade's ultimate victory, in which he slays Nomak with a sword thrust to the heart that manages to get through the bone cage—shown to us in great anatomical detail via a close-up shot of the inside of Nomak's body as the organs are pierced by the sword. This final fight is followed by a rather touching scene in which Blade carries Nyssa, who has been bitten by Nomak, onto a rooftop to await the rising sun, which kills her and prevents her from becoming a Reaper. With the Reaper line thus wiped out, the film then proceeds to a final comic coda in which Blade tracks down and kills a vampire who had escaped him earlier in the film—finding him in a peep-show booth at a London sex shop called (no less) Fuckingham Palace. The film thus ends with a final reminder that this is a film that is meant to be fun and should not be taken too seriously—while also echoing the end of the first film in reminding us of Balde's ongoing international battle against vampires.

BLADE: TRINITY: THE CURSE OF DRACULA

Blade II was an even bigger commercial hit than *Blade*, though critical views were mixed on whether it was really a better film than the original. Given this success, a second sequel was sure to follow, and it did. Snipes again returns in the title role in *Blade: Trinity*, still playing very much the same Blade, though he wears more red and does seem slightly more vampirish in the second sequel, his trademark whisper now punctuated with a greater number of snarls and hisses. Del Toro was also asked to return as director, but was unavailable due to his work on *Hellboy*. Thus, the direction of *Blade: Trinity* fell to David S. Goyer, who at the time had very little in the way of directorial credentials, having directed only the relatively minor drama *ZigZag* (2002). Goyer, however, had an impeccable background as a writer, having scripted the first two *Blade* films, as well as the 1998 cult hit *Dark City*, which has much of the same noirish spirit as the *Blade* pictures. Goyer does a competent job of directing *Blade: Trinity*, though he certainly lacks the visual flair of del Toro. Consequently, *Blade: Trinity* cannot match the visual stylistics of *Blade II*, though (to his credit) Goyer doesn't attempt to match del Toro but instead goes his own route, returning largely to the look and spirit of the original *Blade* film, though his version looks a bit less like film noir and a bit more like science fiction in comparison with the first film. In any case, *Blade: Trinity* seemed to many critics and moviegoers to be a step backward instead of forward, and most reviews of the film were lukewarm at best.

This is not to say that *Blade: Trinity* does not introduce new material to the *Blade* sequence of films. Indeed, it adds a great deal of such material (maybe too much), most of it derived from delving back into the comics from which the character of Blade had arisen. There is even an extensive high-speed car chase early in the film, as if to ensure that it covers all the action-film bases. We return to the original film's scenario of Blade battling against vampires, though the present-day vampires of the film are in this case significantly reinforced when they dig up none other than Dracula himself (played by Dominic Purcell) from his tomb in Syria, hoping to enlist his aid in their battle against Blade—and in their quest to conquer mankind once and for all. This aspect of the film thus ties into the best-known strain of vampire lore in all of Western popular culture, while at the same time drawing upon the fact that Blade and Dracula had often faced each other in various venues in the comics.

Meanwhile, the vampires have tricked Blade into the killing of a human—on videotape, no less—using that evidence and their general influence with the authorities to convince the police and FBI to conduct an all-out military-style assault on Blade's headquarters, where an old and tired Whistler (or maybe Kristofferson is merely tired of the role) has just warned Blade about the danger of trying to fight vampires alone and without allies. Whistler is killed in the raid (this time surely for good), while Blade is captured after a spectacular battle. With Whistler dead, Blade is, as far as he knows, without allies, so the incarcerated hero (undergoing brutal interrogation at the hands of a police psychiatrist who is actually a vampire familiar) seems doomed. The situation changes dramatically, however, when he is rescued by two fellow vampire hunters, the buff-but-sexy Abigail Whistler (Jessica Biel) and the muscular wise-ass Hannibal King (Ryan Reynolds), who turn out to be members of a well-equipped and well-organized group of vampire slayers known as the Nightstalkers. In this sense, though there are substantial modifications, the film once again returns to Blade's roots in the comics, where he, King, and Frank Drake had been organized by Doctor Strange as the Nightstalkers and who subsequently fought vampires in their own *Nightstalkers* imprint of Marvel comics.

Whistler had actually been introduced in a hilarious earlier scene in which she poses as a helpless and vulnerable female with a small baby—just so she can lure a group of vampires into attacking her and then kick their asses big time. The illegitimate daughter of Abraham Whistler, her favorite weapon is a high-tech bow and arrow, and she likes to listen to her MP3 player while she hunts vampires. She was invented for the film (which, after all, needed a female lead), though she roughly corresponds to the character of Rachel Van Helsing (the granddaughter of Abraham Van Helsing), who had appeared in the *Tomb of Dracula* comics. It was decided to replace Van Helsing with Whistler for *Blade: Trinity* to avoid confusion with Stephen Sommers's film *Van Helsing*, which was slated for release a few months before *Blade: Trinity*. Of course, the replacement was entirely appropriate, given that Abraham Whistler was something of a stand-in for Abraham Van Helsing to begin with. Abigail, like Blade, has been trained by her father to fight vampires, and so her group has some of the same expertise as Blade, though he is at first reluctant to join forces with them, regarding them as "amateurs." Meanwhile, as a former vampire himself (though the film does not make his vampire background quite clear), King has some of Blade's physical abilities. Mostly, though, his wise-cracking attitude seems meant as a sort of counterpoint to Blade's laconic dead-seriousness, but the pair never quite come off as a straight man-funny man team.

The Nightstalkers, helped by the blind scientist Sommerfield (Natasha Lyonne), have developed a number of new antivampire weapons, including a "UV arc," something like a cross between a light saber and a Klingon battle blade, whose laser-blade is preposterously stipulated to operate at half the temperature of the sun. Most important to the plot, they are developing a virus (code name Daystar) that will almost instantly kill any vampire with whom it comes into contact. Unfortunately, though, they need a sample of "pure" vampire DNA in order to bring the virus to full strength (and thus able to spread quickly, wiping out the entire vampire race), such DNA apparently no longer being available from the degenerate vampires of today's world. Enter Dracula, here stipulated to be the first vampire and the founder of the entire vampire line. He also is the only remaining vampire with the pure DNA needed to ramp up the power of the antivampire virus. In one of the film's few moments of potential political commentary, the Nightstalkers have heard about Dracula's resurrection, though their information is that he was found in Iraq (rather than Syria), which could be taken as an echo of the Bush Administration's faulty intelligence about Iraqi weapons of mass destruction prior to the 2003 invasion.

Dracula here is a sort of supervampire, who lacks most of the traditional vampire weaknesses and can even go out in direct sunlight. He also has a special skeletal structure that gives him shape-shifting abilities, allowing him to take on different forms, including one particularly monstrous one that looks very much like a science fiction alien, complete with the multihinged jaws of the Reapers from *Blade II*. Unfortunately, despite all of these extra features, the portrayal of Dracula is one of the weaknesses of the film. Dracula is so well known and carries with him such an extensive mythology that any attempt to add to this mythology is fraught with difficulty. This film does not overcome those difficulties. Its Dracula somehow lacks magnitude, seeming more like a thug with superpowers than the regal and mysterious figure he ought to be given the mythical stature that is attributed to him in the film (and in much of the legacy of Dracula lore). The film tries to stipulate that its Dracula, given his abilities, is actually far more frightening than the Dracula of pop culture lore, but never makes that claim convincing. Even his superpowers seem inappropriate, as if the script somewhere got mixed up with that of a science fiction alien-invasion narrative. Indeed, Goyer seems to have attempted to spice up *Blade: Trinity* with a number of science fiction elements, none of which work all that well.

In a similar way, the "conventional" vampires of the film lack the air of creepy supernatural threat that have made vampires so popular as horror-film monsters, partly because this film stipulates that they have grown degenerate and soft, thus the need for Dracula to inject some fresh blood (as it were) into their operation. Wrestler Triple H is okay as their muscle man, Jarko Grimwood, but he again seems more thuggish than truly disturbing. Meanwhile, Parker Posey plays their leader, Danica Talos, as a sort of camped-up bitch who is more annoying than scary. These degenerate vampires could be taken as a commentary on the decadence of the postmodern world, though the film doesn't really seem committed to such commentary. Indeed, the strongest such comment occurs in what might also be the film's funniest scene, in which Dracula walks into a Goth shop and becomes appalled at the commercialization and commodification of vampire myths. Particularly horrified by a display of Count Chocula cereal, he of course kills and feeds on the shopgirl in response. Unfortunately, this motif then drops out of the film, wiped away by the frantic quest for action.

Another problem occurs with the film's other major addition to the mythology of the *Blade* sequence. Here, it is made clear that the vampires have come up with an answer to the problem of where they are supposed to get the human blood that they need for sustenance once they triumph and wipe humanity off the face of the earth. For some time, they have been systematically taking homeless people off the streets, assuming that no one will miss them. They then take their victims to huge, warehouse-like "blood farms," where they are encased in plastic containers and drained of blood, but kept alive for significant periods so that they can produce a continual supply, sometimes as much as 100 pints per person before they die. This motif (strongly reminiscent of the way humans are encased by their machine-rulers in small, womblike compartments to be used as a source of electrical energy in the 1999 sf film *The Matrix*) extends the "milk-factory" motif of the second film. The motif had, in fact, been originally developed by Goyer for the first *Blade* film, but was dropped then because they were unable to come up with a convincing look for the blood farms. Here, the look is reasonably convincing (though still veering dangerously close to the ridiculous), but the blood farms are somehow not nearly as terrifying as they should be, given the potential for this image (like the corresponding image in *The Matrix*) allegorically to address the sense of so many in the real world of contemporary America of being trapped and exploited by a system of forces beyond their understanding.

One reason for the lack of effectiveness of the blood farm motif is probably that it is simply not emphasized in the film, which seems more interested in moving as quickly as possible from one fight sequence to the next than in providing any sort of thoughtful social or political commentary. Or it may simply be that we had already seen basically the same thing done much better in the human battery farms of *The Matrix*, which were much more horrifying, even if they actually made less sense. Ultimately, the quest for action in *Blade: Trinity* seems to have no real direction, which might explain why the filmmakers seem to have had considerable difficulty in coming up with an ending. In the version that was released to theaters, Dracula is killed (of course), but shape-shifts so that he looks like Blade, causing the authorities converging on the scene to declare Blade dead and drop their search for him. This allows Blade to continue his fight against vampires unabated (and opens the way for still another sequel), though Dracula's true motivation is that he believes Blade, lacking the decadence of the other vampires around him, is the key to the future of a new, stronger vampire race. In Goyer's preferred "Director's Cut" ending, Blade ends the film seemingly rising from the dead, with audiences left unsure whether he rises to continue the fight against vampirism or whether he has in fact assumed Dracula's mantle as king of the vampires and founder of a new vampire race. This ending also leaves the way open for a sequel, but the bulk of *Blade: Trinity* suggests that the *Blade* sequence might best be laid to rest—before it becomes a complete parody of its original, darkly serious self, descending into the kind of silliness that plagued the third and fourth films in the Superman, Batman, and Crow sequences.

6

The *X-Men* Film Franchise

Released 2000–2006; Directors Bryan Singer and Brett Ratner

HUMAN EVOLUTION MEETS CULTURAL EVOLUTION: THE BIRTH OF A FRANCHISE

X-Men (2000) followed the success of *Blade* and marked the beginning of a major commitment to film on the part of Marvel Comics. This film not only saw the adaptation of one of Marvel's central comics' franchises to film, but did so in a big way, with a $75 million budget that went well beyond that of *Blade*'s $45 million. At that time superhero films not featuring Superman or Batman had little in the way of a track record of box-office success, but Marvel's investment in the *X-Men* film was a calculated one. For one thing, the X-Men had been one of the most successful superhero teams in the history of the comics, dating back to their debut in their own self-titled comic in September, 1963, and continuing to the time of the film, branching into several different series featuring several different teams of X-Men. The franchise had also already proved popular on television, via the highly successful *X-Men: The Animated Series*, which ran on Fox from 1992 to 1997. The film thus had a sort of built-in audience, some of whom had followed the franchise for decades. It also had plenty of material to draw upon, given the long and varied history of the X-Men comics, with their numerous characters and multiple plot lines. Further, the film's substantial budget, placed in the hands of thirty-five-year-old Bryan Singer, was well spent. Already regarded as one of Hollywood's up-and-coming star directors, largely on the basis of his 1995 film *The Usual*

Suspects, Singer used the budget to hire a superb cast of well-known actors and to produce impressive state-of-the-art special effects. The result was a highly entertaining film with a worldwide gross of roughly $300 million and the beginnings not only of a major new film franchise but of Marvel as a major player in the film industry. This success was a turning point in the history of graphic cinema, leading to a plethora of big-budget films based on the comics, especially those involving superheroes.

The X-Men, created by Marvel pioneers Stan Lee and Jack Kirby, first appeared as the stars of their own comic in *X-Men* #1 in September, 1963. As a superhero team, they thus followed in the footsteps of the Fantastic Four, who had debuted two years earlier, though they had their own unique premise. According to this premise (that clearly grows out of cold war concerns about the potential genetic effects of exposure to radiation), the world has experienced (since World War II) an explosion in the birth rate of mutants (many of them with superhuman powers), potentially suggesting the beginning of a dramatic new phase in the evolution of the human race. Paraplegic mutant telepath Professor Charles Francis Xavier (aka Professor X) gathers together a team of these younger mutants, now teenagers, then trains them to control their powers and to use their special abilities to fight evil, especially that represented by the Brotherhood of Evil Mutants, headed by the powerful mutant Magneto.

Among other things, this premise offers considerable possibilities for social commentary, the xenophobic fear and hatred often shown toward the mutants by "ordinary" humans acting as an allegorical stand-in for racism and other forms of discrimination among humans. This aspect of the premise was also enhanced by the fact that the X-Men comics were among the first to feature a multiracial and multicultural cast of characters when the series was revamped with a new cast of mutant heroes in the 1970s, adding mutants from Africa, the Soviet Union, and Japan, among other places, somewhat along the lines of the crew of the *Enterprise* in the *Star Trek* television series of the late 1960s. Various other changes in the cast of characters occurred over the years; altogether nearly fifty different characters have been designated as members of the X-Men team. Among the original group, two mutants, Cyclops (aka Scott Summers) and Marvel Girl (aka Jean Grey), have remained prominent and are featured in the film. Other prominent members of the X-Men team featured in the film include Wolverine (aka Logan), Storm (aka Ororo Monroe), and Rogue (aka Marie D'Ancanto).

X-Men is a film that seems, in retrospect, to have been overtly designed as the founding work of a franchise. It features a fairly minimal plot and serves primarily as an introduction to the characters and to the near-future world in which they live. Nevertheless, the film was a great success, partly because it strikes such a nice balance between being basically true to the spirit of the comics and making the modifications that are necessary for the translation to film. The success of the film ensured that it would, indeed, be the first in a series, though its follow-up, *X2*, did not appear until 2003, by which time *Spider-Man* had taken superhero films to a whole new level of box-office success. Able to build on the characters and world already established in the first film, *X2* is, on the whole, a more accomplished and more complete film than *X-Men*. The significantly larger budget also made for even better special effects—and paid off with even great receipts at the box office; the film took in more than $400 million worldwide. The second sequel, *X-Men: The Last Stand* (2006), has even more spectacular effects and made even more at the box office, establishing the X-Men sequence as one of the most successful franchises in film history.

MUTANTS OF THE WORLD UNITE—OR NOT

X-Men begins with a voiceover (by Patrick Stewart, who stars as Professor X) explaining how evolution is a very slow process, except that "every few hundred millennia" it leaps forward through a sudden increase in mutations. This beginning thus both sets the stage for the film and removes it from any sort of (now passé) cold war connotations by suggesting that the current outburst of mutations is part of a normal periodic process, not the result of recent human dabbling with nuclear energy and weapons. The film does, however, look back to World War II in that the first actual scene occurs in Poland in 1944, as Nazi soldiers round up Polish Jews to take them off to the death camps. A young boy is left behind as his parents are taken away into a camp. The boy displays strange psychic powers, using his mind to pull at the metal of the gate of the camp, nearly tearing it loose, until he is knocked unconscious by the butt of a Nazi soldier's rifle. This boy, we eventually realize, is Eric Lensherr, who will grow up to become the evil mutant leader Magneto (played in the film by distinguished British actor Ian McKellen). Magneto has tremendous power to manipulate metals via the magnetic forces that he is able to summon through his psychic powers. He has also (presumably due to the psychic consequences of his experiences with the Nazis) become quite bitter, possibly mad; he is determined to use his powers in a war on humanity, because he is convinced (not entirely without reason) that humans, in their treatment of the new generation of mutants, will recreate the treatment of the Jews by the Nazis.

This introductory scene provides a certain psychological basis for Magneto's distrust of humans and is indicative of the way in which *X-Men*, however far-out many of its motifs may be, takes its premise absolutely seriously, with no hint of campy self-consciousness. The evocation of the Holocaust also provides important background to the attempts of humans in the film to limit the freedom and activities of mutants, helping to ensure that the sympathies of filmgoing humans will be with the mutants—or at least with the "good" mutants, as represented by the X-Men. Still, the film's principal villain is both a mutant and a Jewish Holocaust survivor, a fact that complicates any audience identification with mutants via sympathy with the Jewish victims of the Holocaust. Ultimately, while the human fear and potential oppression of mutants is a key part of the backdrop (and the message) of the film, the oppositions in the film are really the old comic book stand-bys: good vs. evil.

After this opening scene, the film immediately cuts to Meridian, Mississippi, in "the not too distant future." Here, we see teenager Marie D'Ancanto (Anna Paquin) kissing her boyfriend, who goes into some sort of seizure as soon as she touches him. Eventually, Marie will become the mutant superhero known as Rogue, who tends (without her own volition) to absorb the strength and abilities of anyone she touches, leaving them in a vastly weakened state that is potentially deadly. As a result, she considers her powers a curse and is one of the most tormented of the X-Men. After this brief introduction to her (without any clear explanation of her powers), the film cuts to a U.S. Senate hearing in which Dr. Jean Grey (Famke Janssen), testifying as a scientist and not as the mutant she in fact is, attempts to assure a Senate investigating committee, led by the pompous demagogue Senator Robert Kelly (Bruce Davison), that mutants are no real threat to humanity. In fact, the real threat is the other way around; she thus opposes Kelly's plan to force all mutants to register as such (as the Nazis forced Jews to register), for fear that mutants, once identified, will become the objects of persecution by humans. Among other things, the depiction of Kelly in the film recalls the real-life career of Senator Joseph McCarthy, a depiction that, among other things, adds communists and other political dissidents to the list of marginalized groups for whom mutants serve as metaphors in the *X-Men* films. In any case, as Kelly enters into a diatribe against mutants, with Professor X looking on with concern from the gallery, he gets an enthusiastic response that suggests just how dangerous he might be to the mutant community.

This scene thus establishes the political situation that is the backdrop to the film. Subsequent scenes establish other basic facts that we need to know, including the fact that Professor X runs an exclusive, high-security boarding school (Xavier's School for Gifted Youngsters) in Westchester County, New York, where young mutants are trained to understand and control their powers. The facility also serves as the secret headquarters of the X-Men, for which the school serves as a cover. We also learn that he and Magneto are old acquaintances, but have now come to a parting of the ways. Professor X believes that mutants and humans can peacefully coexist in a mutually beneficial partnership; Magneto believes that humans, now obsolete but still dangerous, must be entirely subjugated or even destroyed so that mutants can live safely, taking the human race into the next stage of its evolution.

This difference of opinion eventually provides the basic plot of the film, as Professor X and his "good" mutants—led by Grey, Cyclops (James Marsden), and Storm (Halle Berry) and eventually joined by Wolverine (Hugh Jackman) and Rogue—battle to save humanity (and themselves) from the threat posed by Magneto and his "evil" Brotherhood of Mutants—including the shape-shifting Mystique (Rebecca Romijn), the acrobatic Toad (Ray Park), and the vicious Sabretooth (Tyler Mane), a sort of evil counterpart to Wolverine. This basic battle eventually leads to a climactic confrontation at the Statue of Liberty, as the X-Men interrupt Magneto's plan to attack a United Nations Global Summit (described as the "largest single gathering of world leaders in history") that is being held on Ellis Island for the purpose of discussing strategies for dealing with the "mutant problem." Magneto has developed a device (that he has already used on Kelly) that can turn ordinary humans into mutants, and he plans to unleash it on the summit, thereby transforming, in one fell swoop, all of the world's leaders into mutants. To make matters worse, the X-Men have uncovered evidence that these artificially induced mutations can be harmful, or even deadly, and Kelly himself has died as a result of his mutation into a sort of Plastic Man.

Highly symbolic settings such as Ellis Island and the Statue of Liberty suggest, of course, that the treatment of the mutants is a perversion of the ideals of justice and tolerance of difference that the Statue of Liberty and Ellis Island are supposed to represent, but the suggestion is rather halfhearted. This is a film interested in action and special effects, not politics and social commentary. It does, however, attempt to give its portrayal of the X-Men a human dimension, both by emphasizing the fundamental humanity of the mutants, however different they might be, and by providing subplots that focus especially on the personal emotional difficulties that come with being a mutant superbeing. This latter aspect of the film concentrates especially on Wolverine and Rogue. The latter, still an adolescent and dealing with the typical problems of adolescence, must also learn to deal with her newfound powers (that typically activate at puberty). In her case, these powers are particularly isolating in that they mean she is precluded from coming into physical contact with other human beings. Wolverine is older and more cynical, bitter from years of the discrimination he has suffered due to his difference from the human norm. He is also an unusually complex figure. Not only does he have mutant powers (heightened senses, as well as the ability to regenerate damaged cells and thus recover from virtually any wound almost instantaneously), but he has also been the victim of a macabre experiment in which someone has taken advantage of his regenerative powers to somehow infuse his entire skeleton with the virtually indestructible metal adamantium—via an operation that no one without his mutant abilities could have survived. This operation has given him a powerful substructure that also includes the incredibly sharp and tough retractable adamantium claws that are probably his most memorable feature and certainly his deadliest weapon. That he himself suffers considerable pain whenever he uses his claws is indicative of his general tormented state and of the way in which he regards his metallic substructure as a curse, partly because a side-effect of the procedure has been a total loss of memory of anything up to the time he found himself, postexperiment, wandering in the Canadian woods. If Rogue's story is a coming-of-age tale, Wolverine's story is thus a tale of his search for his own identity, as well as his search for the parties who gave him his claws and took that original identity away.

In the course of the film, Rogue (whom Magneto needs in order to operate the machine that will turn the world's leaders into mutants) becomes a member of the X-Men, and the film is to that extent a superhero origin story. Wolverine, though he aligns himself with the X-Men in the film's battles, remains reluctant to join their group, and ends the film going off alone to continue his search for the truth of his past. After all, he is a longtime loner who has trouble trusting anyone, and the ethos of teamwork (including the wearing of matching costumes) that informs the X-Men strikes him as a bit bogus. In addition, his status as a cyborg sets him apart from the other X-Men, though one could argue that Professor X's use of such devices as the mind multiplier Cerebro and even his own wheelchair to extend his personal abilities make him a cyborg of sorts as well. This characterization of Wolverine is consistent with his portrayal in the comics, where he had long been featured in his own self-titled comic and had maintained a somewhat independent status, despite eventually joining the X-Men.

Neither of these "human interest" stories is all that interesting, though Wolverine's complex tale is more effective than that of Rogue. And these stories do at least add enough texture to the action-oriented plot that they help audiences to care about the outcome of the battle scenes, though one could also argue that audiences, being ordinary humans, would naturally side with the X-Men, who defend humanity, against the Brotherhood, who attack it. Of course, defending humanity had long been the mission of the

X-Men—and of superheroes in general—in the comics. One could, however, argue that the basic structural opposition in the film, between the prohuman X-Men and the antihuman Brotherhood, is a problematic one that undermines the film's seemingly liberal (if halfhearted and obligatory) message of tolerance for difference. After all, Magneto and his followers have good reason to fear humans, and one could certainly argue that their vision of a new world, ruled by mutants, has its virtues. Professor X and his charges take the good liberal position that it would do no good to fight the bigotry and intolerance directed against them with more bigotry and intolerance directed against humans. But one could also argue that the X-Men, by defending humans against other mutants, are simply complicit with their own enemies and don't realize who their real friends are, just as the humans who fear mutants (including the X-Men) are unable to understand that the X-Men are their most important defenders. One could even extend this reading to restate the film's message as the very conservative one that we should sympathize with victims of intolerance and oppression unless that take collective action to defend themselves, in which case they need to be dealt with swiftly and forcefully.

MUTANT = GOOD, HUMAN = BAD: THE SIMPLIFIED MORAL UNIVERSE OF *X2*

X2 features the same director and most of the same characters (played by the same actors) as *X-Men* and is very much a direct sequel to that film. However, it takes place in a simplified moral universe in which possible readings of the X-Men as the Uncle Toms of the superhero world are negated by the fact that Professor X and his mutant team are now allied with Magneto and Mystique (Toad and Sabretooth were killed in the climactic battle at the end of the first film), defending mutants against humans. Humans, meanwhile, are presented in *X2* as almost universally ignorant and prejudiced, if not downright evil. *X2* is thus much less conflicted than *X-Men* in its presentation of the mutant team as metaphorical stand-ins for outcasts and misfits everywhere.

X2 again begins with a brief voiceover by Stewart, which prepares us for the mutant-human opposition in the film by warning us that "sharing the world has never been humanity's defining attribute." However, the film proper begins with a bit of misdirection that seems to suggest that mutants are indeed dangerous to humans. In the opening sequence, a mysterious, blue-skinned mutant (played by Alan Cumming) uses his powers of teleportation to infiltrate the White House and attack the president of the United States, easily fighting his way through the president's considerable security team. The mutant, whose pointed tail and ears give a demonic appearance, leaves off the attack, just as he seems on the verge of killing the president. Instead, he leaves his knife stuck in the president's desk, bearing a ribbon carrying the message "Mutant Freedom Now." This sequence, which includes some of the most impressive special effects in the entire film, thus reminds us of the oppression suffered by mutants, but also suggests that humans might be at least partly justified in seeing mutants as a threat to national security, and even to humanity as a whole.

However, we eventually learn that the mutant is one Kurt Wagner (aka Nightcrawler), a German former circus performer. In the course of the film, Wagner joins the X-Men in their battle to save mutants from a genocidal assault by humans. Because of his powers and his strange, even sinister, appearance, Wagner, though a harmless and gentle soul, has always been a radical outsider, mistrusted and feared as a dangerous freak by ordinary humans. It doesn't help that his appearance is made even stranger by the fact that he is covered by strange patterns consisting of self-inflicted scars, via which he has inscribed on his body "angelic symbols," supposedly revealed to him by the angel Gabriel. This scarring combines with the extreme Catholic religiosity of which it is the result, so out of place in the modern world, to separate him even further from mainstream humanity.

Wagner's dramatic Otherness and the poignancy of his rejection by ordinary humans reinforces *X2*'s increased attempt to make the X-Men metaphors for all of those who are hated and feared simply because they are different. Meanwhile, the casting of Cumming, one of Hollywood's most openly gay performers, in the role, subtly suggests that gays and lesbians should be included in the list of those for whom the outcast X-Men are metaphors. This connection is reinforced by the fact that director Singer is himself openly gay and by the fact that the X-Men of the comics have long been read in this way—up to and including the fact that they were joined in 2002 by the powerful mutant Northstar, the first openly gay superhero in mainstream American comics.

The second scene of *X2* occurs in a museum, where Storm, Cyclops, and Jean Grey, all working as teachers at Professor X's school, have taken a group of students on a field trip. Among the students are three teenagers, Rogue, her boyfriend Iceman (also known as Bobby Drake, played by Shawn Ashmore), and the rather bitter Pyro (also known as John Allerdyce, played by Aaron Stanford). As Rogue and Iceman look on, Pyro becomes engaged in an altercation with two human teenagers, one of whom he sets aflame with his mutant ability to manipulate and control fire. Iceman quickly puts out the fire, using his ability to project supercold temperatures, thus freezing the moisture in the air around him. Still, the stage has been set for the way in which these three teens will play a major role in *X2* (though Rogue is actually less important here than in *X-Men*), a fact that both helps younger audiences relate to the film and adds adolescents to the list of outsiders with whose sense of difference the X-Men resonate. In the course of the film, these three must deal with the problems of being an adolescent, here seriously complicated by the problems of being a mutant. These problems seem particularly difficult for Pyro, whose bitterness toward and mistrust of humans makes him a sort of younger version of Magneto, though perhaps the most telling scene in their depiction occurs during a visit to Bobby Drake's family, which only then learns (in a classic coming-out scene) of his mutant abilities. Shocked, his conformist, middle-class parents do not deal well with the news: Mrs. Drake, without irony, asks Bobby if he has ever considered trying not to be a mutant—much in the way such a parent might encourage a gay teenager to try not to be gay.

Soon afterward, we learn that Magneto, captured in the wake of the battle at the Statue of Liberty at the end of *X-Men* is now confined in a high-tech plastic prison where the complete absence of metal makes it impossible for him to use his powers. The film's sequences of Magneto in the prison, where he is tortured and brutalized by his human captors, serve the function of reorienting the moral universe of this film relative to *X-Men* by making Magneto a sympathetic character and by establishing humans as the true villains. Meanwhile, this sequence also makes it clear that the chief individual villain of *X2* is William Stryker (Brian Cox), an army colonel who is also a high-ranking covert agent of the U.S. government. Stryker, a sophisticated scientist, bitterly hates mutants as a result of the fact that his own son's mutant status led to the suicide of Stryker's wife. In the comics, Stryker is a Christian fundamentalist fanatic who believes he is on a mission from God to kill all mutants. That religious element is missing from *X2*, though Stryker is still dedicated to the destruction of all mutants; he is, however, willing to use mutants for his own purposes, including employing them as guinea pigs in his experiments. It was he, for example, who was behind the design of Magneto's prison and who oversees the mutant leader's subsequent brutal interrogation. In fact, we will eventually learn in this film that Stryker was the person in charge of the group that installed Wolverine's experimental adamantium substructure years earlier. It was also Stryker who programmed Nightcrawler to attack the president, hoping that the assault would stir up antimutant sentiments.

Stryker is a classic screen villain: brilliant, ruthless, and utterly without sympathy for those whom he victimizes. The film's depiction of Stryker, which leaves essentially no room for audiences to identify with him, also helps in the rehabilitation of Magneto, who is, in comparison, a highly sympathetic figure. We find, for example, that Stryker has lobotomized his own mutant son, making him a sort of zombie, but leaving him with considerable psychic powers that Stryker can now control for his own purposes. And those purposes are sinister, indeed. Thanks to the attack on the president, Stryker is able to get official approval for an all-out military assault on the Xavier School, which succeeds largely because he has already captured and drugged Professor X and Cyclops, while Storm and Jean are away seeking Nightcrawler. Many of the students are captured, though Wolverine is able to get away with Rogue, Iceman, and Pyro in tow. More importantly, Stryker gets his hands on Cerebro, which he is then able to reconstruct in his secret underground facility at Alkali Lake. Only Professor X can operate Cerebro, but Stryker uses his son's psychic abilities to manipulate the captive Professor X into using the machine to locate all of the world's mutants. The machine then sends out an amplified psychic signal that will kill all of the mutants, but the plan is luckily interrupted when a force of mutants, including the remaining X-Men, Magneto, and Mystique, is able to invade the facility and destroy the machine.

Much of the interest in the action at Alkali Lake concerns the fact that it was at this same facility where Wolverine's adamantium substructure had been implanted years earlier. Thus, as he explores the facility, Wolverine is exploring his own past, the memory of which he at least partly recovers in the process. He also discovers that Stryker's personal bodyguard, Yuriko Oyama (also known as Lady Deathstrike, played by Kelly Hu), is a mutant who has been conditioned for complete obedience to Stryker's authority. Deathstrike has regenerative powers similar to Wolverine's own, which has allowed Stryker to implant her with adamantium as well. Indeed, one of the highlights of the film is a climactic confrontation between Wolverine and Deathstrike, in which the two mutants, endowed with very similar abilities, duel in an evenly matched battle to the death. Wolverine, however, is eventually able to kill her by injecting her with a massive overdose of liquid adamantium. In the end, Stryker is killed and his lab destroyed. Thus, all is relatively well, except that Jean is apparently drowned when a huge dam overlooking the Alkali Lake facility breaks, flooding the entire area.

All in all, *X2* is probably the most successful of all the X-Men films, partly because it is the one in which the opposition between good and evil is most clearly established. It is also the film in which the X-Men serve most effectively as metaphors for outsiders of any kind. Both of these qualities, however, would be substantially diminished in the second sequel, which is, as a result, probably the least successful of the three films, though it has the most spectacular action sequences of any of them—which may account for the fact that, at over $450 million, it took in more in global box-office receipts than either of its predecessors.

KEEPING IT REAL, SORT OF: *X-MEN: THE LAST STAND*

With Singer unavailable due to his work on *Superman Returns*, the helm of the third *X-Men* movie went to Brett Ratner, previously known for his work on music videos and for the two *Rush Hour* Jackie Chan vehicles. Ratner, fortified by a $210 million production budget, does a creditable job of maintaining the franchise, though the third film is much closer in spirit to the first film than to the second. Most of the main cast from the first two films returns, including Janssen as Grey, who has somehow resurrected herself from drowning, only to lose control of her now substantially enhanced psychic powers and go over to the dark side. Indeed, she kills her old lover Cyclops when they first meet after her resurrection. Meanwhile, the clear moral waters of *X2* are significantly muddied, as the X-Men return to their original role of defending humans against other mutants, while Magneto returns to his role of leading the Brotherhood of Mutants against both humans and the X-Men.

X-Men: The Last Stand is set some time after *X2*, at a time when mutants seem to be making progress toward acceptance by humans. For example, the U.S. government has established a cabinet-level Department of Mutant Affairs charged with furthering good relations between humans and mutants. The department is even headed by a mutant, the hirsute Dr. Hank McCoy (aka Beast, played by Kelsey Grammar), one of the X-Men who did not appear in the first two films. Despite such advances, however, Magneto, now at large, still distrusts humans, and still with good reason, as the government is actively engaged in an attempt to hunt down Magneto and his followers. Moreover, a private research lab has developed a new drug (that is produced through some unspecified procedure via a mutant boy who has the ability to negate mutations) that, with a single treatment, causes any mutant to revert to ordinary human form. The drug is supposedly meant to be offered only to mutants who take it willingly, but it has secretly also been made into a weapon that can be delivered via darts fired from special guns, thus transforming even unwilling mutants into humans.

To this extent, humans again function as the villains of the film, though the scientist who developed the antimutant drug, Warren Worthington II (Michael Murphy), lacks the villainy of Stryker. Worthington, too, is the father of a mutant, Warren Worthington III (aka Angel, played by Ben Foster). Angel has large angel-like wings that allow him to fly, though he is at first tormented by the discovery, at the onset of puberty, of his sprouting wings—and even tries to cut them off. In response to his child's torment, Worthington, Sr., dedicates himself to finding a "cure" for mutantism, in a motif that, more clearly than anything else in any of the X-Men films, resonates with the experiences of gays, lesbians, bisexuals, and transsexuals in our own society. After all, numerous conservative commentators, ignorant of the realities of human gendering, have quite often viewed any sort of sexuality outside the straight heterosexual norm to be not only deviant, but a disease for which straight society should seek a cure, thus eliminating "dangerous" sexual misfits in our midst. At least Worthington realizes that mutantism is a genetic condition, not a psychological one, so he is able to focus his research on DNA-altering treatments—though the discovery of the mutant boy who is the key to the treatment seems to have been an accident.

Many mutants decide to take the drug voluntarily, thus ending the torment that their condition has caused them. Rogue is among these mutants who voluntarily alter their very identities in order to be able to lead a more normal life (in her case so that she can enjoy more intimacy with Iceman), though Worthington's son actually refuses the cure. Instead, soaring about the skies of San Francisco, he learns to be at peace with his wings. He saves his father from falling to his death during the film's climactic battle at Alcatraz and ultimately joins the X-Men at the end of the film. Most other mutants resist the cure as well, taking to the streets to demonstrate and to demand that they be left alone to live their lives according to their true natures. Magneto realizes that the antimutation drug may represent the beginning of another all-out war on mutants. He thus raises a mutant army and prepares to assault the heavily fortified Alcatraz headquarters where the treatment is being administered, hoping to destroy existing supplies of the drug and to kill the boy who is its source.

Jean (known as Phoenix since her resurrection, as she was when she was once resurrected from a different death in the comics) now has vast psychic powers that even exceed those of Professor X. In fact, she wins a face-to-face psychic confrontation with her old mentor, causing him literally to disintegrate. With their leader (and Cyclops, his heir-apparent) gone, the X-Men are in disarray, though Wolverine and Storm quickly act to rally their forces. In the meantime, Magneto moves against Alcatraz, with Phoenix and Pyro at his side, along with the virtually unstoppable Juggernaut (Vinnie Jones) and the superfast Callisto (Dania Ramirez). However, Magneto has now lost Mystique, the first mutant to have been involuntarily made human via the new weapon. Indeed, a key moment in the film (and one that is central to Magneto's return to villain status) occurs when Mystique, transformed into a human, is abandoned by Magneto, who now regards her as an enemy, even though she remains loyal to him. Even Pyro seems shocked when Magneto turns his back on his former greatest ally by telling her, "You're not one of us any more." On the other side, with Professor X out of the picture, Wolverine emerges more clearly than ever as the central hero of the film, though here, as a leader of the X-Men, he seems significantly less interesting than when he was a lonely outsider. Storm also has a bit more to do in this film, though the Oscar-winner Berry is still largely wasted in a rather unchallenging role, and Storm never really develops as a fully-formed character.

The cataclysmic battle at Alcatraz, which occurs after Magneto makes the island accessible to his army by using his powers to move the Golden Gate Bridge so that it links the island with the rest of San Francisco, contains some of the most spectacular special effects anywhere in the X-Men sequence of films—or film as a whole. In this battle, Wolverine, Storm, Beast, Iceman, Collosus (a mutant with superhuman strength, played by Daniel Cudmore), and Kitty Pryde (who has the ability to walk through walls, played Ellen Page) lead the handful of remaining X-Men against Magneto and his army (and score an unlikely victory) in what is actually a rather troubling confrontation. In particular, the X-Men kill dozens of their fellow mutants in defense of the antimutant drug that has already shown great potential for abuse. The film seems to go out of its way to make the position of the X-Men seem more tenable by personifying the drug in the person of a defenseless and innocent young boy, whom the victorious X-Men save from death at the hands of their fellow mutants. Yet killing dozens (or even hundreds—the numbers are not clear) of mutants to save one is questionable heroism at best.

As the film ends, the world seems set for a new era of human-mutant cooperation, with Hank McCoy becoming the new United States ambassador to the United Nations. Xavier's school is still in operation, under the leadership of Wolverine and Storm. In the Alcatraz battle, Jean has been killed again (by Wolverine, who loved her, but knew that the true Jean would rather die than wield her power for evil), while Magneto has been rendered an ordinary human via a massive dose of the antimutant drug, administered to him by Beast. In the film's final scene, however, we see him, a lonely old man, playing solitaire chess in a park. Then, concentrating on one of the metal chessmen, he is able to make it move slightly through the force of his will, suggesting that his powers might be returning—and suggesting that he and the X-Men might be returning for another cinematic round, even with so many of the leading X-Men now dead. Granted, the title of *X-Men: The Last Stand* might have made it appear to be the final film in the *X-Men* sequence, but there has, in fact, been considerable talk of still another sequel. In the meantime, a sort of spinoff (rather than a direct sequel) is already in preproduction. *Wolverine*, scheduled for release in 2008, is to feature the *X-Men* character, still played by Jackman. Another spinoff, entitled *Magneto*, has been announced for possible release in 2009.

Batman (Christian Bale) and Lieutenant Gordon (Gary Oldman) set up the Bat Signal in anticipation of trouble to come at the end of *Batman Begins* (2005). [Courtesy of Photofest]

Brandon Lee as the title character in *The Crow* (1994). [Courtesy of Photofest]

Agents J and K (Will Smith and Tommy Lee Jones) prepare to deal with uncooperative aliens in *Men in Black II* (2002). [Courtesy of Photofest]

Blade (Wesley Snipes) prepares to battle a dance club full of vampires in *Blade* (1998). [Courtesy of Photofest]

Storm (Halle Berry) and Wolverine (Hugh Jackman) face danger in *X-Men: The Last Stand* (2006). [Courtesy of Photofest]

Rebecca (Scarlett Johansson) and Enid (Thora Birch) look at life in *Ghost World* (2001). [Courtesy of Photofest]

Police Inspector Fred Abberline (Johnny Depp) studies a London city map in *From Hell* (2001). [Courtesy of Photofest]

Hellboy (Ron Perlman) isn't a very good shot, but his gun uses really big bullets in *Hellboy* (2004). [Courtesy of Photofest]

Tough police detective John Hartigan (Bruce Willis) in *Sin City* (2005), with the vulnerable Nancy Callahan (Jessica Alba) dancing in the background. [Courtesy of Photofest]

Leland (Stephen McHattie) pulls his gun on Tom Stall (Viggo Mortensen), setting in motion the major events of *A History of Violence* (2005). [Courtesy of Photofest]

7

Ghost World

Released 2001;
Director Terry Zwigoff

GHOST WORLD, REAL WORLD: THE COMICS COME DOWN TO EARTH

As the twenty-first century began, the superhero genre remained dominant in both graphic cinema and the comics themselves. On the other hand, there had long been a wide variety of materials and genres in the comics, many of which had made a successful transition to film. It was not, however, until 2001, with the release of *Ghost World*, that the genre of comics based on a realistic depiction of day-to-day life (rather than on the fantastic worlds of superheroes or anthropomorphic animals) came to the big screen. *Ghost World* is based on the similarly titled graphic novel by Daniel Clowes, originally serialized in his legendary alternative comic, *Eightball*. Clowes also cowrote the script for the film with director Terry Zwigoff, whose principal previous credit as a director had been for the 1994 film *Crumb*, a much-admired biographical documentary about cult comics artist Robert Crumb. For his own part, Clowes has made an art form of his explorations, through comics, of the alienation and ennui of postmodern youth, and *Ghost World*, one of his first major efforts in this direction, remains one of the best. It also translates well to film, and the film version—made for a mere $7 million as the mundane subject matter required no fancy special effects or other expensive gimmicks—was a major hit with critics. Roger Ebert, for example, gave the film four stars (his highest rating) in his review, and proclaimed, "I wanted to hug this movie.

It takes such a risky journey and never steps wrong. It creates specific, original, believable, lovable characters, and meanders with them through their inconsolable days, never losing its sense of humor." The film flew under the radar at the box office, where it never received a wide release and grossed less than $9 million worldwide. However, it has since gained attention as a cult favorite and seems to have a growing following on video as the years pass.

Ghost World was not only Zwigoff's first fictional film, but both his and Clowes's first screenplay. Nevertheless, it is an accomplished effort that well captures the spirit of the graphic novel, even if a number of important details are changed in the film version. Zwigoff and Clowes again teamed up for another film adaptation of Clowes's work in the comics, *Art School Confidential* (2006), which has some of the same offbeat charm as *Ghost World*, but is considerably darker and more cynical. It is basically a satire of the art school scene, focusing on aspiring artist Jerome Platz (Max Minghella), who attends the Swarthmore Institute with the avowed goal of becoming the greatest artist of the twenty-first century. Frustrated and thwarted at every turn, Platz is eventually driven to presenting the paintings of an aging cynic known simply as Jimmy (Jim Broadbent) as his own, but these paintings seem to implicate their creator in a series of recent murders, leading to Platz's arrest for the killings. Jim has meanwhile been killed in a fire apparently caused by Platz's careless disposal of a cigarette, so even Platz feels that there is some justice in his own arrest. He ends the film in jail awaiting trial, refusing attempts of his family's lawyer to get him out on bail because he is assured by an opportunistic art gallery owner that his incarceration makes his paintings much more marketable. *Art School Confidential* thoroughly skewers the hypocrisy and pretense of art schools and the art business as a whole, though its rather misanthropic vision ultimately extends to the entire human endeavor, suggesting that the art world may merely be a microcosm of the corrupt world at large.

"ALL THAT IS SOLID MELTS INTO AIR": THE GHOST WORLD OF CONSUMER CAPITALISM

Ghost World opens (brilliantly) with a scene from the 1965 Indian musical *Gumnaam*, which features a high-energy performance (in the style of a 1960s American dance band) of a Hindi dance tune entitled "Jaan Pehechan Ho," featuring vocals by Bollywood legend Mohammed Rafi, who (like the rest of the band) wears semiformal Western dress and a Zorro-style mask. The performance is accompanied by similarly clad dancers, who gyrate joyously to the music, highlighted by the frenetic dancing of Laxmi Chhaya, another Bollywood mainstay. This performance is intercut with shots of a row of identical, characterless suburban houses, television light flickering through the windows. Voyeuristic through-window shots show us, one by one, the universally bored, almost robotic, inhabitants within the houses, culminating with a shot of a teenage girl, Enid (Thora Birch), who turns out to be watching the Indian film on videotape in her bedroom, dancing frenetically along with the dancers on her television.

While it might not be clear at the time, this opening scene, with its slightly eerie sense of cultural displacement, establishes the out-of-kilter tone that will prevail throughout the film. It also nicely captures Enid's sense of being out of phase with her own contemporary culture (or even her desire to be out of phase, thus escaping conformism), which drives her to seek entertainment in exotic viewing such as this obscure foreign film. Enid is given no last name in the film, but her full name in the graphic novel is "Enid Coleslaw," an anagram of "Daniel Clowes," and it is pretty clear that the sensitive, artistic Enid is something of a stand-in for Clowes in both the novel and the film. Convinced that her own culture produces nothing but clichés and ripoffs, she turns to unusual cultural experiences such as the Indian film, apparently unaware that *Gumnaam* itself is a quickly produced ripoff of the then-recent Western film *Ten Little Indians* (1965). *Gumnaam*, in fact, is largely an attempt to mimic, for Eastern audiences, the Western culture that Enid so despises, thus suggesting the difficulty of escaping the gravitational pull of Western culture in the postmodern era of globalization.

Ghost World cuts immediately from this opening scene to a high-school graduation ceremony where Enid and best friend Rebecca (Scarlett Johansson) are among the graduates at the cliché-ridden event. The valedictory address is delivered by a girl in a wheelchair (played by Rini Bell), who was apparently something of a wild girl before an auto accident made her not only a quadriplegic but an arch-conformist and mistress of clichés. She begins her talk by declaring that "High school is like the training wheels for the bicycle of real life," then ends it with the revelation of her own discovery, after her "setback," that "To overcome life's obstacles, you need faith, hope, and (above all) a sense of humor." Enid and Rebecca look on, eyes rolling, and exchange laughing glances, but most of the audience seems to feel that the address sounds fine, though they are anything but inspired.

When the ceremony finally ends, Enid and Rebecca exit the building, then turn and give the finger to their old school—and, for that matter, their old schoolmates. "What a bunch of retards," Enid declares, then focuses her ire on the graduation speaker: "I liked her so much better when she was an alcoholic crack addict. She gets in one car wreck and all of a sudden she's little miss perfect and everyone loves her." Enid's disaffection then quickly turns from an amused irony to horror when she unrolls her would-be diploma only to discover that she has not actually graduated because she earlier failed an art class and thus still lacks that credit, which is needed for graduation.

Enid thus has to repeat the art class in summer school, which doesn't exactly get her first summer as a "free" woman off to a good start. Then again, neither she nor Rebecca has any real plans for the summer—or for the rest of their lives, other than a vague sense that they don't want to do what everyone else does. They have no plans for college, marriage, or careers, though Rebecca does have a job at a local coffee shop, which at least provides her with sufficient income to contemplate moving into her own apartment, which she of course plans to share with Enid. Beyond that, Rebecca and Enid don't have much of a plan for anything, other than hoping to find ways to combat the boredom of suburban life, banding together to face a world full of phonies.

Through most of their lives the main goal of both Enid and Rebecca seems to have been to finish high school, so they are particularly direction-less during this first post-high school summer. The plot of the film takes a turn when the two, hanging out in the new "Wowsville authentic fifties diner" (that they mock for its lack of authenticity), read the newspaper personal ads out of boredom. They find an ad from a man who is trying to locate a "striking blonde" whom he had met in passing while helping her to find her contact lens in an airport shuttle. With nothing better to do, the two call up the man in answer to the ad, claiming to be the blonde, then arrange to meet him for lunch at Wowsville. They then hang out in the diner with their friend Josh (Brad Renfro) and wait until the man shows up, just so they can get a look at him.

The man, Seymour (Steve Buscemi, in the role he was born to play), is pretty much the dorky, middle-aged loser they might have expected him to be, at least on the surface. As he waits for the blonde, Enid in particular begins to sympathize with the man, whom they follow home to his apartment. Eventually, Enid strikes up an acquaintance with the man, with whom she turns out to have a great deal in common—both being lonely outsiders who are appalled by virtually everything in the world around them. Indeed, they become fast friends, as he attempts to introduce her to his passion, collecting old records (especially blues, of which he is something of an aficionado), while she vows to help him find a suitable girlfriend.

The growing relationship of this odd couple (who are nevertheless kindred souls) provides much of the plot of the film, which in this sense departs dramatically from the graphic novel, in which the Seymour figure is one Bob Skeetes, a hack psychic, who has no real relationship with Enid.

The expanded Seymour character in the film, in fact, has a great deal in common with R. Crumb, the subject of Zwigoff's previous film, and one can think of him as a sort of version of what Crumb might have become had he not had his considerable artistic talents. Among other things, this relationship introduces a new element into the friendship of Rebecca and Enid, as Enid spends more and more of her time with Seymour, perhaps the only single male they have ever met who seems to prefer her to the much prettier Rebecca. Left to her own devices as Enid spends more and more time with Seymour, Rebecca begins to find new friends and interests of her own, which only serves to make Enid more miserable than ever.

Life moves on, and high school is indeed over—except that Enid still has to complete that pesky art class, in a motif that does not exist in the graphic novel, where Enid is merely considering going away to art school at Strathmore, the same fictional prestigious art school that features in *Art School Confidential*. In the film, the art class turns out to bury Enid beneath a daily avalanche of clichés and canned wisdom. Ileana Douglas is perfect as Roberta Allsworth, the would-be artist (specializing in "video and performance art") who has now been relegated to teaching art in summer school, a role she pursues with great enthusiasm, investing her charges with a wealth of politically correct encouragement for their creative impulses. She wants, she tells her students, "to find the best way to look within yourself, the best key to your particular lock." She encourages her students to express something important, regardless of how unattractive their works of art might appear. Roberta is clearly earnest and clearly means well, and the satirical depiction of her inability to speak in anything but platitudes and clichés (an especially serious shortcoming for someone who is supposedly a creative artist) is aimed not at her but at the society in which she lives. It is aimed particularly at the whole practice and institution of art education (anticipating the concerns of *Art School Confidential*), which Clowes clearly sees as inimical to the development of genuine artistic creativity.

Roberta is pretty easy to peg, but nice guy Josh remains something of an enigma in the film, partly because he is less recognizable as a "type" than many of the other characters. There are hints that both Enid and Rebecca have something of a crush on him (each has sex with him in the graphic novel), but neither wants to make a move for fear that the other will be jealous. Other than that, we know that Josh works as a convenience store clerk, has his own (rather seedy) apartment, and seems to be friendly with the girls. That we know little else is appropriate and probably intentional on the part of the filmmakers. The lack of development in his character can be taken as a sign that both Rebecca and Enid know little about the opposite sex and that males of all varieties remain something of a mystery to them.

Much of the pleasure of *Ghost World* is in its secondary characters, such as Roberta and Josh, who inhabit the same universe as Enid and Rebecca, crossing their paths, but hardly coming into real contact with them at all. Enid, for example, lives with her father (played by Bob Balaban), himself an apparently lonely soul who cares about his daughter but actually seems to hardly know her. He seems to have no idea, for example, that Enid will be horrified when he resumes his relationship with his old girlfriend Maxine (Teri Garr), and doesn't seem to understand (or perhaps doesn't want to understand) her horror even after she makes it clear, while Maxine's appearance in the film makes it clear that Enid's reaction might be justified. Another important secondary character is Seymour's striking blonde, Dana (Stacey Travis), whom he eventually does meet and with whom he begins a relationship. Dana turns out to be something of a horror herself, not because she is malicious or unattractive, but simply because she has nothing in common with Seymour, other than mutual loneliness. That loneliness, however, drives them together, at least for a time, even though she is virtually the antithesis of Seymour. She has the most ordinary of thoughts and tastes (including, worst of all, in music, as when she attempts to entice Seymour to dance to insipid—at least to him—pop music); she even attempts to remake Seymour by changing the way he dresses. She tries (not very successfully) to develop an interest in Seymour's beloved blues music, but she "never cared for" the Laurel and Hardy movies that are one of Seymour's enthusiasms, because she can't understand why "the fat one has to be so mean to the skinny one."

Ghost World takes the trouble to make even extremely minor characters interesting. After all, in their own lives, they are the major characters. Thus, we get the distinct feeling that characters such as Maxine or the "Satan worshipping" couple that Enid becomes fascinated with might have interests, opinions, and problems of their own if we were only to find out more about them. The same goes for the band of record collectors of which Seymour is a member, many of whom may actually be quite different from Seymour himself. We see no details about the lives of any of these collectors other than Seymour, but it is clear that all of them are lonely, alienated souls, attempting to fill emotional holes in their lives by collecting records, which serve for them as fetishistic objects. They can thus be taken as emblems of consumer capitalism as a whole, in which the alienation that is a natural consequence of a capitalist economic system is central to the creation of an unfulfillable desire that is crucial to the operations of that system, driving individuals to attempt to compensate for the lack of genuine human relationships by acquiring commodities that can never substitute for such relationships. In this sense, the record-collecting motif in *Ghost World* (a motif that is absent in the graphic novel) is crucial to the film's subtle satirical engagement with the world of modern consumer capitalism.

Among the film's interesting marginal characters one might also number the sad old man, Norman (Charles C. Stevenson, Jr.), who sits daily on a bus-stop bench waiting for a bus whose route has long been discontinued. One imagines him a widower, possibly deranged by the loss of a beloved wife, but certainly disconnected from reality. There's also the waiter at Wowsville with the Weird Al Yankovic haircut who happens to actually be named Al (Ezra Buzzington), much to the delight of the girls. He also seems to be a bit weird—and seems to know it. Thus, when the girls ask if they can call him "Weird Al," he simply replies, "I'd imagine so." Finally, some of the funniest scenes in *Ghost World* involve the antics of a shirtless redneck, Doug (Dave Sheridan), who delights in displaying his six-pack abs, twirling his nunchuks, and generally tormenting the Greek manager (Brian George) of Josh's convenience store, taunting the immigrant about being a foreigner, urging him to "learn the rules" of life in America. For his part, the manager is repeatedly driven to the verge of apoplexy by Doug's taunts, much to the amusement of the girls, though a thoughtful look at these hilarious scenes reminds us that both Doug and the Greek manager are, in their own ways, outsiders like the girls or Seymour and his collector friends, with some of the same sense of loneliness and emptiness in their lives. The same might be said for the misanthropic John Ellis (Pat Healy), who is even made interesting in the film, despite the fact that his attitudes are so unattractive. He loves to torment the Jewish Enid with antisemitic taunts, but also supplies her with exotic materials such as the videotape of *Gumnaam* that she watches at the beginning of the film. *Ghost World* is, ultimately, an extremely kind-hearted film—much more so than the somewhat more cynical graphic novel on which it is based. It may have a certain amount of fun at the expense of its cast of offbeat characters, but it also maintains a constant sympathy for the plight of these characters, all of whom are, ironically, in the same boat despite their common sense of not fitting in with anyone else. They are all, in fact, losers, but that very notion serves itself as an acerbic comment on the competitive ethos of capitalism and of the toxicity of a system that separates individuals into categories of winners and losers, rather than simply appreciating each individual on his or her own terms.

It is certainly the case that Enid and Rebecca have absolutely no real connection with any of these minor characters who populate their world. The two girls observe everyone they meet with complete detachment, almost like bird-watchers viewing rare species of birds—indeed, the people they observe might as well be members of another species. The problem, however, is not with Enid and Rebecca, but with the world in which they live, which makes it difficult for anyone to connect with anyone else. The two girls do connect with each other and have, all through school, banded together to survive the phoniness of the highly artificial world they find around them. Still, in the film's strongest and saddest comment on the difficulty of establishing and maintaining any sort of human connection in the contemporary capitalist world, even these two fast friends begin to grow apart after graduation. Indeed, while the girls enter the world after high school with the intention of sticking together no matter what, they in fact move in virtually opposite directions. Rebecca, focused on the rather ordinary consumerist dream of having her own apartment (and thrilling at such features as a fold-down ironing board in the apartment she eventually finds) is really much more conventional than Enid. For one thing, Rebecca is more physically attractive than Enid, so that—in a world in which feminine beauty is one of the most valuable commodities of all—it is somewhat easier for her to fit in. For another thing, Enid possesses a greater amount of artistic talent, which—in a world that does not value genuine originality—only makes it harder for her to fit in, even as her greater sensitivity makes it more painful for her not to.

Enid tries to break free of the banality of her everyday life by observing as many strange characters as possible, using her creativity to draw sketches of them in her sketchbook, while making up imaginary stories about them. Meanwhile, Enid has flunked high school art—and that she is so uninterested in her summer makeup class—just goes to suggest how far from any encouragement of genuine creativity such classes really are. In one of the film's most complicated sequences (and one that does not appear in the graphic novel), Enid achieves her greatest success in the summer class by presenting a work of found art, not one she has created herself. This found art is the former logo of "Coon Chicken Inn," now Cook's Chicken House, for which Seymour works in low-level management. The logo is a highly racist blackface caricature of the head of a grinning African-American porter that Seymour has recovered from his company's archives and that he shows to Enid. Shocked and horrified that such blatant racism could once have existed, Enid concludes that the logo could be a valuable statement about the history of racism in America and about the possibility that, by ignoring this past, we are simply perpetuating racism in more subtle forms.

Roberta, much to Enid's surprise, absolutely gushes over this piece of found art and concludes that Enid is her most brilliant student. She thus decides to recommend Enid for a scholarship to art school. Unfortunately, the attendees at the class art show that marks the end of the summer class react to the logo in a knee-jerk politically correct manner, demanding that this obviously racist emblem be removed from the show. It is, and Enid is given a failing grade for the class (thus losing her scholarship), over Roberta's objection. The film thus scores a point against the superficial sort of political correctness that would simply demand that all signs of racism be removed from view, rather than bringing them out into the open where they can be discussed frankly and perhaps dealt with, rather than ignored.

This motif gains importance from the fact that is based in reality: the blackface caricature was in fact the prominently featured logo of the Coon Chicken Inn franchise, which operated a number of restaurants in the United States from the 1920s to the 1950s—including a popular restaurant in Hollywood that opened in 1930. That chain closed in the late 1950s (and did not continue as Cook's Chicken), but the very fact that this now shocking logo was accepted without comment for so many years makes a striking point about American cultural history. *Ghost World*'s prominent use of this motif helps to reinforce this point, somewhat in the vein of the various racist images featured in Spike Lee's *Bamboozled* (2000), while the repression of this image by Enid's school provides a telling commentary on our inability to deal with such aspects of our past, thus allowing the ideas behind them to survive, in a more subtle form, in the present.

Of course, Enid's central attempt at finding an authentic alternative to everyday suburban life involves her relationship with Seymour, the unusual nature of which is clearly part of the attraction for her. Granted, she and Seymour do have a great deal in common beneath the surface, though it is telling that Enid's principal explanation for her attraction to him is her declaration that "he's the exact opposite of everything I hate," rather than anything positive that she can cite about him. For his part, the fortyish Seymour seems uncertain and uncomfortable about the relationship from the beginning, presumably because of the large age difference between himself and Enid. He thus does not view her as a possible partner in romance, choosing (despite his supposed rejection of bourgeois conformity) to allow the expectations of society to determine the parameters of acceptable relationships.

Dana, on the other hand, is a socially acceptable partner, and Seymour immediately switches his attentions from Enid to Dana once the latter comes into his life, leaving Enid to feel that she has been abandoned by both Seymour and Rebecca. This intense sense of abandonment leads Enid to a champagne-aided seduction of Seymour. For his part, once this dreaded line has been passed, Seymour seems to be able to envision a genuine romance with Enid. As a result, he immediately breaks off his unfulfilling two-month relationship with Dana, presumably so that he can be with Enid. In the world of conventional Hollywood film, this unlikely couple might then have made a life together, living happily ever after, despite the unconventional nature of their bond. *Ghost World*, however, is not a conventional Hollywood film. Enid, having finally had sex with Seymour, concludes that, in reality, he is not an appropriate mate for her and immediately turns away from him.

In response, Seymour concludes (partly due to a suggestion by Rebecca) that Enid and Josh have been having sport with him. He goes to Josh's convenience store and begins to wreck the place in a fit of anger, then winds up in a clinic after he gets into a tussle with Doug, who becomes the store's unlikely defender. Enid visits Seymour as he recuperates and assures him that she genuinely admires him and that he is "like, my hero." But Enid and Seymour are nevertheless estranged, as are Enid and Rebecca, who is moving away from Enid and toward coming to terms with life in the "real" world after high school. Enid, though, still refuses to give in to the inauthenticity of this world, which she still thinks is a sham. As long ago as 1848, in the *Communist Manifesto*, Karl Marx and Friedrch Engels argued that the drive for constant innovation that is central to capitalism makes all human relationships fleeting and insubstantial, so that "all that is solid melts into air." Enid, less consciously and more instinctively, has much the same insight, recognizing that the consumerist, conformist world that she finds around her is indeed a ghost world where virtually nothing is really what it appears to be.

As the film nears its conclusion, Enid is more lonely and more uncertain about her future than ever, while her two friends have, in their separate ways, demonstrated the difficulty of being genuinely different in the postmodern world. Rebecca has given in to the drive toward conformism, while Seymour has been crushed beneath the weight of his own difference. On top of everything else, he has been busted at work because of the incident at the art show involving the Coon's Chicken logo. He now apparently finds himself living with his mother and attending sessions with a quack therapist. Yet the film ends with a moment of enchantment as Enid sees the supposedly out-of-service bus pick up Norman and take him out of town. In the film's last scene, Enid, carrying a single small bag for luggage, returns to the bus stop and boards the ghostly bus herself, presumably to go away to seek a new life elsewhere. At least, this ending seems to suggest, it might be possible for an unconventional person to find success in life (or at least to survive) without selling out. After all, Daniel Clowes has become a leading figure in the world of alternative comic books—and has now even broken into the world of Hollywood.

On the other hand, the ending is highly enigmatic. *Ghost World* is a sort of bildungsroman that lacks the conventional resolution (at least in English literature) of the genre, in which the protagonist matures and grows to the point that he or she is able to function comfortably within the bounds of polite society. In this, the film and the graphic novel are highly reminiscent of the ending of James Joyce's *A Portrait of the Artist as a Young Man* (1916), in which promising poet Stephen Dedalus, unable to fit in within the stifling confines of colonial Ireland, simply leaves at the end of the text. It is not clear, though, whether Dedalus will accomplish anything as an artist. Indeed, by the time of Joyce's subsequent novel, *Ulysses* (1922), the aspiring poet has returned to Ireland, still having achieved essentially nothing as an artist. One can imagine a similar fate for Enid. Then again, Joyce went on to become one of the most respected authors in literary history, providing even more evidence than Clowes that artists can sometimes transcend stultifying backgrounds.

8

From Hell

Released 2001; Directors Albert Hughes and Allen Hughes

FROM HELL TO HOLLYWOOD: SHERLOCK HOLMES COMES TO WHITECHAPLE

From Hell is a comic book series written by Alan Moore and illustrated by Eddie Campbell that appeared in serial form over the period 1989 to 1998. It was published as a single-volume graphic novel in 1999. *From Hell* is a complex and erudite retelling of the story of Jack the Ripper, the notorious murderer who killed and mutilated a series of London prostitutes in 1888, then disappeared from the scene, never to be officially captured or identified. Partly because he was never caught—and partly because of the sensational nature of the killings, which received an unprecedented amount of press coverage at the time—Jack the Ripper has, over time, become a legendary figure, and speculation about his identity and motives has become a cultural phenomenon of its own. *From Hell* is a meticulously researched work that draws heavily upon Jack the Ripper lore, especially the work of conspiracy theorist Stephen Knight, who specialized in rumors that the Ripper killings were part of a plot involving the Freemasons. However, it also includes elements from numerous other sources in the long legacy of speculation about the killer. The main text is even supplemented by extensive footnotes that explain the sources of much of the (often strange and incongruous) material. As such, it is one of the more complex works of Moore, a writer noted for the complexity of his work in the comics. It is also a highly political work that is less interested in Jack the Ripper killings themselves than in the social, historical, and political climate that would make such a phenomenon possible. It uses the killings as the occasion for a complex meditation on politics, power, and class inequality, doing so in a way that is bitterly critical of the corruption, brutality, and inequity of late Victorian England, a society that has often been held up as a locus of now-lost old-fashioned virtue. In particular, it draws upon a legacy of rumors that the killings had been part of a large conspiracy reaching up into the highest echelons of the British government (including Queen Victoria herself).

Given its complexity and potentially controversial nature, *From Hell* would not, at first glance, seem to be a prime candidate for film adaptation. Nor did the Hughes brothers, known for their gritty depictions of urban African American life in such films as *Menace II Society* (1993) and *Dead Presidents* (1995), seem likely candidates to perform such an adaptation. On the other hand, the film does focus on life in the slums of London, and the Hughes brothers have themselves stated that they saw it as a sort of "ghetto" film. In addition, the Hughes brother made *From Hell* (with its central focus on the travails of Victorian prostitutes) coming off the making of *American Pimp* (1999), a documentary dealing with the lives of prostitutes. Further, the Jack the Ripper case had already been the inspiration for a long line of books (fiction and nonfiction) and films—and had even made numerous appearances in the comics. In any case, having secured the services of the versatile Johnny Depp to play the lead role of Police Inspector Fred Abberline, the Hughes were able to get the backing of a major film studio (Twentieth Century Fox) and to secure a $35 million budget for what did not at all seem to be a sure box-office hit. In fact it wasn't a commercial success, making back less than $32 million at the domestic box office, though it had more success internationally and was ultimately able to pull in nearly $75 million in worldwide receipts. The film also drew considerable praise from critics, who were particularly impressed with its compelling and richly atmospheric depiction of the slums of late Victorian London.

Moore, as is usually the case with film adaptations of his work, was not impressed with plans for the film and refused to collaborate on the project. Campbell had certain creative differences with Moore during the production of the comics, especially surrounding the depiction of Victoria, whom Moore saw as a considerably more sinister and cold-hearted figure than did Campbell. But he, too, complained that the film had removed most of what was interesting about the comic—even though its depiction of Victoria is closer to his conception than to Moore's (which prevailed in the comic). It is certainly the case that numerous elements of the graphic novel have been eliminated in the film, though such eliminations are always necessary in any adaptation of such a complex work. Moore, however, was particularly upset about Depp's (and the film's) characterization of Abberline, which actually *adds* several elements not present in the graphic novel. For one thing, Abberline (a real historical figure who was in fact placed in charge of the detectives investigating the Jack the Ripper murders) is simply a more prominent character in the film, no doubt largely because of the Hollywood truism that films need central protagonist figures with whom to identify—and because an actor of Depp's stature needs an important role to play. In addition, Abberline in the graphic novel is a rather ordinary police inspector, distinguished primarily by the fact that he is more honest than most of those around him on the force. In the film, however, Abberline is an opium addict whose psychic visions supposedly help him to solve crimes. There seems to be no real historical basis for this depiction (and Moore saw it as a pointless distortion of his work), though it may have been derived from the suggestion in the graphic novel that Abberline is well acquainted with the famous Victorian psychic Robert James Lees, about whose involvement in the Ripper case there have long been rumors. Indeed, the novel opens and closes with frame scenes in which Lees and Abberline look back on the Ripper case from the point of view of 1923. However, the graphic novel stipulates that Lees is in fact a charlatan whose powers are pretended as a way of gaining attention for himself, while the film suggests that Abberline's powers might be real. This suggestion does add certain resonances to the film, as does the portrayal of Abberline as a drug addict, which extends Michael Caine's portrayal of Abberline in the 1988 made-for-TV film *Jack the Ripper* as an aging alcoholic whose work on the Ripper case causes him to give up drinking. A more important connection may involve the way the film's depiction of Abberline links him to that best-known of all Victorian detectives, Sherlock Holmes, also known as a devotee of the opium pipe. This link is also strengthened by the film's depiction of Police Sergeant Peter Godley (Robbie Coltrane) as Abberline's sidekick, very much in the mode of Holmes's Watson. The Holmsian link can also be seen in the way the film makes the story much more a whodunit than was the case with the graphic novel, a change that was in fact the central complaint of Campbell, who felt that the transformation of the story into a more conventional murder mystery detracted from its social and political commentary.

The attempt of *From Hell* to make Abberline a sort of Sherlock Holmes figure may owe something to the influence of the 1979 thriller *Murder by Decree*, in which Holmes and Watson investigate the Jack the Ripper slayings in a plot taken largely from Knight's book *Jack the Ripper: The Final Solution* (London: Harrap, 1976). Other films that link Holmes to the Jack the Ripper case include *A Study in Terror* (1965), which also features

Holmes and Watson in pursuit of the Ripper. Among numerous other films focusing on the Ripper story, *Time after Time* (1979) and *Bridge across Time* (1985) both bring Jack the Ripper into the contemporary world of the films, suggesting an ongoing fascination with the figure. Indeed, *From Hell* often seems aware of its place in this long line of Jack the Ripper films, many of which took considerable liberties with the source material. This self-conscious intertextuality may also explain some of the differences between the film (that is mediated through so many other films) and the original graphic novel.

CSI: *LONDON* MEETS *MEDIUM* VIA THE X-FILES

As if to emphasize Abberline's drug use, the film begins with a scene of the policeman preparing and smoking an opium pipe, interspersed with the beginning titles. Then the first post-title sequence (with time and place identified via on-screen captions) takes us to the Whitechaple district of 1888 London. A saucy young prostitute, Mary Kelly (Heather Graham), walks jauntily along a crowded, busy street in a scene that emphasizes the poverty and squalor of the area. The dangerous nature of life in Whitechaple is also suddenly emphasized as Mary is accosted by two street toughs, who drag her into an alley and threaten her life, unless she and her friends, fellow prostitutes, pay the protection money that they owe to the Nicholls Gang, which the men represent.

The scene thus immediately establishes both the difficulty and the danger of everyday life for the "unfortunate" women of the Whitechaple district, a fact reinforced by two other scenes that follow in quick succession, in which Mary and her friends are shown first sleeping while sitting on a bench, held upright by a rope, then washing up in a public trough out on the street. The film thus touches on some of the same kind of social commentary that is contained in the book, though it does so in a relatively superficial and perfunctory way—and one that is somewhat undermined by the fact that though the other prostitutes do look a bit beaten up, Mary herself looks much more fresh-faced and beautiful than one would expect of someone with such a hard life, however young she might still be.

At this point, we meet another relatively healthy and wholesome-looking prostitute, Ann Crook (Joanna Page), though Ann has a reason for her hale and hearty appearance. It seems that she has, for some time, been involved with an affluent lover, who has now become her husband and with whom she has had an infant daughter, Alice. Ann leaves the baby in the care of the other prostitutes while she goes off for a romantic rendezvous with her artist husband, Albert (Mark Dexter), who has supposedly been away in France to sell some of his paintings. Mysterious men, led by the sinister Ben Kidney (Terence Harvey), an agent of the notorious Special Branch of the police, burst in on Ann and Albert as the two are having sex, then unceremoniously spirit the two of them away in separate carriages, while some of the men stay behind to trash the flat.

We gradually learn that Albert is actually Prince Edward Albert Victor, the grandson of Queen Victoria (Liz Moscrop), who has (through a series of intermediaries who shield her from the details) actuated a plan not only to break up Ann and Albert but to eliminate anyone who knows about their relationship, even though Ann and her circle of friends do not know Albert's true identity. Meanwhile, Ann is lobotomized and placed in an insane asylum, while Albert, suffering from syphilis, is safely stowed away to drift toward death. This aspect of the film (and the graphic novel) is based upon longstanding legends that have to do with the notorious nature of the prince's private life, though it does not quite match historical fact, in which the prince lived on for several years (and got involved in several more scandals) before his death. For example, he was dispatched to India in late 1889 after his involvement in the Cleveland Street male prostitution scandal earlier that year—an event the investigation of which was led by the historical Abberline. True to his reputation for scandalous behavior, the prince became involved in an affair with a married woman while in India, possibly fathering a daughter. He died in 1892, officially of pneumonia as a complication of influenza, though rumors that the actual cause was syphilis have long circulated.

In the film, Abberline has to be fetched from an opium den (by Godley), so that he can take charge of the investigation of the recent brutal slaying of prostitute Martha Tabram (Samantha Spiro), which is quickly followed by the killing of four other prostitutes, including Polly (Annabelle Apsion), Annie Chapman (Katrin Cartlidge), Liz Stride (Susan Lynch), and Kate Eddowes (Lesley Sharp). In most cases, the bodies of the victims are ritually mutilated in a way that suggests (at least to Abberline) considerable surgical skill and knowledge of human anatomy. Abberline concludes (as have most subsequent Ripperologists) that the Tabram killing was different from the others and not the work of the killer (or killers) who would become known as Jack the Ripper.

In the most canonical version of the Jack the Ripper story, the killer's fifth victim was Mary Kelly. However, in the film (and the graphic novel), Mary escapes, fleeing London and leaving her lodgings to another woman, who then becomes the Ripper's fifth victim, made unrecognizable by his mutilation of the body. In the novel, she simply flees, absconding with money loaned her by Abberline. The film, however, is given a more romantic ending. Mary collects young Alice, then returns to her native Ireland to assume an idyllic seaside existence. She hopes that Abberline will come to join her, but he refuses to do so for fear that the powerful forces behind the killings may still have him under surveillance and could follow him to Ireland, thereby discovering that Mary is still alive. He decides to remain alone in London to protect Mary. However, hopelessly in love (though he barely knows her), he eventually commits suicide via a drug overdose, ending his suffering at last—and presumably keeping Mary permanently safe.

This romanticized ending is typical of the Hollywoodization of numerous elements of the graphic novel, perhaps in an apparent effort to make the dark and bloody subject matter more palatable to modern-day audiences who might also have relatively little interest in the details of the conspiracy theory put forth in the film. The film also seeks to add entertainment value by quickening the plot and by adding moments of special suspense—as when Abberline is abducted and nearly killed by Kidney and another Mason. The film is thus far less thought-provoking than the book—a situation that is typical of film adaptations of graphic novels and conventional novels alike. It also goes for a certain hipness via occasional MTV-style quick-cut editing and fast motion. The casting of the supercool Depp in the lead role added a certain hipness as well, as did the use of a song ("The Nobodies") by Marilyn Manson as the closing theme. Finally, the film attempts to overcome the fact that young American audiences (the biggest single source of box office revenue) might not be all that interested in the political implications of the graphic novel. After all, the corrupt political system described in the story is more than a hundred years old, and the film does far less than the graphic novel to suggest that this system is not unique but in fact typical of governments in general, including those that are still in power today. Thus, though the film does cite the claim, traditionally attributed to Jack the Ripper, to have "given birth to the twentieth century," the context of the film makes this claim appear to be more a reference to the violence and bloodshed that marked the twentieth century than to any comment about political systems. That the political system involved is British, not American, also distances it from American movie audiences, as opposed to the graphic novel, which (written by a British author and drawn by a British artist) was largely aimed at a British audience to begin with.

The graphic novel also includes a much more extensive treatment of the theory that the Ripper killings were engineered as part of a secret plot by the Freemasons, a theory that was especially espoused by Knight, who also wrote a well-known exposé of what he saw as various Masonic conspiracies. As put forth in the film, the Masons are essentially a sort of old boy's club, in which various rich and powerful men join forces to further their own common interests. They are, in fact, officially horrified when one of their members, the surgeon Sir William Gull (Ian Holm), takes seriously the mystical elements of Freemasonry. It is, in fact, Gull who is Jack the Ripper, and his killing of the prostitutes is part of an official conspiracy endorsed by the British government. It is, however, Gull's own idea to mutilate the bodies in ritualistic fashion. In response, he is lobotomized by the Masons (as Ann Crook had been before him), then left mindless and drooling in a dreary asylum. The novel treats the Masonic material much more extensively and delves much more deeply into the possible meanings behind Masonic participation in the Ripper killings, aspects that the filmmakers apparently felt would be of little interest to their audience.

Perhaps because so many elements of the graphic novel are absent from the film, some of the elements that are present come more clearly into focus. For example, the postmodern mixing of genres that is present in both media seems much more clear in the film, though this may also be partly due to the fact that filmgoers are accustomed to films that fit into easily identifiable genres. To begin with, the film builds its central plot much more upon the model of the detective story than does the graphic novel, as when several scenes focus on Abberline's Holmsian analyses of crime scenes as he attempts to deduce the identity of the killer from forensic analysis. At one scene, for example, he notes that the victim's throat has been cut, but that there is no arterial spray on the nearby wall, leading to the conclusion that she was killed elsewhere, then brought to the site where the body was found. He also notes that the victim's clothes are dry, though it had rained through the night; he thus concludes that she had been killed indoors, possibly inside a carriage, which then brought her to the current crime scene. As a result, multiple men must have been involved in the crime, because (at least according to Abberline's reasoning) it would take at least one to drive the carriage and another to do the actual killing. Finally, finding on the scene the leftover stem from a cluster of grapes, he deduces that the killing was not done by the Nicholls Gang but by someone of more affluent means, who used the (then very expensive) grapes to lure the woman to her death.

In such scenes, Abberline not only again recalls the work of Sherlock Holmes, but looks forward to the kind of modern forensic investigations that have gained popular interest in such recent television series as the *CSI* cluster of programs, which emphasize the highly scientific analysis of crime scene data. On the other hand, Abberline also claims to have seen all of this information in one of his visions, bringing in a supernatural element that anticipates other recent popular programs, such as *Medium*, in which a woman with psychic powers uses her ability to contact the dead to provide crime-solving information to the police. This aspect of *From Hell* draws upon a strand of Jack the Ripper lore that has long suggested some sort of paranormal involvement, though in this case no particular supernatural powers are attributed to Gull; indeed, though he himself seems to feel that he is conjuring with powerful mystical forces, the film clearly suggests that he is simply mad. These hints of the presence of forces beyond those present in the physical world combine with the particularly gruesome nature of the killings and the brooding atmosphere of Whitechaple at night to make *From Hell* a kind of horror film, drawing particularly on the horror subgenre of slasher films.

From Hell is also a psychological drama that focuses on the travails of Abberline as he attempts to deal with the difficulties of investigating the Ripper case in an environment in which so many powerful official forces are determined to ensure that the case will not be solved. In particular, the film hints that Abberline's drug addiction arises from his attempts to cope with the fact that his wife and newborn infant both died in childbirth a little over two years earlier. This aspect of the drama also intersects in significant ways with the love-story subplot, in which Abberline finds a special connection with Mary Kelly that allows him at least the hope of filling an emotional void in his life he had thought could never again filled. His decision to forego any chance of happiness with Mary so that she can remain safe thus takes on a special poignancy, as does his final suicide—an event that does not occur in the graphic novel, which features scenes of Abberline many years later, looking back on the Ripper case, having retired in comfort on the proceeds gained from his agreement not to press his investigation.

Abberline in the novel thus gives in to the corruption he finds around, even if he does not actively participate in it, a fact that still gives him great guilt decades later—though not so great that he is unwilling to live comfortably in the home that his compliance bought him. The critique of the rottenness of Victorian society is far more central to the book than to the film, though it is certainly the case that the film also participates extensively in the general of conspiracy films and political thrillers. After all, the film at least indicates that the Ripper case involves a conspiracy that reaches all the way to Victoria herself and that particularly involves the Freemasons. Virtually every high-placed official or powerful individual that we see in the film turns out to be a member of the Masons, who are thus able to exercise a tremendous amount of political power behind the scenes, suggesting the presence of shadowy forces behind the public façade of government. This aspect of *From Hell* thus resonates with the conspiracies put forth in contemporary works such as television's *The X-Files* (that ran from 1993 to 2002). It also looks back to the great political thrillers of the 1970s, such as Alan J. Pakula's *The Parallax View* (1974) and *All the President's Men* (1976), Francis Ford Coppola's *The Conversation* (1974), and Sydney Pollack's *Three Days of the Condor* (1975), a connection that suggests ways in which Jack the Ripper did indeed give birth to the twentieth century. Meanwhile, the Masonic elements of the conspiracy depicted in *From Hell* also look forward to such films as *National Treasure* (2004) and *The Da Vinci Code* (2006).

Finally, *From Hell* is an historical drama that (while it lacks the richness of the Victoriana that is introduced by Moore into the graphic novel) continually reminds us of its historical setting. It even takes the trouble to introduce one scene featuring Joseph Merrick, the famed Victorian medical curiosity featured in David Lynch's film *The Elephant Man* (1980), whose title was taken from the appellation by which Merrick was widely known in late 1880s London. The film's atmospheric re-creation of Victorian London adds significantly to its impact and to its vague hints (though not so insistently as the graphic novel) that late Victorian England was a crucial historical turning point and that the corrupt nature of this society contributed mightily to the often ugly turns taken by history in the twentieth century.

From Hell gains considerable energy from its postmodern combination of the detective and horror genres, along with elements derived from the psychological drama, political thriller, and historical drama. Add to this fact the film's extremely unconventional protagonist and subject matter and the result is a highly unusual film that is extremely difficult to categorize, a fact that no doubt contributed to the film's less than stellar commercial success, given that film marketing is typically aimed at specific audiences who want to see specific types of films. Nevertheless, the film remains one of the most interesting and unusual examples of graphic cinema yet produced.

9

The *Spider-Man* Film Franchise

Released 2002–2007; Director Sam Raimi

HERE COMES THE *SPIDER-MAN*

The introduction of Spider-Man in Marvel Comics' *Amazing Fantasy* in August of 1962 proved to be a landmark in the history of superhero comics and a key event in the comeback of Marvel on their way to becoming a major player in the comics industry. Teenage characters had long been featured in superhero comics as a way of attracting adolescent readers, though these characters (Batman's Robin is the leading example) were typically mere sidekicks of more adult heroes. Even young Billy Batson, the alter ego of Captain Marvel, seemed to be transformed into an adult whenever he summoned his magically endowed superpowers. Spider-Man, though, was not only the alter ego of teenager Peter Parker, but also remained a teenager (with a full array of adolescent problems) even when in superhero mode. Given spider-like superpowers as a result of the bite of a radioactive spider, the geeky teenager Parker thus became an ideal fantasy figure for millions of teenage readers. The character was an immediate hit, soon receiving his own comic imprint, *The Amazing Spider-Man*, which began publication in 1963 and went on to become Marvel's best-selling series.

Spider-Man survived the various travails of Marvel and the comics industry as a whole to remain one of the most popular and recognizable superheroes in the comics over the next four decades. Among other things, he consistently remained a younger and hipper alternative to such established heroes as Superman and Batman, even though he did slowly mature over the years, eventually becoming a married high school science teacher. In the intervening time, Spider-Man had been featured in several different Marvel imprints, generally starring in at least two to four different titles each month. He became Marvel's signature character and most valuable property, leading the way in Marvel's expansion from the comics into other media.

Spider-Man first came to television in a self-titled animated series that ran for three years on ABC beginning in 1967 and featured the catchy "Spider-Man, Spider-Man, does whatever a spider can" theme song, one of the best-known themes in television history. Several other television incarnations followed, including a live-action series, *The Amazing Spider-Man* (starring Nicholas Hammond as Spider-Man), which ran for fifteen episodes in 1978–1979, amid a spate of live-action superhero series that debuted on CBS that year. That series scored solid ratings, but was much criticized by fans of the comics, including Spider-Man cocreator Stan Lee. *Spider-Man: The Animated Series*, executive produced by Lee and Avi Arad, ran for five seasons from 1994 to 1998 as part of Fox's Fox Kids afternoon block and was much more true to the spirit of the original comics.

Given his status as the flagship superhero of the Marvel Comics universe, it is not surprising that Spider-Man's arrival on the big screen in 2002 was one of most hyped and eagerly anticipated cinematic events in movie history. It also became one of the biggest hits in movie history, hitting the $100 million mark in domestic box-office receipts in a mere three days, at that time an all-time record. However, the path to this success had been a difficult one. As early as 1985, a bankrupt Marvel auctioned off the film rights to Spider-Man to Cannon Films in an effort to generate quick cash. The project bounced around from one company to another, going through numerous aborted scripts (including one by *Terminator* and *Titanic* director James Cameron, at one point attached to direct the film). It also went through various bankruptcies and rights litigations among the various companies involved, until Marvel, having reacquired the rights, sold them to Sony Pictures in 1999. Production of the film then moved forward as a joint venture between Sony and Marvel, finally leading to the release of *Spider-Man* in 2002, under the direction of Sam Raimi, previously best known as the director of the *Evil Dead* low-budget cult horror films, though he had also tried his hand at a sort of superhero film with *Darkman* (1990).

The film version of *Spider-Man* stayed relatively true to the original comics, with a few new elements (some derived from the recent Marvel imprint *Ultimate Spider-Man*) to keep the film up to date for contemporary audiences. For example, the spider that bites Peter Parker and gives him his powers has now been genetically engineered rather than irradiated. All in all, though, the film's protagonist is still pretty much the same old (or same young) Spidey, with souped up computer-generated special effects that allow him to participate in some of the most spectacular action sequences ever brought to film. The result smashed numerous "fastest-to" box-office records on the way to a total worldwide gross of over $800 million, split roughly evenly between domestic and international receipts. That success virtually ensured the appearance of a sequel, and *Spider-Man 2*, with the same director and same main cast, did indeed appear in 2004. Though the sequel lacked the fan anticipation and the sense of a breakthrough in superhero filmmaking that accompanied the original, it was nearly as successful at the box office, bringing in nearly $800 million in worldwide receipts. In addition, the second film also received even better reviews than had the first, which had already been well received by critics. Numerous commentators declared *Spider-Man 2* to be the greatest superhero film ever made.

Superhero comics are, by their very nature, larger than life, featuring over-the-top characters and scenarios that make no claim to being realistic but that very well might be the closest thing we have to mythology in the contemporary world. Virtually all screen adaptations of such comics have attempted to tone them down a bit, making them more realistic and giving the heroes more human qualities—for fear that a direct translation of the original comics would appear campy and preposterous on the big screen. In this sense, Spider-Man was the perfect superhero for film adaptation because Marvel had from the very beginning attempted to make him seem more human and more realistic than previous superheroes. It should probably thus come as no surprise that the Spider-Man films have been the most successful superhero films in history, though it was probably also a good thing that it took so long to bring Spider-Man to film, allowing special-effects technology to catch up with the potential of the character. With early box-office results from *Spider-Man 3* (released May 4, 2007) looking as spectacular as those of its predecessors, the franchise promises to remain one of the most lucrative properties in the entire film industry for years to come, even if some aspects of the third film suggest that the franchise needs a rest for a while.

THE *SPIDER-MAN* FORMULA: SUPERHEROES, SUPERVILLAINS, AND A TOUCH OF ROMANCE

The first *Spider-Man* film combines an origin story with an account of Spider-Man's battle with the Green Goblin, one of the most prominent supervillains to have appeared in the *Spider-Man* comics. For example, the Green Goblin had been featured as Spider-Man's antagonist in perhaps the best-known series of *Spider-Man* comics in history: the three issue sequence of *The Amazing Spider-Man* that appeared in 1971 featuring a drug-related theme that caused it to fail to receive the Comics Code seal of approval. The story, produced at the request of the U.S. Department of Health, Education, and Welfare, had a clear antidrug message, but the rigid Code forbade all reference to illegal drugs in the comics. Marvel published the sequence anyway, the sky didn't fall, and the power that the Comics Code had long had over the industry was broken forever, paving the way for the eventual appearance of far more interesting and adult-oriented stories in the comics in the years to come.

Like the comics, the film version of *Spider-Man* is set in New York City, which serves as an immediate announcement that this superhero will exist in a more realistic world than that of Superman's Metropolis or Batman's Gotham City. The casting of Tobey Maguire, best known for sensitive, character-driven roles in such films as *The Ice Storm* (1997) and *Wonder Boys* (2000), in the title role is also telling because it suggests the importance of the greater detail and reality with which Spider-Man's alter ego, Peter Parker, is treated in the film (and the comics), as opposed to the relatively superficial characterization of alter egos such as Clark Kent in the Superman tradition. Indeed, there is a fundamental difference between Spider-Man and Superman in this respect. Superman is the *real* identity of the character, while Clark Kent is a sort of artificial and superficial identity, fabricated for convenience. In the case of Spider-Man, Peter Parker is the real identity, and Spider-Man is the disguise, a situation that is emphasized by the fact that Spider-Man wears a mask, whereas Superman does not (though Clark Kent does, in the form of his trademark eyeglasses). Further, Spider-Man remains essentially the same person even when he is in superhero mode, whereas Clark Kent is completely transformed when he becomes Superman.

The recent television series *Smallville* is an exception in Superman lore in that it presents teenager Clark Kent as the primary identity of its main character, just growing into the powers that will eventually allow him to become Superman. In short, that series has abandoned the usual dynamic between identities that informs the Superman story and essentially opted for the Spider-Man scenario instead, thus suggesting a recognition of the greater appeal of the latter. It is no accident that *Smallville* cocreators Alfred Gough and Miles Millar were the cowriters of the script for *Spider-Man 2*, suggesting the affinity between the worlds of *Smallville* and Spider-Man, with their emphasis on the human side of their superheroes, even if (as in the case of Clark Kent) the hero isn't biologically human.

Indeed, much of the success of the *Spider-Man* movies can be attributed to this humanization of the central character, which is furthered through the fact that roughly half of the running time of the first film takes place before Parker actually becomes Spider-Man, while about half of the second film takes place during a period in which Parker has lost his powers and returned to a normal life that had been seriously disrupted by his duties as a superhero. The first film opens with a voiceover in which Parker declares that the story we are about to see is a "story about a girl," one Mary Jane Watson (Kirsten Dunst), Parker's next door neighbor, with whom he has been in love since early childhood. This declaration makes Mary Jane very much the center of Peter's life in a way that Lois Lane could never have been the center of Superman's life. It also suggests the extent to which Peter's personal and very human desires and dilemmas will be foregrounded in the film, as opposed to superhuman battles against evil and heroic struggles to save the world. Mary Jane's personal life (compressed from a more complex background in the comics) is given depth as well, as when we (and Peter) see her being abused by her loutish father, who accuses her of being on the way to becoming a tramp like her mother, who is apparently no longer on the scene. Indeed, while Spider-Man will battle (and defeat) the Green Goblin, a formidable supervillain, in the film, even in that sense he remains a sort of local hero. One senses in the film that he is saving not the world or at least America (as Superman tends to do) but just New York. Spider-Man is a scaled down superhero who sometimes (as in the second movie) uses his superpowers for such down-to-earth tasks as attempting (unsuccessfully) to deliver pizzas on time. It is thus much easier for audiences (especially the young audiences who dominate at the box office) to identify with him, even when he is in superhero mode, not to mention when he is in his day-to-day mode as the absentminded science geek Parker, shunned by the popular crowd in high school and bullied by star athletes such as Flash Thompson (Joe Manganiello), Mary Jane's boyfriend.

The opening minutes of the first *Spider-Man* film are particularly impressive for the amount of information and development that are poured into relatively little screen time. In the very first scene of the first film we see Peter (who has a serious problem with punctuality even before becoming Spider-Man) running to try to catch a school bus for which he is late as usual. The students (and even the driver) are highly amused by his predicament, though Mary Jane finally convinces the driver to stop to let Peter on the bus, whereupon no one (even a geeky girl with glasses like his own) will let him sit with them and he is eventually tripped (while distractedly staring at Mary Jane) and sent sprawling into the aisle floor. The bus, it turns out, is headed for Columbia University, where students from Peter's high school are touring the science department on a field trip. Science geek that he is, Peter seems to be one of the few students who are genuinely interested in the various displays they see on the trip. Meanwhile, an aspiring photographer, he also attempts to get some pictures from the trip for the school newspaper, though he is repeatedly thwarted by bullies who maliciously jostle him just as he is about to take a picture.

These first few scenes thus provide an excellent capsule introduction to Peter's character. They also introduce Mary Jane, Peter's friend Harry Osborn (James Franco), and Harry's wealthy father Norman Osborn (Willem Dafoe), a brilliant scientist (specializing in nanotechnology research) and founder of Oscorp, a multimillion dollar technology company. These early scenes also serve very efficiently to recount Spider-Man's familiar origins when Parker is bitten (just after the ten-minute mark) by a genetically modified spider while viewing an exhibit on spiders. We are next treated to a brief tour of the Oscorp research labs, where it turns out that Pentagon funding for a major "human performance enhancement" treatment developed by Norman Osborn is currently in jeopardy, experimental applications of the treatment to rats having caused "violence, aggression, and insanity" in at least one case. Parker, meanwhile, staggers home from the field trip, feeling ill from the spider bite, greeted by the elderly Aunt May (Rosemary) and Uncle Ben Parker (Cliff Robertson), who have raised him and with whom he lives. Peter collapses upstairs in his room at the fifteen-minute mark.

We know, of course, that the scrawny Peter is in the process of being transformed into Spider-Man, though there is no actual indication of this fact in the film to this point. In an interesting parallel construction, we observe the genesis of the Green Goblin even as Peter lies unconscious in his bedroom. Osborn, now in traditional mad scientist mode, is desperate to prove that his human enhancement treatment works and thus save his company's government funding. Therefore, he decides to undergo the treatment himself as a demonstration of its effectiveness. The treatment sends him into convulsions, but he emerges with superhuman strength and agility, though he does seem murderously unhinged. Quick cut back to Peter, who awakes to discover that he no longer needs his glasses and that he has suddenly sprouted a muscular physique. Characteristically, Peter has no thoughts of using this new strength to fight crime: his first thought (as signaled by the fact that he looks out his window to see Mary Jane next door in her bedroom) is that, all buffed up, he might now be able to win the love of Mary Jane.

All of this occurs in the first nineteen minutes of the film, though the pace slows a bit at this point, as Peter gradually discovers his new powers and evolves into Spider-Man, while Norman Osborn becomes the Green

Goblin, possessed by a sort of evil entity that arises as a result of his experimental human performance enhancement treatments. In the intervening time, Peter finally stands up to and defeats Flash, while continuing to focus on trying to win the heart of Mary Jane, as when he enters a match with a professional wrestler to try to win money to buy a cool car with which to impress her.

In this match, Peter appears as the "Human Spider," wearing a makeshift costume that is an important first step toward becoming Spider-Man. Though not yet fully in possession of his spider powers, he predictably wins the match, but is cheated out of the money he was supposed to earn by the event's promoter. When the promoter is subsequently robbed at gunpoint, Peter gets revenge by passing up a chance to stop the robber. In a crucial development, the fleeing robber subsequently kills Uncle Ben (or so we are led to believe). When Peter captures (and apparently kills) the killer, he realizes that the thug is the same man who had robbed the promoter. This realization spurs Peter, tormented by feelings of guilt over his uncle's death, to decide to devote his newfound powers to fighting crime, though he does not fully take on his Spider-Man persona (and costume) until nearly an hour into the film, when he foils a robbery at a Chinese deli. By this time, Osborn has become the Green Goblin, aided by a high-tech flight suit and glider that allow him to zip about the skies of New York (and to blow up a rival research facility), while Peter and Mary Jane have graduated from high school. Mary Jane has broken up with Flash and his now dating Harry, who now shares an apartment with Peter.

With all of this background now in place, Spider-Man embarks on a one-man crusade against crime, generating considerable controversy, though the people of New York are generally more enthusiastic about his heroism than are the police and other city officials, who tend to regard his vigilante campaign as a public menace. Meanwhile, in a development that provides one of the most direct examples of dialogue between the Superman and Spider-Man stories, a third-rate New York newspaper, the *Daily Bugle* becomes a central player in the evolution of Spider-Man's public image. For reasons that are unclear (except that perhaps it might generate sensationalism and sell newspapers), *Daily Bugle* editor J. Jonah Jameson (J. K. Simmons) declares a vendetta against Spider-Man, attacking him in the press as a felon and danger to the public safety. Echoing Clark Kent's employment by the *Daily Planet*, Peter (desperate for money because his activities as Spider-Man make it difficult for him to hold a job) becomes a freelance photographer for the *Daily Bugle*, which he supplies with photos of Spider-Man in action.

A little more than halfway through the film, Osborn's Green Goblin persona (a name coined by Jameson to help sell papers) launches an all-out campaign of terror against New York after Osborn has been ousted from his post as the CEO of Oscorp by its board of directors. For a time, Osborn and the Green Goblin exist as rival personalities within the same body, but the Green Goblin persona, a sort of Mr. Hyde to Osborn's Dr. Jekyll, gradually wins out. He begins by killing Oscorp's board of directors, then goes on to try to take control of New York. The film thus moves from its first half, the story of the origin of Spider-Man (and the Green Goblin), to its second half, a high-octane action film featuring the titanic running battle between Spider-Man and Green Goblin, with the latter terrorizing New York and the former seeking to defend it, despite the efforts of the Green Goblin to convince Spider-Man join him in taking over the city and amid growing public suspicion (fueled by the *Daily Bugle*) that Spider-Man and the Green Goblin are two of a kind.

Spider-Man, of course, is hampered in the struggle against the Green Goblin by distractions like saving babies from burning buildings. Peter also has to worry about protecting his loved ones (especially after Osborn begins to suspect his identity as Spider-Man). Indeed, in keeping with the more personal vein that marks the *Spider-Man* films, the hero spends much of his time simply seeking to save Mary Jane, who is (of course) abducted and threatened by the Green Goblin. This leads to their final battle, a spectacular special-effects extravaganza in which Mary Jane is saved and Osborn is killed, though we discover in *Spider-Man 2* that the evil entity that caused him to become the Green Goblin lives on. Also significant during this last battle is the way various ordinary New Yorkers rally to Spider-Man's aid, establishing his status as a hero of the people. In a possible reference to the September 11, 2001, bombings of the World Trade Center, one of them says, "You mess with one of us, you mess with all of us!"

Spider-Man seems to be ending in high Hollywood fashion as Mary Jane declares her love for Peter and gives him a passionate kiss. But Peter, afraid that a relationship with him will bring Mary Jane into constant danger such as that she has just faced from the Green Goblin, backs away, telling her he can only offer her friendship. In a crucial development, he has thus foregone his central dream as Peter Parker so that he can continue his career as Spider-Man. Seemingly finalizing his commitment to a life as a superhero, he tells us in his final voiceover, "Who am I? I'm Spider-Man."

Of course, leaving the romantic tensions between Peter and Mary Jane unresolved also preserves that continuing motif for use in the sequel, which was already planned, even before the vast commercial success of the first film. (Maguire, for example, signed a contract to do three *Spider-Man* films even before the first was made.) *Spider-Man*, however, was a tough act to follow, and *Spider-Man 2* was clearly in danger of falling prey to the sequel syndrome, offering audiences little that they hadn't already experienced. However, it avoided that pitfall and remained a strong and interesting film, partly because its significantly higher budget allowed for substantially better special effects. The second film also profited from the further development of the main characters and the establishment of a clever dialogue with the first film (one of several reasons the second film is definitely funnier than the first). *Spider-Man 2* also does a better job of capturing the spirit of the tradition of superhero comics, perhaps due to the efforts of screenwriters Michael Chabon (an important novelist and a writer of comics in his own right) and the *Smallville* team of Gough and Millar.

Spider-Man 2 also adds interest through the introduction of a motif possibly borrowed from *Superman II*, in which Peter temporarily loses his powers. However, whereas the virtually omnipotent Superman gives up his powers willingly for love, Spider-Man apparently loses his powers through the much more prosaic path of simply suffering from burn-out, given the stress of his nightly duties fighting crime, which are making it increasingly difficult for him to hold a job or keep up with his studies as a college science major. Indeed, Spider-Man begins to lose his powers twenty-nine minutes into the film, when his web-shooting powers vanish, causing him to fall from a great height—one of three nasty falls he takes in the film thanks to his failing powers.

Up to this point, the film's most important superhero action moments occur in the memorable opening sequence that shows Peter, in danger of losing his job as a pizza delivery man, swinging through the skies of New York as Spider-Man, trying to make a delivery on time. The scene is largely comic, though it has serious results for Peter: he misses by three minutes and loses his job, which he really needs because he wants to stop taking pictures of himself as Spider-Man for the *Daily Bugle*, given their anti-Spider-Man editorial stance. Indeed, Peter's ongoing money troubles form an important subplot of the first half of the film, further establishing that Spider-Man is a much more human superhero than predecessors such as Superman. Soon afterward, we learn that Peter is on the verge of flunking a science class with his favorite professor because he's been missing class and not doing assignments. The implication is clear: the burden of being Spider-Man, which had already caused him to have to give up a life with Mary Jane at the end of the first film, is getting to be too much for Peter, who is, after all, still a very young man. Nevertheless, he continually remembers Uncle Ben's onetime admonition that "with great power comes great responsibility" and tries his best to persevere, putting so much stress on himself that he eventually burns out and loses his powers.

For a while, Peter experiences the loss of his powers as a glorious relief. For one thing, he no longer carries the burden of feeling that it is his personal duty to fight crime and save citizens from various dangers. In one scene, he witnesses a mugging and does nothing: it's no longer his problem. In addition, Peter is now able to get to class on time, do his homework, and generally begin to fulfill his potential as a brilliant science student. Perhaps more importantly, he is now able to envision a normal life with Mary Jane, though she herself has moved on, making great strides in her acting and modeling careers and establishing a serious romantic relationship with astronaut John Jameson (Daniel Gillies), the handsome son of none other than Jonah Jameson.

Unfortunately, while Peter may be able to do without Spider-Man, New York suddenly needs a superhero more than ever when a science experiment gone bad once again produces a menacing supervillain. This time, brilliant physicist Otto Octavius (Alfred Molina), one of Peter's personal heroes, falls prey to his own experimental contraption when a high-tech set of four artificially intelligent telescoping mechanical arms controlled directly by his brain gets out of whack and starts to control him instead, sending him on a destructive binge through the city. Spider-Man, of course, attempts to stop him, sputtering powers and all, especially after the villain takes Aunt May hostage during a bank robbery attempt that is foiled by Spider-Man.

Soon afterward, his powers continuing to fail, Peter decides to retire from the superhero business, leaving his Spider-Man suit in a dumpster. However, in a scene that echoes the one in the first film in which Spider-Man saved a baby from a burning building, Peter, even without his spider powers, manages to rescue a small girl from a similar conflagration. He is, however, unable to rescue another victim left in the fire. This event helps him to realize that the people of New York need a hero like Spider-Man, a realization reinforced when Aunt May, now a Spider-Man fan (though she has no idea Peter is Spider-Man), discourses on the symbolic importance of heroes, "courageous, self-sacrificing people, setting examples for all of us." This speech (which, among other things, serves as a sort of capsule defense of the whole superhero genre) inspires Peter to work to regain his powers, even if it will mean once again giving up his quest for Mary Jane.

Speaking of quests for Mary Jane, Spider-Man seems to regain his full powers soon afterward (just over an hour of running time after his powers first began to fail), largely due to the necessity of rescuing his true love from Octavius (now known as "Doctor Octopus," or simply "Doc Ock"), who has abducted her as part of an attempt to lure Spider-Man to him. It seems that Dock Ock needs rare tritium to fuel an experimental fusion reactor that is crucial to his research, and it turns out that the research division of Oscorp (that has been funding his work) has an ample supply. Harry Osborn, who now heads this division, still bears a grudge against Spider-Man for killing his father, so offers to supply Dock Ock with the tritium if he will bring a captive Spider-Man to him.

After a spectacular running battle that features Spider-Man's memorable Superman-like attempts to stop a runaway train, Doc Ock manages to capture the hero (though the New Yorkers on the train once again stand up for him), who is exhausted from stopping the train. Spider-Man is taken to Harry and Doc Ock leaves with the tritium, after which Harry unmasks Spidey. Stunned to find Peter under the mask, he is unable to follow through on his plan to kill Spider-Man, who then escapes and resumes his attempt to save Mary Jane—and to save New York, assuming that Doc Ock's newly refueled fusion reactor will probably get out of control and blow up half the city. Amid some of the most spectacular special effects ever put on film, Spider-Man defeats Doc Ock and shuts down the reactor, saving both New York and Mary Jane.

In the process, Spidey unmasks himself so that he can appeal to Octavius man-to-man to help him stop the reactor, which he does, regaining control of his tentacle-like smart arms and sacrificing himself to save the city. Meanwhile, Spider-Man's true identity is revealed to Mary Jane, who suggests (perched with him on a giant spider web high in the air) that deep down, she had always suspected as much. Peter once again gives her the Spidey-can't-have-a-girlfriend speech, then lowers her to the ground. Below, she is greeted by John Jameson and returns to his arms, but looks longingly back up at Spider-Man, who slips on his mask and swings away into the night. Meanwhile, back at his posh apartment, Harry is confronted by the ghost of the Green Goblin, then discovers the flight suit and glider in a secret room. He is now prepared to become the New Green Goblin in the next sequel.

Spider-Man 2 is given a fairly conventional Hollywood happy ending. We cut to the church where Mary Jane is preparing to marry Jameson, but she leaves him stranded at the altar, dashing away *Graduate*-like in her wedding gown to Peter's apartment, where she declares that "I can't survive without you." Danger or not, she wants to be with him—and to save him as he has so often saved her. They start to kiss, but a siren interrupts them and he has to rush off as Spider-Man—with her knowledge and blessing. As the film ends, he swings through the skies of New York, whooping with glee in a symbolic moment that enacts the element of fun that is crucial to all the *Spider-Man* films.

Spider-Man 2 features more comic moments than the first *Spider-Man*, as in the classic vignette in which, his powers failing, Spider-Man has to take an elevator, which he shares with a man (played by comedian

Hal Sparks) who thinks he is simply an ordinary guy wearing a Spider-Man costume. When the man suggests that the suit looks uncomfortable, Spidey replies, "It gets kinda itchy. and it rides up in the crotch a little bit, too." The second *Spider-Man* film also features more moments of poignant drama than the first, as when Peter finally confesses to Aunt May his feelings of responsibility for the death of Uncle Ben. The love story between Peter and Mary Jane is significantly stepped up as well, with the added element of her impending wedding to John Jameson posing a considerable complication. Finally, Doc Ock himself is a much more interesting figure than the Green Goblin had been in the first film, partly because Molina's nuanced performance (as opposed to Dafoe's over-the-top performance in the first film) well captures the fact that Octavius is a good man who becomes a villain only because he is under the control of an evil artificial intelligence.

Such strengths allowed *Spider-Man 2* to be at least as successful as *Spider-Man*, despite the fact that it was necessarily less original. Of course, the initial *Superman* and *Batman* sequences, which paved the way for all future superhero film franchises, both also did well in their first sequels. However, both fell prey to the third-time's-a-disaster curse and fell off dramatically in quality after the first two films, descending into pointless silliness. Both of those franchises changed creative teams between the second and third films, of course, while *Spider-Man 3* maintained the same director and producers, though with different writers, director Raimi, his brother Ivan, and Alvin Sargent. Moreover, as if specifically aware of the danger of descending into camp, *Spider-Man 3* takes itself more seriously than the previous films and moves in the opposite direction of camp by going for a much more epic feel than its predecessors. Not only is it substantially longer (with a runtime of 140 minutes) than the first two films, but it features not one, but three supervillains—and Spider-Man is superpowered throughout. Indeed, the highly ambitious *Spider-Man 3* seems designed to be the most epic superhero movie since the first *Superman,* which is ironic, given that, while the first two *Spider-Man* films seemed to invite comparison between their protagonist and Superman, the Spider-Man of *Spider-Man 3* seems much more analogous to Batman. Spider-Man is here even given a personal theme (written by Danny Elfman) that seems to intentionally mirror Elfman's earlier theme music for Batman. Perhaps because of this turn, *Spider-Man 3* does not entirely succeed as a film epic, at times seeming as if the filmmakers were attempting to cram more into the film than it could really bear.

Spider-Man 3 begins on an upbeat note. Spidey is now almost universally beloved by New Yorkers (except for Jonah Jameson, of course); his superhero exploits having become a regular part of the life of the city. Even the police love him after he heroically rescues Gwen Stacey (Bryce Dallas Howard), the daughter of a police captain, from a near-fatal accident. Meanwhile, Peter Parker has found a way to balance his secret superhero life with his regular day-to-day activities. He's still a bit short of cash, but he's making straight A's in his college classes and things are going well with Mary Jane—so much so that, as the film begins, he is preparing to pop the question, encouraged by Aunt May, who touchingly gives him her own engagement ring to pass on to Mary Jane.

There are, however, dark clouds on the horizon. Mary Jane, having finally made it to Broadway, is fired after one performance due to negative reviews and her career seems headed down the tubes just as Spider-Man's is reaching an all-time high. She's also jealous of what seems to her to be a budding relationship between Peter and Gwen, though there's really nothing there; Gwen seems tossed in as a reference to her more important role in the comics and really has nothing to do in the film. Meanwhile, Harry still knows that Peter is Spider-Man and still wants revenge for the death of his father, spurred by the influence of the Green Goblin entity. So he becomes the New Green Goblin—now mostly clad in black, actually, suggesting a darker (and less campy) turn in the character. Early in the film, he attacks Peter on the street and they engage in a high-speed battle through the streets and alleys of New York, the first time we have seen Peter use his superpowers in battle while not clad in the Spidey costume. It's a very effective sequence, probably the most exciting action sequence in the film, which is something of a structural problem, given that the film still has two hours to go. In any case, Peter ultimately wins the battle, nearly killing Harry in the process and leaving Harry with amnesia about recent events, going all the way back before the death of his father.

As a result, Harry returns to his old amiable self, removing the Green Goblin from the equation, at least for a while, though he soon recovers his memories, becomes evil again, and has to be defeated by Spider-Man once more. In the meantime, smalltime thug Flint Marko (Thomas Haden Church), escapes from prison and flees into a physics research facility, where a high-energy particle experiment transforms him into the Sandman, an entity who is able to take on Marko's normal human appearance, but who is constituted of sand, which he can manipulate into virtually any shape or consistency, from rocklike hardness to a wispy cloud that flies through the air. He can also take control of any sand with which he comes into contact, transforming himself into a huge, hulking sand monster. Marko/Sandman is a classic villain from the *Spider-Man* comics (he first appeared in 1963 and subsequently appeared many times), but he never quite works in the film. The depiction of his origin as a supervillain is here particularly unconvincing, while the attempt to add moral complexity to the character (he loves his small daughter and repeatedly claims to be a good man who has just had bad luck, though he also turns out—maybe—to be the true killer of Uncle Ben) is not very convincing.

In any case, Spider-Man repeatedly battles Sandman in the course of the film, though the villain becomes particularly dangerous when he joins forces late in the film with Venom, another classic supervillain from the comics. Venom is an evil alien symbiote that crashes to earth in a meteor (something of a science fiction cliché) and soon takes Peter Parker as his first host, transforming him into black-suit Spider-Man, thus partaking of the Jekyll-and-Hyde motif that informs most of the villains in the *Spider-Man* film world. The symbiote also transforms Peter into a would-be swinger, somewhat in the mode of the effect of red Kryptonite on Clark Kent in *Smallville*, though here treated in a lighter mode. Indeed, Peter's experiences in this mode provide some of the film's chief comic moments, though they are never really quite as funny as they could have been. The film's funniest sequence, in fact, involves not Bad Peter but the campy bad-French-accent cameo by Bruce Campbell (the cult-favorite star of Raimi's *Evil Dead* films) as a maître d'. By this film, of course, Campbell's cameos are obligatory in *Spider-Man* films (he appears in all three), but this one is probably the funniest of the lot, even if it is also the most out of step with the tone of the rest of the film.

In the meantime, Spider-Man eventually shakes off the symbiote, which subsequently takes unscrupulous aspiring *Daily Bugle* photographer Eddy Brock (Topher Grace) as its next host. Brock is thus endowed with Spider-Man-like powers; however (presumably because Brock was fairly evil to begin with), the Brock-hosted Venom is far more evil than black-suit Spider-Man had been. This new superevil Venom teams up with Sandman to terrorize New York, starting, of course, by kidnapping and menacing Mary Jane. Spider-Man seems overmatched by the teamed-up villains, but manages to defeat them with the help of the New Green Goblin, who has another swing back toward benevolence just in the knick of time. The final four-man superbattle is clearly designed to be the most spectacular special-effects battle ever put on film, but it never quite works, partly because it is so ambitious that it strains the abilities of available technology, thus looking a little bit *too* computer-generated. The writing is also a bit lame, too, so that the outcome is somehow both unbelievable and entirely predictable. Spider-Man wins, Harry/Green Goblin and Venom are destroyed, and Sandman (having received Peter's forgiveness for killing Uncle Ben) flies off on a passing breeze, possibly surviving to fight again in another film. In the end, Peter and Mary Jane are together again, though their on-again off-again relationship is beginning to get a bit tiring by this point.

Venom is the most interesting and effective villain in *Spider-Man 3*, though its portrayal is actually one of the film's structural weaknesses. Spider-Man vs. Venom probably deserves a film of its own, with the presence of the other supervillains here becoming something of a distraction. Indeed, there is in general too much of everything in *Spider-Man 3*, and the entire franchise definitely seems to be straining at the seams in this third film. At times, it seems as if Raimi and his team are trying to cram everything possible into one last film, yet there are still enough loose ends (and still plenty of unused material from the comics) for more films. Indeed, the film's spectacular box-office success means that there will be considerable pressure to produce still more sequels. There are, in fact, already rumors as of this writing that Sony is in discussion with David Koepp, principal writer of the first *Spider-Man* film (and of the upcoming fourth *Indiana Jones* film), to produce a script for *Spider-Man 4*, while other rumors suggest that Sony is interested in cutting a second three-picture deal with Raimi and the franchise's principal performers. In addition, the huge commercial success of *Spider-Man 3* suggests a market for the ongoing production of graphic cinema in general, which shows no signs of slowing down as of this writing.

10

Road to Perdition

Released 2002;
Director Sam Mendes

LONE GANGSTER AND SON: THE GENESIS OF *ROAD TO PERDITION*

Road to Perdition, based on the similarly titled graphic novel by the prolific mystery writer Max Allan Collins, was one of the major films of 2002. Despite its source in the comics, the film is anything but cartoonish. In fact, *Road to Perdition*, which is first and foremost a gangster film, is presented in a mode of gritty realism that fits in well with the long tradition of American gangster and crime films. However, the beautifully photographed film is a little bit slicker and smoother than most such films (and certainly than the violent and brutal graphic novel on which it is based). Even though it required relatively little in the way of special effects, *Road to Perdition* nevertheless had a production budget of roughly $80 million, partly because of its big-name, big-money cast, including such Hollywood megastars as Tom Hanks and Paul Newman, the latter of whom garnered an Oscar nomination for Best Supporting Actor for his role in the film. The supporting cast also featured such prominent actors as Jude Law, Stanley Tucci, Jennifer Jason Leigh, and Daniel Craig, who would go on to become the next James Bond in *Casino Royale* (2006). *Road to Perdition* was directed by Sam Mendes, in his followup to *American Beauty* (1999), which had won multiple Oscars, including Best Film and Best Director for Mendes. *Road to Perdition* got less recognition than *American Beauty*, but it did receive several Oscar nominations in technical categories; it was the last film to be photographed by famed cinematographer Conrad L. Hall, who won a posthumous Oscar for Best Cinematography for the film. Finally, *Road to Perdition* grossed a very respectable $180 million worldwide and garnered generally positive reviews. In short, released the same summer that *Spider-Man* became one of the biggest box-office hits of all time, *Road to Perdition* was another landmark in the history of graphic cinema, indicating the extent to which films based on comic books and graphic novels had become part of the Hollywood mainstream. The success of the film also spurred Collins (whose big break as a writer of comics came when he was tabbed to take over the writing of the *Dick Tracy* comic strip from creator Chester Gould in 1977) to follow his original graphic novel with several sequels. These include two conventional novels, *Road to Purgatory* (2004) and *Road to Paradise* (2005), as well as a sequence of three graphic novelettes, published together as *Road to Perdition 2: On the Road*, all of which take place within the time frame of *Road to Perdition*, providing support for the original story.

Much of Collins's introduction to the graphic novel explains the background of that original story. He particularly acknowledges his considerable debt to the classic Japanese manga epic *Lone Wolf and Cub*, written by Kazuo Koike (and subsequently published in English translation in the U.S. by Dark Horse comics as a massive twenty-eight-volume sequence). Indeed, Collins describes his work as being "in part ... an unabashed homage" to *Lone Wolf and Cub*, which tells the story of a lone samurai who seeks retribution, accompanied by his infant son, after his betrayal by his shogun. *Road to Perdition* transplants much the same story to the context of 1930s gangster culture, which might explain some of the success of its adaptation to film. After all, the *Lone Wolf and Cub* epic was itself the basis for a series of six highly successful Japanese films, which Collins calls, in his introduction, "probably the finest movie series ever to be derived from comics."

The fact that the graphic novel itself was importantly influenced by other works of film and television also made it something of a natural for film adaptation. For example, Collins notes that his graphic novel was crucially influenced by such works as the 1950s American television series *The Untouchables* (that is about the Chicago mob scene of the 1930s), Arthur Penn's film *Bonnie and Clyde* (1967), and the Hong Kong cinema of John Woo, including *Heroes Shed no Tears* (1986), which contains Woo's own homage to *Lone Wolf and Cub*. Ultimately, however, Collins concludes that the most important source of all for *Road to Perdition* was American history itself, and both the book and the film are very much period pieces that draw in important ways on their setting in the early 1930s. In this sense, *Road to Perdition* is typical of Collins's crime fiction, much of which is set in the past, typically revolving around real historical crimes or mysteries. For example, his longest running series of crime novels involves the efforts of fictional Chicago private investigator Nathan Heller to solve famous real-world mysteries from the 1930s and 1940s, meanwhile meeting up with a variety of well-known historical personages. Collins himself suggests, in the introduction to the graphic novel, that much of his work, including *Road to Perdition*, falls within the subgenre of "true-crime fiction." Actually, this particular graphic novel depends less heavily on real historical events than do the Heller novels, though it does feature appearances by real historical figures such as Frank Nitti and Eliot Ness (the latter of whom is absent in the film version), while including an important engagement with its historical context, an engagement that is less richly realized in the film. The graphic novel of *Road to Perdition* is thus not only a work of gangster fiction, joining a rich American cultural tradition, but also a work of historical fiction, vividly evoking a period of the American past that has loomed particularly large in the popular American imagination, partly because of the Depression and partly because the early 1930s were the heyday of near-legendary organized-crime bosses such as Al Capone (and Nitti). The film version is also very much a period piece, though it mentions fewer real historical events than does the graphic novel and places less emphasis on issues such as the role of immigrants in American society at the time of the story's action. Indeed, the film's access to American history is doubly mediated: not only does it derive its historical basis via the graphic novel, but it represents the 1930s (and especially the gangster culture of the 1930s) through a whole panoply of films and television series that deal with the same material.

DIRTY BUSINESS, CLEAN PHOTOGRAPHY: SANITIZED BRUTALITY IN *ROAD TO PERDITION*

Road to Perdition is a beautiful film that clearly deserves its Best Cinematography Oscar. On the other hand, the very quality of the film's lighting and photography sets it apart from the relatively gritty look of the gangster films that were actually made in the early 1930s, such as *Little Caesar* (1931), *Public Enemy* (1931), and *Scarface* (1932). The film is also much smoother and slicker looking than the noir crime films of the 1940s and early 1950s, which also form an inescapable part of its cinematic background. This difference is particularly significant because the black-and-white artwork of the graphic novel version of *Road to Perdition* is closer in style and spirit to film noir than to the novel's own film adaptation. In addition, this stylistic difference in the film version of *Road to*

Perdition is matched by a general movement toward softer and less brutal content. Thus, though a fine film in its own right, *Road to Perdition* is definitely a sanitized version of its source novel, indicating the way in which mainstream Hollywood film, with so many millions of dollars at stake, tends to shy away from the kind of extreme and experimental material that is often the lifeblood of the comics, more of a niche form that can be produced much more economically than film and therefore need not attract such a broad audience in order to be a success.

The film version of *Road to Perdition* begins with scenes from the childhood of young Michael Sullivan, Jr. (Tyler Hoechlin), who first introduces the film with a voiceover narration that identifies the setting as the winter of 1931. We see the twelve-year-old Michael selling newspapers, having a snowball fight with younger brother Peter (Liam Aiken), and struggling with math homework, with which his kindly mother Annie (Leigh) promises to help him after dinner. There are, however, darker hints in these scenes that remind us that we are not about to see a simple collection of nostalgic Norman Rockwellesque scenes from Midwestern American life—even if the film is, in fact, much kinder and gentler than the graphic novel. For one thing, Michael attempts to sell his papers to a group of workers who drearily trudge past him two abreast, like exhausted automatons, toward their latest shift at a local factory. At least these men have jobs (something of a boon in 1931), but their approach to the factory suggests the mind-numbing, back-breaking nature of the work they will be expected to perform there. On the other hand, it would be a mistake to take this scene as an announcement that we are about to see a highly political film exploring the exploitation of workers, especially within the special context of the early Depression years. In fact, this motif essentially disappears after this initial scene, other than extremely vague hints that Michael's father, Michael, Sr. (Hanks), justifies his work as a mob hit man at least partly by the fact that he has a family to feed in the difficult economic climate of the Depression.

There is also a hint of darkness in this early sequence when young Michael sees his father beginning to undress after his own day's work, removing items from his clothing that include a loaded pistol. This moment is enhanced by the fact that the father seems so mysterious. Indeed, the elder Sullivan seems extremely tight-lipped and repressed, hardly speaking to his own son, to whom he is clearly a distant and mysterious (though possibly romantic and heroic) figure.

The atmosphere of the film is further established in the next scene, which occurs at a wake (attended by Sullivan and Michael, Jr.) being held at the home of the seemingly jovial John Rooney (Newman). Rooney himself delivers a speech reminiscing about the dead man, Danny McGovern, but containing an anecdote about how the man, when playing high school football, once tackled his own quarterback and thus lost a big game. "Mistakes," Rooney concludes (in what seems to be a sort of veiled reference to the cause of McGovern's death), "we all make 'em." This speech is immediately followed by a eulogy that is delivered by Finn McGovern (Ciarán Hinds), Danny's brother, who begins by thanking Rooney for hosting his brother's wake, then is overcome with emotion and bitterness, which he turns against Rooney, telling him, "You rule this town as God rules the earth. You give and you take away." The crowd at the wake hastily interrupts, applauding the speech but also drowning it out, while McGovern is quickly hustled out to a waiting car by a group of men that include Sullivan.

It is clear by this point that Rooney, who seems a kindly soul, is a rich and powerful man but also a dangerous one. It is soon obvious that he is the kingpin of the local mob and that Sullivan works for him as his chief enforcer. Further, it becomes clear that Danny was apparently killed because Rooney believed he was stealing from him. We are also introduced early on to Rooney's only son, Connor (Craig), who seems bitter and perhaps insane, or at least dangerously unstable. Soon after the wake, young Michael stows away in the back of his father's car as the elder Sullivan goes with Connor on a "mission" to "talk to" Finn McGovern. During that conversation, Connor loses his temper and suddenly shoots McGovern, forcing Sullivan to gun down McGovern's two henchmen in the ensuing battle, while the shocked Michael, Jr., looks on.

By this point in the film, the events that trigger all of the subsequent action of the film have been put into place. For those familiar with the historical background invoked by the graphic novel and film, it is also clear by this point that *Road to Perdition* takes considerable liberties with the real-world historical events upon which it is based. John Rooney, for example, is based on John Looney, a real crime boss in Rock Island, Illinois, in the early part of this century. Indeed, the character is called John Looney in the graphic novel, making the connection absolute. However, while the events that make up the plot occur in 1930 in the novel and in 1931 in the film, the fact is that most of Looney's career in Rock Island crime occurred before 1912, when he was forced to flee the city in the wake of events related to the Market Square Riot, a bloody civil disturbance incited by his lieutenants in the wake of a run-in between Looney and the city's mayor. Looney remained away at his ranch in New Mexico until 1921, when he returned to Rock Island and resumed his criminal enterprises, now enriched by a lucrative bootleg business in light of the beginning of Prohibition. Looney's second career in Rock Island was short, however. The murder of a Looney rival, William Gabel, in 1922, led to a gang war that culminated in the gunning down of Looney's son, Connor, in October 1922.

Looney himself was indicted soon afterward, again fleeing to New Mexico, where he was arrested in 1924. He was convicted in 1925 and served nine years in prison—which means that he was in prison (and Connor was dead) at the time of the events related in *Road to Perdition*. Those events, however, are closely related to the killing of Gabel and the subsequent gang war, though Michael Sullivan (O'Sullivan in the graphic novel) is not a real historical figure. Gabel, in fact, appears (and is murdered) early in the novel, though he is replaced by Finn McGovern in the film.

Road to Perdition moves the historical events on which it is based from the early 1920s to the early 1930s in order to take advantage of the greater resonance of the later period in the American cultural imagination. Collins also introduced such well-known figures as Nitti and Ness (though only Nitti appears in the film) into his narrative in order to take advantage of their fame (via works such as *The Untouchables*) and in order to introduce a new dimension by having the powerful Capone mob provide protection to Connor Looney/Rooney through much of the story, even though the real Connor was killed several years before Capone rose through the ranks to take the leadership of Johnny Torrio's Chicago mob in 1925. (The real Looney, by the way, died of tuberculosis in 1947, at the age of eighty.)

The main plot of *Road to Perdition* is set into motion (and moves away from historical reality) when Connor decides that young Michael, as a witness to the killing of McGovern, must himself be killed. Knowing that Sullivan will never stand by and let his son be killed, Connor (apparently without the knowledge of the elder Rooney) arranges to have the elder Sullivan killed as well. The plans of the Rooneys go awry, however. Connor kills Annie and Peter Sullivan, but Michael escapes. Sullivan, Sr., meanwhile, shoots his way out of the ambush set up by Connor and manages to spirit his remaining son out of town. What follows is an extended campaign of revenge in which Sullivan seeks to kill Connor, only to find that the killer is protected first by his father, then by Nitti (Tucci) and the Capone gang in Chicago.

John Rooney, disgusted with his son's behavior, protects him out of family loyalty. Nitti, one of Capone's top lieutenants, seems to sympathize with Sullivan's position and to have little regard for Connor. He does, however, have tremendous regard for the profits that accrue to the Capone gang from their business dealings with Rooney and his gang. Therefore, he reluctantly agrees to protect Connor (describing it as "protecting our interests"), turning down Sullivan's request that he turn a blind eye and Sullivan's offer subsequently to put his considerable skills to work for the Capone gang. Gangster films such as *The Godfather* (1972) have suggested that organized crime, at least up until it became a business like any other beginning in the 1970s, contained an element of romance and even honor, with family connections and other personal loyalties often taking precedence over the quest for profits. Mob families are thus figured as genuine communities of a precapitalist kind that is largely unavailable in the contemporary world. In addition, films such as *Bonnie and Clyde* have seen "unorganized" gangsters such as Clyde barrow as romantic outlaw figures, battling to establish an authentic individual identity amid the routinization and alienation of the modern capitalist world. *Road to Perdition* rejects both of these positive visions of American crime. Nitti places monetary gain above all else in managing his corner of Capone's empire, caring little for honor or justice. For his part, Sullivan, while treated sympathetically, is hardly a romantic figure. His campaign of retribution for the killing of his wife and son is grim and methodical, pursued without pleasure and out of a sense of obligation to his family rather than striking blows for justice.

Sullivan's campaign is also bloody at times, though far less bloody in the film than in the graphic novel. Mostly, however, Sullivan aims at striking blows against the finances of the Capones, recognizing that the only way he can secure the cooperation of the Capones is to see to it that protecting Connor costs them more money than they can gain from continued good relations with Connor's father. Sullivan and Michael thus begin to travel around the Midwest, seeking banks where Sullivan knows the Capone gang has stashed illegal, off-the-books deposits. He then robs the banks, but takes only the dirty Capone money, meanwhile making sure that Nitti and the Capones know full well who is doing the robbing.

What Sullivan does not know is that, even before his bank-robbing campaign, Nitti has contracted a hired killer to kill both him and Michael, even though Rooney, reluctantly approving the plan to kill Sullivan, has insisted that the boy be left unharmed. This killer, Harlen McGuire (Jude Law), is a minor (unnamed) figure in the graphic novel, appearing only at the end. In the film, however, McGuire is a major presence in the second half of the film, stalking the Sullivans as they travel about the Midwest. The portrayal of McGuire adds an entirely new and very dark element to the film. Described as a "gifted" killer, McGuire clearly takes glee in killing. Fascinated with death, he pursues a parallel career as a photographer, specializing in taking photos of the bodies of the victims of recent violent killings, including killings he himself has performed. The latter photos he apparently sells to private customers, suggesting a dark and depraved world inhabited by shadowy and perverted figures who take (potentially sexual) pleasure in the violent deaths of others.

This lurid element adds a dimension to the film that is missing in the graphic novel; it serves in particular to make Sullivan a more sympathetic figure in comparison to his genuinely loathsome antagonist. Sullivan had been a killer and mob enforcer long before he embarked on his Robin

Hood-like campaign of lifting mob money from banks, but it becomes much easier for audiences to identify with his position when he is contrasted with McGuire, who takes such pleasure in the kind of killing that Sullivan does only reluctantly and as a matter of necessity. In general, the film seems to go out of its way to downplay Sullivan's history of violence, dropping altogether the graphic novel's frequent references to the fact that he is known as the Archangel of Death because of his legendary prowess in killing.

In addition, Sullivan does far less killing in the film than in the graphic novel, which also tends to make him more sympathetic in numerous other ways. The very casting of such as a well-known (and well-liked) actor as Hanks in the role certainly facilitates this project, though it also in part necessitates it. After all, audiences might be disturbed to see the usually sympathetic Hanks as a cold-blooded killer—and mainstream Hollywood film (of which *Road to Perdition* is definitely an example) is not generally given to trying to disturb its audiences. Young Michael's obvious admiration for his father is one of the key elements that make it easier for audiences to accept Sullivan as the hero of the piece, partly because the opening and closing voiceover narrations establish Michael's point of view as the central point of view in the film.

During their travels, Michael continually reads from an illustrated novel about the Lone Ranger, and it is clear that Michael sees his father as a figure in the mold of that legendary hero, inviting audiences to do likewise, suggesting an archetypal image that might help audiences identify with the mysterious Sullivan. In addition, there are more specifically sentimental attempts to garner sympathy for Sullivan because of his relationship with Michael. After all, a boy's love for his father contains an irresistible sentimental appeal, of which the film takes maximum advantage. Thus, the film includes archetypal father-and-son experiences such as Sullivan teaching young Michael to drive. Similarly, one of the film's central sentimental moments occurs as the Sullivans take refuge with a kindly old rural couple while Sullivan recuperates from a bullet wound suffered at the hands of McGuire. As Sullivan and the farm woman watch young Michael working in the farmyard, she turns to Sullivan and tells him, "He dotes on you," something that is obvious to her but something that Sullivan has apparently not realized before. He watches his son, considering the statement, then is unable to suppress a small and fleeting smile that steals across his face. He is clearly pleased, even though it is made clear in the course of the film that the last thing he wants is for Michael to follow in his footsteps and to lead a life of crime and violence. That evening, Michael has a bad dream and emerges from bed to find his father going over some account records he has taken from Capone's foppish accountant. "Math, huh?" asked the boy. "Yeah," says Sullivan, "I always hated it." "Me, too," says the boy. This potential moment of bonding is then solidified as Sullivan looks at the son about whom he knows so little, then asks with obvious awkwardness, "So, what do you like?" When the subsequent conversation turns to the murdered Peter, Michael finally poses the question that has apparently bothered him for years, asking his father, "Did you like Peter more than me?" Sullivan assures him that he didn't, to which Michael responds that Sullivan seemed to treat his two sons differently. Sullivan, surprised at this information, thoughtfully replies, "Well, maybe it was because Peter was just, such a sweet boy, you know? And you, you were more like me. And, I didn't want you to be. I didn't mean to be different." "Okay," says Michael, then says goodnight, ending the conversation with a hug that cements the growing bond between father and son.

When Sullivan returns to his study of the account records, he discovers evidence that Connor has been embezzling from his father for years. When he takes this evidence to the elder Rooney, however, Rooney simply responds that he knows all about Connor's thefts and that he still refuses to authorize the killing of his own son, however murderous and corrupt the younger Rooney might be. Thus, Rooney's loyalty to his son resonates with the growing bond between Sullivan and Michael, reinforcing the sentimentality of the film's exploration of father-son relationships and making Rooney a more sympathetic figure as well (even though the real Looney was by all accounts a murderous thug with little in the way of honor or decency).

Rooney further points out that both he and Sullivan are murderers and thieves as well. He begs Sullivan to walk away and to drop his campaign of revenge, so that he can at least have a chance to start a new life elsewhere and to keep Michael from becoming a killer as well. Sullivan's tragic flaw is that he is unable to follow this advice; he feels honor bound to continue his quest to kill Connor, no matter what the consequences. Then, on a dark, rainy night, he mows down an entire squad of Rooney's henchmen, in an oddly choreographed gunbattle accompanied by somber music, but otherwise silent—in perhaps another attempt to make Sullivan's actions seem less shockingly violent. Sullivan then confronts and kills Rooney, who tells him in resigned farewell, "I'm glad it's you."

With Rooney dead, Nitti not only gives Sullivan the go-ahead to kill Connor, but even supplies him with Connor's whereabouts. After all, the Capones do not wish to do business with such an unstable individual, and with Connor out of the way they can take over Rooney's operations for themselves. Sullivan joylessly guns down Connor, without fanfare and aplomb, as the latter sits in a bathtub. He then grimly walks away, believing that the entire affair is ended at last—as perhaps might audiences unfamiliar with the graphic novel. The two Sullivans travel to the home of the boy's aunt and uncle, here located in a picturesque setting on the shore of Lake Michigan near the town of Perdition (though Perdition in the novel is actually located in Kansas). The boy seems set to begin a new life here, complete with the big, affectionate dog who greets them. Nitti, however, has not called off McGuire, who has killed the aunt and uncle and still lurks within the house. In a shocking moment (set in a large, eerie, virtually empty room decorated almost entirely in white), McGuire fatally shoots Sullivan as well. As the killer sets up to photograph the dying Sullivan, Michael appears and prepares to shoot McGuire. However, after a sustained and suspenseful moment in which Michael hesitates to pull the trigger, Sullivan himself summons the strength to shoot down McGuire, thus saving his son from becoming a killer. "I couldn't do it," Michael says, apologetically. "I know," says Sullivan, proudly and happily, just before dying in his son's arms.

In his final voiceover, Michael assures us that he never again held a gun, thus following his father's wishes that he would not follow his road. A quick denouement (absent from the graphic novel) shows Michael returning to the old (childless) farm couple with whom he and his father had stayed earlier. The implication is that he will now receive an idyllic upbringing, something like that given Clark Kent on the Kent Farm in Smallville. The final scene at the home of the aunt and uncle has also been substantially modified in the film, which again seeks to temper the brutality and hardcore violence of the graphic novel, in which young Michael does, in fact, shoot down his father's killer, while the story ends soon afterward, with no kindly farm couple on the scene to care for the young boy.

The film, in good Hollywood fashion, thus provides a sort of manufactured happy ending, as Hollywood films are wont to do. That the film version of *Road to Perdition* is so sanitized relative to the graphic novel should probably come as no surprise, given the financial realities involved. That it is nevertheless a fine work of art suggests that these realities, while foreclosing certain avenues of artistic expression, still allow and enable others. The film version of *Road to Perdition* is certainly much more beautiful than the graphic novel, but the gritty art of the novel has its own aesthetic virtues as well—and is probably more consistent in spirit with the historical reality on which both the novel and the film are based. Similarly, the content of the graphic novel is much more true to the reality of the aspects of American history on which it is based, while the greater sentimentality of the film allows it to explore certain emotional avenues more fully than does the graphic novel. Rather than judging the absolute merit of one version as opposed to the other, it is probably best simply to note that the film and the graphic novel of *Road to Perdition* are different works of art in different media. Each has its own separate virtues and is designed to appeal to different audiences with different tastes; both are successful in doing so.

11

American Splendor

Released 2003; Directors Shari Springer Berman and Robert Pulcini

INDIE COMICS, INDIE FILM

American Splendor is the very epitome of the underground comic, and the 2003 film based on it is a quintessential example of the independent film. Begun in 1976 by creator and author Harvey Pekar, the comics are essentially a series of vignettes from Pekar's own life, ranging from his travails in various working-class jobs, to (sometimes quite intimate) accounts of his difficult personal life, to self-referential accounts of the production of the comic itself. As a down-to-earth, realistic account of everyday working-class life in modern America, *American Splendor* differs dramatically from most other comics and graphic novels, which have been dominated by stories about superheroes and ultranoir crime stories. Though never very widely read (at least before the release of the film adaptation), Pekar's work has gained a substantial cult following and a great deal of positive critical attention. His work thus represents a genuine landmark in the history of comics, demonstrating the viability of comics about realistic, everyday topics and paving the way for later authors, such as Daniel Clowes, who have worked in the same vein.

Pekar began producing *American Splendor* in 1976, in collaboration with artist Robert Crumb, who would go on to become a legend in the underground comics world in his own right. Over the years, the artwork has been produced by a variety of different artists, sometimes with dramatically different styles—and dramatically different depictions of Pekar himself. Indeed, the varying styles of the art constitute one of the most interesting and often remarked aspects of the series. Though gradually building a loyal following (and obtaining greater visibility through Pekar's appearances in the late 1980s on *Late Night with David Letterman*), *American Splendor* remained a relatively obscure series throughout its initial run, which included seventeen issues published between 1976 and 1993, mostly self-published by Pekar, reportedly at considerable financial loss. Beginning in 1994, Pekar produced additional issues of *American Splendor* for Dark Horse Comics, moving more into the mainstream of the comics industry, though maintaining very much the same flavor in his actual work. It was also in 1994 that Pekar and third wife Joyce Brabner wrote the graphic novel *Our Cancer Year*, illustrated by Frank Stack. The novel details Pekar's (successful) year-long battle with cancer, very much in the vein of *American Splendor*, though it is not officially part of that sequence. *Our Cancer Year* won the 1995 Harvey Award (given annually for achievement in the comics) in the category "Best Graphic Album of Original Work," adding to Pekar's growing critical reputation.

The 2003 film adaptation of *American Splendor* (based on a number of stories from the comic series, as well as *Our Cancer Year*) was directed by little-known documentary filmmakers Shari Springer Berman and Robert Pulcini. It was a fairly low-budget effort that grossed less than $8 million worldwide and received only limited distribution. Nevertheless, with Indie king Paul Giamatti in the lead role (supplemented by several inserted appearances by the real Pekar as himself), the movie received considerable positive critical attention. Roger Ebert, for example, gave it a full four stars, calling the film "magnificently audacious." Among numerous awards and award nominations, *American Splendor* won a prize at Cannes for Berman and Pulcini's innovative combination of the resources of film and the graphic novel, while the Berman-Pulcini script won an Oscar nomination for Best Adapted Screenplay.

All of this attention brought Pekar much more into the limelight and led to much more commercial success, even if he remained the sour pessimist he had always been. Pekar has also experienced an outburst of creativity and productivity since the making of the film—partly because the end of the filming roughly coincided with his retirement from the VA Administration, thus freeing up more time to work on his writing. His subsequent published works have included a special volume entitled *American Splendor: Our Movie Year* (2004), an account by Pekar and Brabner of the impact of the making of the film on their lives. Pekar then entered the real mainstream of comics publishing with *The Quitter* (2005, released under the Vertigo imprint of DC Comics), which continues his typical autobiographical vein, now focusing on his early years. Pekar also produced a special four-issue *American Splendor* miniseries for DC Vertigo in 2006. He has even branched out to produce nonautobiographical works, such as *American Splendor: Unsung Hero* (Dark Horse Comics, 2003), about the Vietnam war experiences of Robert McNeill, an African American coworker of Pekar during his years as a file clerk at the Veterans' Administration hospital in Cleveland. Finally, *Macedonia* (due out from Villard Books in the summer of 2007), cowritten by Pekar and student activist Heather Roberson, details Roberson's experiences traveling in Macedonia to a country that veered close to civil war during the Balkan conflicts of the 1990s, but avoided all-out violence.

The film adaptation of *American Splendor* has been much praised for its ability to capture the spirit of the comics on which it is based, and in particular for the way it is able to mimic the ability of the comics to blur the boundary between fiction and reality in a highly effective (and very postmodern) way. In so doing, the film adaptation also blurs the boundary between the two media of film and the comics, as when it directly incorporates artwork from the comics into the film. This latter effect is not present in the comics themselves, of course, but it is highly in keeping with the way in which the comics challenge conventional cultural boundaries in general.

THE LIFE AND TIMES OF HARVEY PEKAR: NO SUPERHEROES NEED APPLY

In the opening scene of *American Splendor*, set in 1950, an eleven-year-old Harvey Pekar (Daniel Tay) joins a group of neighborhood kids who are out treat-or-treating on Halloween. All of the other kids are dressed as superheroes (Superman, Batman, Robin, and Green Lantern). Young Harvey, however, goes simply as himself, no special costume required. Interrogated about his lack of a costume by a neighborhood woman who answers the door to hand out candy, young Harvey simply replies, "I ain't no superhero, lady. I'm just a kid from the neighborhood, all right?" The symbolism here is pretty easy to decode, this scene serving as an anticipation of Pekar's later entry into the world of comics, a world that had long been dominated by stories about superheroes, but in which he made his mark by the straightforward presentation of stories that are simply slices of his own life and the lives of his acquaintances.

Young Harvey, frustrated by the universal assumption that kids have to have costumes on Halloween, stalks away without candy, mumbling under his breath about the stupidity of everyone. The scene then morphs into a shot of the adult Harvey (Giamatti), similarly walking through his neighborhood looking frustrated and perplexed. Titles in the style of the comics, including some actual panels from an early Crumb-drawn sequence in which Pekar introduces himself, foreground what will be the film's ongoing dialogue with its source. An inserted panel that features a photograph of the actual Pekar with a speech balloon reading, "But hey, I'm also a real guy" also indicates the way in which the film will mix fiction and reality, very much in the mode of the *American Splendor* comics, except that the film now has the extra dimension of self-consciously mixing the world of film with the world of the comics. Another Crumb-style cartoon Pekar then indicates the film's awareness of this dimension via a speech balloon that reads, "An' now this guy here's playin' me in a movie." The cartoon Pekar points to the next comic-style frame, which contains film footage of Giamatti (as Pekar) walking along a Cleveland street.

This display of a scene from a film inside a comic-book frame perfectly sums up the overall strategy of this film, which seeks to combine the resources of the two media as seamlessly and effectively as possible. Subsequent frames contain captions that contain various credits, gradually moving into the actual beginning of the film, with Giammati's Pekar walking along the street while the real Pekar provides a voiceover narration that introduces the character, while warning audiences that if they are looking for "romance, or escapism, or some fantasy figure to save the day, guess what? You got the wrong movie." As this narration ends, the film cuts to a studio setting in which we see Pekar delivering the voiceover, meanwhile getting into a discussion with Berman about the narration and about the film in general. By this point it is clear that *American Splendor* will be an unconventional film that breaks many of the rules of Hollywood cinema, taking its formal and stylistic cues more from the comics on which it is based than from any previous models in film. Then, just as this real Pekar complains that all the takes are beginning to cause him to lose his voice, the film cuts to a scene from 1975, in which Giammati's fictional Pekar is in a doctor's office, seeking treatment for chronic laryngitis.

The laryngitis motif is greatly compressed in comparison to its treatment in the vignette "An Everyday Horror Story" from the *American Splendor* comic, used here partly to set up the later treatment of Pekar's bout with cancer (here he's convinced that the laryngitis is caused by throat cancer, though the doctor assures him otherwise). The scene in the doctor's office also helps to establish that Pekar is in a bad second marriage: he tells the doctor that his wife finds him a social embarrassment because his laryngitis makes him unable to converse properly. Pekar then returns home to find his wife, an academic, packing her things to move out, complaining that their "plebeian lifestyle just doesn't work for me anymore." He tries to dissuade her, but can't talk because of the laryngitis, adding to his frustration. She walks out of the apartment and out of the film.

The next scene, again narrated by the real Pekar, shows us Giammati's Pekar at work as a file clerk in the Cleveland Veterans' Administration Hospital. One of the most important aspects of the *American Splendor* comics is their treatment of life in the workplace for such lowly individuals as file clerks, whose boring and banal work routine certainly differs dramatically from that of comic-book superheroes. Indeed, such workers are seldom represented in American culture as a whole, which tends to shy away from workplace tedium as a topic, generally showing characters doing their actual work only if they are involved in exciting and dangerous jobs (cops, private eyes, astronauts), rewarding professional jobs (doctors, lawyers, professors), or creative, fulfilling jobs (writers, musicians, actors). Pekar's work is not physically dangerous or demanding, nor is it rewarding or creative. In fact, it is demeaning and mind-numbingly routine; he can do his work without having to even think about what he is doing, which means that he is free, while at work, to agonize over the considerable woes of his private life. This job does, however, bring Pekar into contact with a number of colorful coworkers, several of whom are featured in the comic. Particularly important in the film is Toby Radloff (Judah Friedlander), a self-declared nerd with Asperger's syndrome (or perhaps borderline autism), whose various fascinations and obsessions provide a certain amount of comedy. However, this character (in the comics and in the film) is presented not with mockery but with a genuine touch of warmth and sympathy, reminding us that even the most marginal of us are still people, worthy of kindness and respect. The treatment of Radloff is also indicative of the streak of compassion and generosity that runs through Pekar's gruff and often seemingly misanthropic grumblings in the comics, adding an element that is one of the secrets to the appeal of his work.

Interviews with the real Pekar are sprinkled throughout the film, as he discourses on various topics (such as his penchant for collecting jazz records) in ways that nicely illuminate the various brief vignettes that make up much of the main narrative (many of which include the real Pekar's voiceovers). These highly episodic vignettes are very similar in structure to the comics, which tend to include brief, episodic segments with little or no continuous plot lines tying them together. In the film, however, the episodic segments are supplemented by three main continuous plot arcs that give greater coherence to the overall work. One of these details Pekar's production of the *American Splendor* comics themselves, with a special focus on the beginning of his friendship with Crumb, leading to their initial collaboration on the project. These self-referential segments work particularly well with the generally self-conscious nature of the film as a whole, which foregrounds its own construction from its source material in the comics.

Particularly central to this construction is the film's self-conscious blurring (again, following the comics) of the boundary between fiction and reality. Thus, in addition to the voiceover narration and the inserted segments featuring the real Pekar, the film directly incorporates video-tape footage of two of Pekar's appearances on the Letterman show. The film also includes brief appearances by other real people who appear as characters in the film, including Radloff and Brabner, whose appearances demonstrate, among other things, that Friedlander and Hope Davis (who plays Brabner) have nailed their real-world characters to a tee. Radloff's appearances include actual footage from the promotional spots that he (having gained their attention because of his association with Pekar) shot for the MTV cable network in the 1980s. Pekar, however, reacts negatively to Radloff's MTV experience, realizing that his friend is simply being made fun of—much as Pekar feels he himself has been an object of fun on the Letterman show. Watching one of Radloff's MTV spots, Pekar has an "epiphany," telling us in a voiceover that "real salt-of-the-earth people like Toby and me were getting co-opted by these huge corporations. We were getting held up and ridiculed as losers in the system. What can I say," he concludes, "it was the eighties, man."

Thus, in one of the film's few openly political commentaries, Pekar gives a nod to the social and political climate of the 1980s, the decade of Reaganism, corporate greed, and general lack of sympathy for the little man. This point in the film is also important because of its indication of Pekar's own self-image. When he sees the seemingly dimwitted Radloff being made fun of by slick media types at MTV, his immediate response is not only to sympathize with Radloff, but to identify with him. In his own mind, Pekar is not a sophisticated artist and intellectual masquerading as a file clerk. He really *is* an ordinary file clerk, who simply happens to have certain creative talents and intellectual abilities. Herein lies one of the secrets to the success of *American Splendor* in both the comics and the film: Pekar may be an intellectual, but he is an organic intellectual who genuinely belongs to the working class, rather than merely sympathizing with it. He observes and comments on working-class life from the inside, not from the perspective of an outside observer.

This epiphany also leads to the film's narration of one of Pekar's own rare overtly political gestures in its presentation of the controversial August 31, 1988, Letterman show appearance during which Pekar, angered by his insight concerning Radloff's MTV appearances and distracted by the recent discovery of a testicular lump signaling his cancer, comes out swinging with a criticism of the conflict of interest he sees in the owner-ship of the NBC television network by a giant conglomerate like General Electric Corporation—that had recently been involved in several question-able dealings in the state of Ohio. All the while, Pekar wears a tee-shirt reading "ON STRIKE AGAINST NBC," in reference to the unsuccessful seventeen-week strike against NBC by members (mostly television writ-ers) of the National Association of Broadcast Employees and Technicians in 1987. NBC stayed on the air during the strike (as did Letterman), filling necessary positions vacated by the strike with nonunion workers. Pekar's tee-shirt thus suggests his solidarity with the striking workers (and with the working class in general), at the same time suggesting Letterman's culpability in strike-breaking (a suggestion Pekar made openly in his ac-tual appearance, though that aspect of the appearance is omitted from the film). Letterman, in turn, has little patience with Pekar's truculent com-ments, explaining that "this is a comedy show" and essentially rushing him off the air. Pekar is subsequently banned from the show—which actually seems fine with him.

Interestingly, the film's presentation of this last Letterman appearance features a recreation of the sequence, with Giamatti as Pekar and an actor playing Letterman. The combination of this recreated appearance with the earlier appearances shown via actual footage nicely complements the film's general blurring of the boundary between fiction and reality, though in this case it was really a matter of necessity, rather than postmodern art. NBC restricted the footage of the last Pekar appearance immediately after the actual show, so that it was never again broadcast and was unavailable to the filmmakers at the time they were making the film.

American Splendor also includes a love story, as any good Hollywood film is supposed to do. But this isn't your typical Hollywood film, and its love story involving the "courtship" and marriage of Pekar and his third wife, Brabner, is definitely not your typical Hollywood romance. This plot arc begins a little over a third of the way through the film, after several other sequences have established just how painfully lonely Pekar really is in the wake of his second divorce. Brabner starts out as an *American Splendor* fan working in her own comic-book store in Wilmington, Delaware. When one issue sells out before she gets a chance to read it, she contacts Pekar to try to get another copy. They strike up a relationship, and eventually she comes to visit him in Cleveland. Sparks don't exactly fly (this isn't *You've Got Mail*) and the two seem ill-suited for one another (or for anybody else) in obvious ways. For example, she is a "notorious reformer," and he is about as set in his ways as a person can get. He thus doesn't bother to clean his preposterously messy apartment before she arrives, not wanting to give her a false idea of what she might be getting into. At first, the two seem more annoying to one another than anything else, partly because they are both equally incompetent at courtship rituals. For example, each has a tendency to say whatever is on his or her mind. When Brabner arrives in Cleveland, Pekar's first words to her announce that he has had a vasectomy. When they go to dinner (at a restaurant neither of them appears to like), she discourses on her "borderline health disorders," including numerous food allergies that give her "serious intestinal distress." The two divorcées are also equally lonely, however, and in many ways they seem oddly suited to one another—or at least equally ill-suited for anyone else. Despite it all, they start to make out on his couch back at the apartment after dinner, whereupon Brabner is overcome by nausea and has to rush off to the bathroom to throw up—apparently because of the dinner, not the kissing. Finally, realizing that further courtship is pointless because they're both so bad at it, Brabner simply declares that they should "skip the whole courtship thing and just get married," if only to minimize further nuisance.

Oddly enough, the two misfits turn out to be a perfect match—or at least as perfect as they can be given their mutual low expectations from relationships and life in general. Thus, Brabner's proclivity for making snap diagnoses of the personality disorders of virtually everyone she meets (including diagnosing herself as clinically depressed and Pekar as obsessive-compulsive) meshes quite nicely with Pekar's own perceptive, but highly critical observations on just about everything he sees. Indeed, the relationship is strong enough to help carry them through the third important plot arc, taken from *Our Cancer Year*, which narrates the experience of Pekar and Brabner as they face his testicular cancer together. The sour, pessimistic Pekar seems ill-equipped to deal with cancer and the debilitating treatments he must undergo. Indeed, at first Pekar does seem ready simply to give up and die. Brabner, however, comes up with the perfect strategy for dealing with this most terrifying of illnesses: they write *Our Cancer Year* together—though only after she has considerable difficulty convincing him to do it.

In the way Brabner and Pekar work together in the fight against cancer (a fight the film implies he could not have won without her support), the third (cancer) plot arc merges with the second (love story) plot arc. And, given that the production of a graphic novel is their central strategy in the battle against cancer, these two plot arcs merge with the first, self-referential, plot arc as well, tying all of the film's themes neatly together in its final half hour. The collaboration of Pekar and Brabner with an artist called Fred (James McCaffrey) on *Our Cancer Year* also brings a new dimension to their relationship. Fred repeatedly brings his daughter Danielle (Madylin Sweeten) along with him for work sessions at the couple's home. As a relationship grows between Brabner and Danielle, Fred begins to realize that Danielle would have a better life living with Brabner and Pekar than with himself or his unstable ex-wife. Danielle thus joins the couple, completing their family, their mutual bond cemented by the announcement that Pekar has successfully defeated cancer.

Pekar and Brabner do, in fact, have a foster daughter named Danielle who came to live with them during this period. However, *Our Cancer Year* was actually illustrated by talented cartoonist Frank Stack, who is not Danielle's father. Stack was replaced in the film by the fictional Fred to supply an explanation for Danielle's presence, though the actual circumstances under which Danielle came to live with family are not disclosed in the film at the request of Pekar and Brabner. The story of Danielle's arrival is thus fictionalized in the film for perfectly legitimate personal reasons. However, the film's fudging of the facts in this instance is very much in keeping with the blurring of the boundary between fiction and reality that is so central to the film as a whole. Like the necessary reenactment of the controversial Letterman appearance, this aspect of the film thus represents a piece of found art—much like virtually everything in the *American Splendor* comics.

The film ends with one last symbolic blur as we see Giamatti's Pekar, walking along a Cleveland street, suddenly morph into the real Pekar walking along the same street. Pekar's voiceover narration explains that he is now ready for retirement from his job as a file clerk, but that he still has plans for a full life. "Sure, I'll lose the war eventually," he acknowledges. "But the goal is to win a few skirmishes along the way, right?" The film then cuts to Pekar back at his desk at the VA hospital, leading to footage of Pekar's actual retirement party, which begins as Radloff brings in the cake, followed by Brabner, Danielle, and a group of Pekar's VA coworkers. The film shows Pekar at the party, seeming genuinely touched by the well wishes of his family and friends. The film then ends as Pekar, Brabner, and Danielle share a group hug, followed by a final shot that shows the cover of *American Splendor: Our Movie Year* sitting on a cluttered desktop beside a half-eaten piece of cake. The film's final seconds thus perfectly sum up and recapitulate all that has come before, combining Pekar's work life and family life with a final reminder of his artistic life—juxtaposed with a mundane piece of partly consumed food as a reminder of how down-to-earth his art really is.

12

Hellboy

Released 2004; Director Guillermo del Toro

THE COMIC FROM HELL: FIGHTING FIRE WITH FIRE

By combining the superhero, action, and horror genres with a liberal dose of comedy, *Hellboy* is a film that gets a great deal of mileage out of postmodern intergeneric dialogue. In this sense, it is very much in the tradition of the *Blade* films, and it is no coincidence that *Hellboy* was directed by Guillermo del Toro, who had also directed perhaps the finest of the *Blade* films. Then again, del Toro's previous career had prepared him to direct *Hellboy* in a number of ways. In addition to directing *Blade II*, del Toro had established a reputation for himself as the director of stylish, high-quality horror films, with such efforts as *Cronos* (1993) and *The Devil's Backbone* (2001). Del Toro had also demonstrated his ability to combine genres in the 1997 science fiction/horror flick *Mimic*, his first effort at Hollywood film. *Mimic*, essentially a warmed-over version of the highly successful *Alien* films, doesn't quite come together to produce the terrifying sense of menace that informs the *Alien* films, but it does show some of the visual flair for which del Toro has become justifiably famous, culminating in the spectacular visuals of the adult fairy-tale *Pan's Labyrinth* (2006), which won Oscars in the crucial visual achievement categories of best cinematography, best art direction, and best makeup.

Del Toro was also especially well prepared to direct *Hellboy* because he was a devoted fan of the Mike Mignola comics on which the film is based. Indeed, he had already employed Mignola as an artistic consultant on *Blade II*, a role for which Mignola himself had preparation from serving as an illustrator for Francis Ford Coppola's stylish vampire flick *Bram Stoker's Dracula* (1992), even before the appearance of the first *Hellboy* comic in 1993. Del Toro's appreciation of the *Hellboy* comics is also evident in his introduction to *Hellboy: Conqueror Worm* (2003), one of a series of graphic novels in which the individual *Hellboy* comics have been collected, beginning with *Hellboy: Seed of Destruction* (1994, new edition 2004), which provides the primary source material for the film. In his introduction to *Conqueror Worm*, del Toro declares Mignola a "genius" and declares himself a "groveling fan" who has often tried to imitate Mignola's visual style in the design of his films. Because of his interest in the comics, del Toro jumped at the chance to direct the film adaptation, foregoing offers to direct both the third *Blade* film and the guaranteed megahit *Harry Potter and the Prisoner of Azkaban* in order to concentrate on *Hellboy*.

The choice was a good one. *Hellboy* offers precisely the kind of opportunities for visual flair and over-the-top storytelling for which del Toro's considerable talents seem best suited. *Hellboy* itself is one of the richest and most inventive additions to the world of comics in the past decade or so. The title character is a large, red, wisecracking demon from hell who was brought to earth as an infant by Nazi occultists seeking supernatural aid for their cause during World War II. The young demon was subsequently snatched from the Nazis by Allied forces, then raised within the top-secret Bureau for Paranormal Research and Defense (BPRD). The grown-up Hellboy is a cigar-chomping, beer-swilling, junk-food-eating smartass, who uses his formidable strength, toughness, and array of supernatural abilities to help defend humanity from the forces of evil. This basic idea is itself not all that different from the Blade motif of a half-vampire defending humans from vampires, the X-Men motif of mutants defending ordinary humanity from other mutants, or even the Superman motif of an alien defending humanity from various threats. Still, Hellboy, whose supernatural powers are combined with a down-to-earth blue-collar view of the world, is in fact a considerably more colorful and multidimensional figure than Blade, Wolverine, or Superman. In addition, he is aided by other paranormal creatures in the BPRD that fight against a diverse array of enemies, ranging from the original Nazis, to other demons from hell, to a variety of villains drawn from the mythology and folklore of various cultures from around the world. This scenario thus offers virtually limitless possibilities, which are further enhanced by the way Mignola draws upon such earlier works as classic 1930s pulp adventure stories, the horror stories of such authors as Edgar Allan Poe and H. P. Lovecraft, and a variety of earlier comics.

The film version of *Hellboy*, made for roughly $66 million (though it looks more expensive than that), pulled in just under $100 million in worldwide box office receipts and so was only a moderate success, though it has also done well in DVD rentals and sales. The film also got mixed reviews from fans and critics. For Roger Ebert, *Hellboy* is refreshing in that, based on a comic book, it also "feels like a comic book." Further, it is "vibrating with energy and you can sense the zeal and joy in its making." Critic Scott Holleran, on the other hand, found the film a jumbled mess, arguing that it "suffers from a sluggish pace, confusing narratives and weak plot." Still, the film had enough supporters and made enough money that talk of a sequel was almost immediately in the works. It is certainly the case that the *Hellboy* comic series includes far too much (and too many types of) material for a single film. Indeed, given that the film draws only upon the first graphic novel compilation (out of, so far, a total of five), there was plenty of published material available for the founding of an entire franchise. In addition, the comics themselves have branched out to include stories written by writers other than Mignola, as well as an array of conventional novels, so the pool of available material is quite large. The 2004 live-action film has already been followed by two feature-length made-for-television animated films, *Hellboy Animated: Sword of Storms* (2006) and *Hellboy Animated: Blood and Iron* (2007), both voiced by many of the same actors who appeared in the original live-action film, including Ron Perlman as Hellboy. In addition, a second live-action theatrical film, also to be directed by del Toro, is scheduled for release in 2008, while an array of comarketed video games, action figures, and so on has also extended the reach of the franchise.

NATURE VS. NURTURE: "OUR" DEMON VS. "THEIR" DEMONS

In many ways, the central question addressed by the *Hellboy* film is the old one of nature vs. nurture. Hellboy has been born and bred for demonic purposes—which are revealed in the course of the film. He is literally a creature from hell, though in this case it is a somewhat unconventional (the cosmology of *Hellboy* is unique to its own universe, drawing upon numerous Christian and non-Christian traditions) hell that seems (though this isn't entirely clear) to reside somewhere deep in outer space. Thus, Hellboy is also a sort of alien in one of the many examples of the way the film frequently verges on becoming science fiction, but never quite does. However, Hellboy has been raised by humans and treated well by the humans closest to him, particularly the kindly Professor Bruttenholm (pronounced "Broom," played to perfection by John Hurt), who regards Hellboy as his son. Thus, even though Hellboy has little contact with the general population, from whom his very existence has been kept a secret, and even though that population would probably regard him with fear and loathing if they knew about him, Hellboy's sympathies and loyalties are clear. Nurture here wins out over nature (answering the question posed by Bruttenholm at the beginning of the film, "What makes a man a man?"), and Hellboy stands as a staunch defender of humans from the supernatural evils that (unbeknownst to the humans) constantly threaten them.

Moreover, through his association with the BPRD, which is itself a secret branch of the FBI, Hellboy is an agent of the U.S. government, so his allegiances are vaguely American. He is, however, no Superman-style defender of truth, justice, and the American Way. For one thing, he goes about his battle against evil with more boredom than enthusiasm, seeming more annoyed than anything that he has to disrupt his routine to fight against his fellow demons and other supernatural threats to mankind. In addition, he is devoted not to abstract principles or large public causes, but simply to those around him. His loyalties are mostly personal, especially to Bruttenholm and those he knows personally within the BPRD, which includes a collection of one-of-a-kind misfits with unusual powers, and thus is the only place where Hellboy even vaguely fits in. To this extent, *Hellboy* is vaguely reminiscent of *X-Men*, whose various mutants seek community together when they are unable to find a comfortable place in the outside world.

Chief among the misfits at BPRD in the film is Abe Sapien (physically played by Doug Jones, but voiced by David Hyde Pierce), a sort of fish-man with psychic powers, and Liz Sherman (Selma Blair), a beautiful, but troubled, young pyrokineticist, with whom Hellboy is madly in love and who receives a greatly expanded role in the film relative to the comics, making it possible to work a love-story subplot into the film that is absent in the comics. Bruttenholm has a greatly expanded role in the film as well, which allows for much more exploration of the father-and-son motif in the relationship between Hellboy and the professor. This aspect of the film introduces a certain sentimentality that is not quite true to the spirit of the comics. In general the introduction of both Hellboy's romantic love for Liz and his filial love for Bruttenholm seem aimed toward humanizing the red demon, making him more emotionally vulnerable and thus more sympathetic to filmgoing audiences.

However, the film's wisecracking Hellboy is in most ways reasonably true to the spirit of the character in the comics, and it would be hard to imagine an actor better suited to the role than Perlman, though the very fact that the character is played by a human actor (albeit with a substantial amount of makeup and prosthetics) necessarily makes him seem more human than he is in the comics. Given del Toro's admiration for the comics, it should also come as no surprise that the film tries to stay true to the comic in other ways as well, even though the plot is modified substantially from the *Seed of Destruction* graphic novel. Thus, while the film is Hollywoodized in several ways, such as its humanization of Hellboy's emotional life, it never turns its back on what makes the comics special, and it should be noted that Mignola was an active (and enthusiastic) participant throughout the making of the film, serving as coexecutive producer and visual consultant.

Still, the entire film is less dark and frightening than the comics, with greater emphasis on humor (as opposed to supernatural threat and violence), perhaps in quest of the PG-13 rating that made it easier to attract more youthful audiences. Further, in addition to the added human elements in Hellboy's relationships with Liz and Bruttenholm, the film introduces an entirely new human character who is not present in the graphic novel, in the person of neophyte FBI agent John Myers (Rupert Evans). Stipulated to be "pure of heart" (over his own objections), Myers provides the central point of identification for audiences of the film, who follow him as he joins the BPRD and begins to learn about its mission and personnel, much as audiences themselves must get oriented within the world of the film, which is so different from their own. Hellboy is clearly the central character in the film and he is presented in a highly sympathetic way. Still, as a red-skinned (and virtually indestructible, at least physically) demon from hell, he necessarily has less in common with viewers than does Myers, a clean-cut, good-hearted human, with normal human weaknesses.

Hellboy begins with a very effective introductory scene set on an island off the coast of Scotland in 1944 that quickly establishes Hellboy's origin in a Nazi plot to recruit supernatural reinforcements from hell—on the presumption that Satan and his minions would sympathize with the similarly evil Nazis. Nazis, of course, are staple villains of the comics, dating back to the 1930s—and especially to World War II, when numerous American comics featured battles against Nazis as part of a program to support the American war effort. Here, they have set up shop near the spooky ruins of an old abbey and are attempting to open a portal into hell in the middle of the night while a thunder storm rages around them. This stereotypical and potentially campy setting is beautifully filmed and treated with complete seriousness, though the whole scene is given a further bizarre twist due to the fact that the Nazis encamped off Scotland are led by none other than Grigori Rasputin (Karel Roden), the notorious Russian mystic and advisor to Tsar Nicholas II. The historical Rasputin was assassinated in 1916, but the film's Rasputin turns out to have the ability to return from the dead thanks to a pact with demonic forces from beyond the grave. Rasputin is, in fact, apparently killed again in this opening scene, only to be resurrected by his surviving minions sixty years later, after which he goes on to become the principal villain of the film, becoming a sort of over-the-top version of Batman's Ra's Al Ghul. In particular, Rasputin institutes a plot to force Hellboy to help him bring about an apocalypse that will leave earth under the rule of the Seven Gods of Chaos (aka the Ogdru Jahad), currently trapped in deep space and unable to return to earth, where they once reigned. The Seven Gods of Chaos seem to be Mignola's original creation, though they are attributed in an on-screen epigraph at the beginning of the film to the mystical text *De Vermis Mysteriis*, a fictional creation of the writer Robert Bloch (himself a professed fan of the *Hellboy* comics) and later incorporated by Bloch's mentor, the legendary horror writer H. P. Lovecraft, into his Cthulhu mythos.

All of this sounds a bit far-fetched, of course, though it is also the case that it has some basis in fact. Many top Nazi leaders, especially SS head Heinrich Himmler (who, in the comics, recruits Rasputin to work for the Nazis), were known to have an interest in the occult. Further, also among the Nazi leaders in the opening scene is one Karl Ruprecht Kroenen (Ladislav Beran), described as "Hitler's top assassin and head of the Thule Occult Society." The Thule Society was a real organization, founded by German occultist Rudolf von Sebottendorf in 1918, which became one of the forerunners of the Nazi party. Though Hitler officially cut ties with the Thule Society soon after the founding of the Nazi party in 1920, rumors have long abounded of further links between the society and the Nazis and of various occult activities within the Nazi ranks. Mignola builds upon these rumors in the comics, and del Toro follows suit in the film, though he adds numerous elements, including making Kroenen a deadly, supernatural clockwork cyborg killer, as opposed to the same figure in the comics, who is more of an officious bureaucrat.

It is a tribute to both the graphic novel and the film adaptation of *Hellboy* that neither succumbs to the disastrous silliness that some of its basic scenarios might easily have produced. For example, even Rasputin is given a human dimension in the film through his relationship with the woman Ilsa (Bridget Hodson), a Nazi officer who is totally devoted to Rasputin and for whom he seems to have genuine (though apparently nonsexual) feelings as well. Further, though Rasputin is allied with extremely dark forces, there are suggestions in the film that he truly believes that his quest for the apocalyptic annihilation of the current human civilization could be the necessary beginning to a better world of the future.

In fact, both the film and comic versions of *Hellboy* handle the material in such a way that it never really feels as ridiculous as it easily could have, though each employs different strategies in order to achieve this effect.

The *Hellboy* comics work because they take the material absolutely at face value, proceeding as if it makes perfect sense, while at the same time illustrating the stories with distinctive artwork that both reinforces the narratives and contains a slight wink to the reader to acknowledge that *Hellboy* is a fun romp through world mythology that should not be taken *too* seriously. In short, in the comics the writing is serious, while the visuals are just a bit over-the-top. To an extent, the film is just the opposite. Though numerous frames of the film might almost have been taken directly from panels of the comics, the impressive visuals of the film represent the story in a more realistic way, and Guillermo Navarro's cinematography treats the material with absolute respect. The serious look of the film is also enhanced by del Toro's decision to do as much with actors, makeup, and models as he possibly could, keeping the computer generated elements of the film to a minimum. But the script is full of jokes and wisecracks, giving the film a slightly campy air that serves to invite audiences into the joke that this is a fun film that *of course* should not be taken too seriously.

Viewers of the *Hellboy* film are constantly invited to think of themselves as being playfully in on a secret that others do not know. The opening scene in Scotland leads directly into the opening credits, which include numerous shots of extracts from newspapers and tabloids, establishing the fact that Hellboy has, over the years, become a sort of urban legend, a shadowy figure whose existence has long been rumored, despite official government denials. This sequence thus adds a dimension that is lacking in the comics (in which Hellboy is a public figure) by linking Hellboy to various mythical figures (such as Big Foot) and to various conspiracy theories, such as the persistent claims that the government has covered up evidence of the presence of extraterrestrials on earth. Here, of course, filmgoers are presumably aware that, within the world of the film, Hellboy does exist, just as viewers of the *Men in Black* films (with which *Hellboy* has much in common) know that the shadowy Men in Black organization exists within those films. We therefore know that the rumors of Hellboy's existence are true and that the government denials are false, a knowledge that adds irony and humor to a scene that follows soon afterward in which a Larry King-like television hosts interviews oily, officious government bureaucrat Tom Manning (Jeffrey Tambor), identified as the Head of Special Operations for the FBI. Here, in a bit of light-hearted satire of the media and of government stonewalling, Manning looks straight into the camera and categorically denies the existence of Hellboy and the BPRD, followed by an immediate cut (accompanied by humorous music) to a building that is identified by on-screen text as the BPRD headquarters, in Newark, New Jersey (though the building is actually located in Prague, where most of *Hellboy* was shot).

We arrive with Myers at the headquarters, and then follow him on his first entrance into the building and through his initial voyage of discovery as he begins to realize just how strange his new assignment really is. Descending into a high-security bunker, Myers is given a succinct explanation of the role of the BPRD by Professor Bruttenholm, its leader: "There are things that go bump in the night. We are the ones who bump back." Myers meets the amazing Abe Sapien and is then even more amazed when he is introduced to Hellboy, to whom he is to serve as the new principal human liaison. Hellboy's first words are addressed to Myers as the latter examines a *Hellboy* comic book. "I hate those comic books," says Hellboy. "They never get the eyes right." This amusing moment ostensibly announces that the *Hellboy* film takes place in a different world from the comics and that the comics in fact exist within the world of film. But of course it primarily serves as another wink to the viewer, who knows perfectly well that the film is based on the comics. It also provides a special in-joke for readers of the actual comic, who are here placed in a privileged position because of their familiarity with the film's source material.

Myers takes all of this pretty well in stride, just as the audiences who are supposed to identify with his point of view must grant the film its far-out premise, suspending their disbelief, in order for the story to work at all. By this point it is clear that Hellboy lives an extremely circumscribed existence in which he is kept in his underground lair to keep his existence a secret from the public, then brought out only in emergencies when his talent for fighting monsters is needed to save a humanity that will never know it has been saved. He fills his days watching television, eating huge amounts of junk food, and attending his vast collection of pet cats. We then get a further view of this existence when an emergency does, in fact, arise, and we learn that Hellboy goes out on his missions inside a specially equipped garbage truck that disguises the true nature of its highly functional interior. This interior is a sort of combined scientific laboratory and chamber of magic (which, in addition to various sorts of electronic gadgetry, also contains items related to magic and the occult, including bottles of various potions and cages of live black roosters).

Hellboy is, after all, a supernatural being, though one with considerable institutional support from the U.S. government. However, though Hellboy does seem to own a variety of amulets and reliquaries, he relies relatively little on magical gimmicks in his fight against evil. Nor does Hellboy generally like to use the various high-tech weapons developed by the scientists at the BPRD. Much of his charm as a character comes from the fact that he is such a down-to-earth, working-class sort of supernatural being. Not only does Hellboy go about in a garbage truck, but his most important weapon in battling against supernatural evil is a large but rather ordinary-looking hand-gun (he isn't a very good shot, but it uses really big bullets), while he also has a proclivity for pummeling his opponents with his massive right hand, which is made of an indestructible variety of supernatural stone.

Hellboy's first mission in the film is to a library, where several security guards have been killed and a statue destroyed. There, Hellboy encounters the demon Sammael, a "Hound of Resurrection," which is virtually impossible to defeat, because it simply comes back from the dead after being killed. This encounter leads into an extended and highly impressive fight sequence between Hellboy and Sammael that spills out of the library onto a busy computer-generated city street and down into the subways of, presumably, New York, including water-drenched abandoned areas of the subways, directly echoing the subterranean settings of del Toro's *Mimic*. What is particularly impressive about these scenes is that Sammael is mostly shot in live action, with actor Brian Steele in a high-tech rubber suit, even though the demon looks like the kind of extreme creature that would surely be generated by computer. Some of the Sammael scenes are computer generated, of course. Indeed, some of the most cutting-edge filmmaking technology involved in the making of *Hellboy* involves the way in which computer-generated versions of several of the characters are merged seamlessly with their live-action counterparts.

By the time Hellboy finally defeats Sammael once and for all (by burning him to a crisp, because "I'm fireproof, you're not"), it is clear that the demon has already laid numerous eggs that will soon produce large numbers of demons like himself. The love story between Hellboy and Liz has also been put into place. Liz, troubled by her inability to control her powers as a "firestarter" (a term she hates), has left the BPRD to try to pursue a normal life on the outside, though the fact that we first see her as an inmate in a mental hospital suggests that she has had only limited success. She seems to feel that putting Hellboy and the BPRD behind her is crucial to her attempt at normalcy, while Hellboy pines away, watching old videos of her and thinking of her constantly. He also becomes comically jealous when she is befriended by Myers, though it is pretty clear to viewers that the straight-laced Myers is not for her. In fact, it is clear that Hellboy and Liz are perfect for one another. After all, she has a tendency to burst into flames at the onset of strong emotion, while he is the one person who wouldn't be damaged by such an event. Indeed, this fact is emphasized at the end of the film in the predictable but perfect romantic climax, in which Hellboy and Liz, reunited, ardently kiss, causing her to ignite, engulfing them both in flames that symbolize the heat of their passion.

Hellboy's other great experience of love, his devotion to the father figure Bruttenholm, is also developed intermittently in the first half of the film, which makes it clear that however unconventional their relationship, we are meant to understand that the professor and Hellboy love each other as much as any father and son could—though one could certainly ask whether Hellboy is in fact being exploited by the U.S. government with Bruttenholm's full participation. But this is a fun film and an action film, and we are clearly not expected to interrogate such aspects of the film to any significant extent, even though del Toro does attempt in numerous ways to given Hellboy himself an emotional depth that goes beyond his portrayal in the comics. The relationship between Hellboy and the professor, meanwhile, is given added poignancy by the fact that (unbeknownst to Hellboy) Bruttenholm is in the final stages of terminal cancer and must soon die. As it turns out, he dies even sooner than that, killed by Kroenen, who, in the meantime, has joined with Ilsa to resurrect Rasputin and resume their quest, aided by Sammael's offspring, to bring about the apocalyptic destruction of the earth.

Eventually, as the film moves into its final act, Hellboy and the BPRD pursue Rasputin and the demon eggs to Russia, accompanied by Liz, whose attempt to live a normal life has been derailed by Rasputin, who has caused her to explode violently into flame, largely destroying the Bellamie Mental Hospital. With Bruttenholm dead, they are also accompanied by Manning, who seems to have assumed temporary command of the BPRD, even though he has no real understanding of the work they do, which he regards with contempt and distaste. Indeed, one of the numerous subplots in the film involves the contrast between Hellboy's free-wheeling, individualistic style and the repressed, by-the-book style of Manning. Hellboy's style wins out, of course (individualism generally wins out over bureaucracy in American film), and by the end of the film Manning has learned a new appreciation for Hellboy and his talents.

In the final segment of the film, the good guys are determined to stop Rasputin and his minions once and for all, while it eventually becomes clear that Rasputin has intentionally led them to Russia, where he plans to use Hellboy for the purpose for which he was originally created: to use his right hand as a key to open permanently (by magical means) the gate to hell that Rasputin had temporarily opened by technological means at the beginning of the film. By this point, the plot of *Hellboy* is beginning to get a bit ragged, and the final segment of the film bounces about from one battle to the next (inside a sort of haunted castle in Russia), seemingly at random, offering numerous opportunities for impressive high-action sequences, but providing little else in what is the least interesting segment of the film, even if it includes the most spectacular special effects.

Hellboy battles the Sammael offspring and is nearly killed, saved only when Liz ignites to destroy them all—like their parent, they are not fireproof. In the aftermath, however, Rasputin captures Hellboy and Liz; he even nearly succeeds in securing Hellboy's cooperation in opening the gate to hell, using Liz as leverage. The big red hero momentarily resprouts the demon horns that he normally keeps ground down so he will fit in better with humans. However, it comes as no surprise whatsoever that Hellboy pulls back from the edge, saves Liz, and mortally wounds Rasputin, winning one final cataclysmic battle against a particularly large and powerful tentacled monster that emerges from the dying Russian mystic's chest (recalling the chest burster of *Alien*). All the while, Hellboy maintains his usual demeanor, complaining that "I'm gonna be sore in the mornin'" after he blows up the monster, showering himself with monster slime. In the process, the monster apparently finishes off both Rasputin and Ilsa, after the two have a touching last moment together. Kroenen has already been killed by Hellboy, so the film's villains have been wiped out. Meanwhile, Liz is sent back from the land of the dead (after Hellboy issues a harsh don't-make-me-come-over-there warning) and the film ends as the two share their flame-embroiled kiss.

During the kiss, Myers (in voiceover) reiterates the what-makes-a-man-a-man theme of the film, which has already made clear that it is not where one comes from but where one goes in life that determines who one is. The final kiss tops off the film with a feel-good moment, followed by the beginning of the ending titles, briefly interrupted by a final inserted comic scene of Manning, lost in the haunted castle and apparently "accidentally" left behind by Hellboy, Liz, and Myers, who seem to have already departed. This last moment leaves filmgoers with a final note of levity. We thus get one last reminder that, while the world has nearly ended and many deaths have ensued, it has all been in fun.

13

Sin City

Released 2005; Directors Robert Rodriguez and Frank Miller

ADAPTATION BECOMES TRANSPLANTATION: *SIN CITY* ON FILM

Sin City was a genuine landmark in the evolution of graphic cinema, a revolutionary first effort at translating the aesthetics of a graphic novel (or, in this case, novels) directly into film. Using techniques made available by recent advances in digital video shooting and processing technology, maverick Hollywood outsider Robert Rodriguez conceived of the idea of bringing Frank Miller's legendary series of ultranoir graphic novels to film in a way that would closely match the distinctive look and feel of Miller's work. The graphic novels are used essentially as storyboards for the film, and numerous frames of the film can be recognized as virtual reproductions of specific panels from the novels. Even the dialogue and voiceover narration is taken almost verbatim from the graphic novel. In short, as Roger Ebert put it in his highly enthusiastic Chicago *Sun-Times* review, the film is not really an adaptation of a comic book but "a comic book brought to life."

The result is a decided aesthetic success on its own terms, though the very fact that the film so closely reproduces the extreme style and content of the *Sin City* graphic novels necessarily means that it is not for everyone. For example, J. Hoberman, in his *Village Voice* review of the film, found its reproduction of Miller's style "overwrought." The film, according to Hoberman, is all style and no substance, ultimately lacking any sort of human interest. "Watching *Sin City* is like spending two hours in a state-of-the-art wax museum," Hoberman concludes. "Rodriguez loves his material so much that he embalmed it." Ebert, however, felt that just about everything about the film worked perfectly, describing it as a sort of film noir nightmare and arguing that it "plays like a convention at the movie museum in Quentin Tarantino's subconscious."

Tarantino's films, especially *Pulp Fiction* (1994), are certainly among the progenitors of this exercise in the celebration of pulp noir culture, and Rodriguez's friend Tarantino even guest-directed one sequence of the film, if only to give him a chance to try out first hand the innovative digital filmmaking technologies that Rodriguez employed in generating the film. But there is nothing else in film history that looks and feels quite like *Sin City*. The only thing that really resembles the *Sin City* film is the sequence of *Sin City* graphic novels, so much so that it is difficult to imagine that anyone could like the film who doesn't like the graphic novels (that could certainly be—and have been—criticized as overly violent, misogynistic, and totally lacking in any sort of redeeming social vision). Of course, some would say (if unfairly) the same about the entire tradition of film noir, in which *Sin City* clearly participates, though the Rodriquez-Miller film is particularly extreme, violent, and brutal, even by film noir standards.

Before the production of *Sin City*, Miller had done some work in the film industry, such as serving as a screenwriter for *Robocop 2* (1990) and *Robocop 3* (1993). However, those films were genuinely awful, which might have contributed to his reluctance to endorse the idea of adapting any of his work in the comics to film, feeling that the film version would not be able to do justice to his original vision. Indeed, Rodriguez had to do a substantial selling job to convince Miller to allow him to adapt *Sin City*, perhaps the single most important work in Miller's entire career. To do so, Rodriguez even went to the extent of filming a test scene (which still appears in the final film as a sort of prologue before the opening titles) to show Miller that he intended to make a film that was extremely true to Miller's original style and content. Miller, obviously, was convinced, and the film was made—with his active participation. Indeed, Miller participated so actively that Rodriguez insisted on listing Miller as the codirector of the film, even though that insistence got Rodriguez into hot water with the Director's Guild of America, which refused to waive its standard rule that films can have only one director, causing Rodriguez to resign from the guild. Miller was enthusiastic about the results of his collaboration and is also codirecting the sequels *Sin City 2* and *Sin City 3*, both scheduled for release in 2008. Miller also authorized the film adaptation of his graphic novel *300*, directed by Zack Snyder and released in 2007. Miller himself, extending his new participation in the film industry, has signed on to direct a screen adaptation of Will Eisner's graphic novel *The Spirit*—an expressionistic work that has been called "the *Citizen Kane* of comics" and that is one of the most important predecessors of Miller's own work.

BLACK HEARTS AND GREEN SCREENS: THE DIGITAL NOIR OF *SIN CITY*

Sin City is an impressive demonstration of the latest in digital film-making technology. It employs a strong list of A-list actors doing their things in front of a green screen, after which the distinctive atmospheric backgrounds that constitute Sin City itself (it's actually called "Basin City," but the shortened form is clearly more appropriate) are added in by Rodriguez with his whiz-bang personal computer. As such, the film could be seen more as an exercise in and demonstration of filmmaking technology than an attempt at the kind of compelling storytelling that is typically associated with the best Hollywood films. Much, in fact, has been made of the film's experimental techniques, as described in detail in Miller and Rodriguez's own companion book, *Sin City: The Making of the Movie* (published by Rodriquez's own Troublemaker Studios, 2005). However, *Sin City* is far more than a simple laboratory experiment in filmmaking technology. It is a highly entertaining film that careens about with zany and malicious energy, much like the graphic novels themselves. Moreover, in the case of *Sin City*, the seemingly artificial technology of the film is well matched with the material at hand, which is already artificial, divorced from reality, with which it comes into only the most distant of contact, mediated through Miller's graphic novels, which are already mediated through the entire noir tradition. Miller's novels represent not reality, but noir representations of reality, and Rodriguez's film is a representation of Miller's representations. Further, Miller has long insisted that the *Sin City* novels are intended as explorations of character in which plot and setting are entirely secondary. Sin City, as Miller would have it, is not a place but a state of mind. As a result, Rodriguez's filming (actually videoing) technique, which foregrounds top-notch human actors and then generates the backgrounds after the fact to support the work of those actors, seems perfectly suited to the source material. Much of the success of the film lies in its appreciation of the way the various elements of the graphic novels—the extreme hardboiled writing style; the dark black-and-white visuals, with few shadings of gray; the larger-than-life characters; the shockingly violent events—work together in a careful balance. The film includes all of these elements and does so absolutely without reservation, making no attempt somehow to tone them down for the cinema.

For example, the actors of *Sin City*—virtually the only "real" things in the film—are themselves processed through a panoply of extreme makeup, outrageous prostheses, over-the-top costumes, and after-the-fact digital enhancements before they appear in the film. Most notable in this sense is Mickey Rourke as the brutish and powerful Marv, rendered pretty much unrecognizable by the heavy facial makeup and prostheses that make him a dead ringer for the character from the graphic novels, a lowly outcast from society with superhuman strength and toughness, but with limited intelligence and only the most tenuous of grips on reality. Marv also has a soft spot for the ladies and a sense of chivalry that spills well over into the condescending. Indeed, one of the most problematic aspects of *Sin City* is the way in which so much of the material from its multiple plot lines involves strong men defending weak and helpless women, in a kind of adolescent male fantasy of sexual power. Granted, the film does feature some strong and formidable women—primarily the deadly prostitutes who rule the Old Town section of the city—but the very fact that these woman are prostitutes makes their portrayal problematic as well.

The multiple plot lines of *Sin City* (each of which is derived from a different graphic novel) are interwoven freely, creating a nonlinear structure that has reminded numerous critics of *Pulp Fiction*. This structure also places the film within the postmodern film form that critic Alissa Quart (writing in *Film Comment* 41 (4) (2005), pp. 48–51) has called "hyperlink cinema," in which multiple narratives intertwine in a single film, allowing (and requiring) viewers to jump about in time within a story and from one story to another much in the way they jump about among Web sites on the Internet. *Pulp Fiction*, as I note in my book *Postmodern Hollywood* (Praeger, 2007), is perhaps the most prominent and influential example of hyperlink cinema (p. 13). However, in the case of *Sin City*, it should also be noted that the virtually randomized chronology with which the different plot lines are intermixed also resembles the scrambled chronology of the original graphic novels, each of which features a similarly nonlinear plot, while the novels themselves are not published in chronological order. In fact, the nonlinear plotting of *Sin City*, in both the graphic novels and the films, really goes beyond that of *Pulp Fiction* or most other examples of hyperlink cinema, which typically allow the viewer to reassemble the pieces into a coherent, chronological whole, even if they also suggest that there would be little point to doing so. In the case of *Sin City*, however, the pieces never quite fit—slight inconsistencies and bits of missing information make it impossible to rearrange the events of the film in exact chronological sequence.

The two-disk "extended" edition of *Sin City* on DVD acknowledges the flagrant lack of regard for chronological sequence in the film by providing, on the second disk, recut and extended versions of each of the film's three main story lines (plus the prologue), each of which is accessible—intact without interruptions from the other plot lines—from a central menu. Viewers can thus watch any one of the plot lines all the way through, but these plots still seem fragmented and almost arbitrary. Moreover, the fact that the different plot lines can be viewed in any order further emphasizes the lack of any real narrative coherence. This is a film of striking images, not compelling story lines, providing an excellent example of the postmodern lack of regard for narrative sequence, while at the same time enacting Miller's own professed desire to make Sin City a place in the mind, with no real-world location or temporality.

The precredit prologue is taken from the short story "The Customer Is Always Right," one of several brief vignettes from the *Sin City* sequence, collected in the single volume *Booze, Broads, & Bullets.* This opening sequence nicely sets the tone for the rest of the *Sin City* film, even if it is one of the quieter and less extreme scenes in the film. Here, Josh Hartnett plays a hit man who has been engaged by a beautiful blonde (Marley Shelton) to kill her so that she can avoid an even worse (though unspecified) fate. The scene is shot on a high balcony, seen from the rear, so that the city's grim skyline provides a perfect backdrop to the action. It begins as the woman walks out to the railing, soon to be approached by the hit man, who narrates the scene in voiceover. "She shivers in the wind like the last leaf on a dying tree," he tells us as he approaches her. He utters soothing words to her, they embrace, and he shoots her, after which she drops dead to the balcony floor. There are no reprieves in Sin City.

Voiceovers, as in this opening scene, are heavily used throughout *Sin City*, just as they often are in film noir. In the case of this film, the scripts of the voiceovers are lifted largely intact from the graphic novels, in the amped-up hardboiled-style that Miller has perfected for the series, reminiscent of the distinctive style of hardboiled detective-fiction writers such as Raymond Chandler. However, this already extreme style is pushed here to even greater heights, in what could easily have turned into self parody, but doesn't—because the style is entirely appropriate to the world of Sin City and to the events being described.

The first third or so of *Sin City* is dominated by the first plot line, taken from *The Hard Goodbye*, the first in the sequence of *Sin City* graphic novels. It features Rourke as the hulking Marv, a man so ugly and mis-shapen (and ill-behaved) that normal people tend to flee at his approach. He is so unattractive that even prostitutes shun his company, though we eventually learn that he is a friend and sometime protector to beautiful young Nancy Callahan (Jessica Alba), a stripper who dances in Kadie's, a lowlife saloon frequented by Marv and other rough types, but who has nevertheless managed to maintain her stereotypical innocence and purity through it all. In fact, in one of the rare instances in which the film tones down the material of the graphic novels, Nancy is actually more pure in the film than in the novels, with the demure Alba opting to keep her top on during her striptease sequences, as opposed to the topless Nancy of the graphic novels. Nancy, as a character, really belongs in the film's third plot line, and her brief appearance in the first plot line is typical of the way characters often cross over from one of the film's stories into another.

Marv is not really as bad as he seems, we are told: he was just born in the wrong century. In an anticipation of the themes of Miller's graphic novel *300* (1999, adapted to film in 2006), a voiceover narration delivered by private detective Dwight McCarthy (Clive Owen), a major figure in the film's second plot line, tells us that Marv doesn't fit in in the modern world but "would be right at home on some ancient battlefield swinging an axe." As this first story opens, Marv finds himself seduced by the stunningly beautiful Goldie (Jaime King), whose golden hair and red lips are so dazzling that they shine through the basic black-and-white of the film, providing one of the numerous touches of color (the most common are splashes of red blood) that add emphasis—just as they do in the graphic novels. Goldie is absolute feminine perfection and "smells like angels oughta smell," Marv tells us. After a night of passion (on a heart-shaped bed, also red), Marv awakes to find Goldie dead beside him, apparently murdered by a killer so silent and quick that he was able to slip into the room and kill her (leaving her perfect body unmarked in the process) without disturbing even the light-sleeping and usually hyper-alert Marv. What's more, Marv has been set up. Large numbers of heavily armed police immediately arrive at the scene to arrest him for the murder, leading to one of the film's most outrageous action scenes as Marv fights his way through the police and escapes so that he can pursue the real killer on his own.

Marv, in fact, dedicates the rest of his life to finding Goldie's killer, even after he learns that she had been a prostitute and even after it becomes clear that she had come to him in the hope that he could protect her from the danger that was following her. After all, as he explains, "she was nice to me," an event so rare in his life (especially from someone so beautiful) that this one night becomes his central experience. In the subsequent manhunt, Marv leaves a trail of bodies in his wake, while he himself survives a variety of assaults, including being run down by a speeding car and shot numerous times. He also runs afoul of the prostitutes of Old Town, led by Goldie's twin sister Wendy (also played by King), though he is ultimately able to win them over to his side by convincing them that he loved Goldie and had nothing to do with her death. The real killer, as it turns out, is one Kevin (Elijah Wood), a heartless killer with superhuman speed and reflexes, who has the chilling habit of imprisoning beautiful women and then slowly removing various body parts for his own consumption. Meanwhile, the creepy, bespectacled Kevin is the ward and chief henchman of the aging Cardinal Roark (Rutger Hauer), top man in the city's Catholic church, a member of the city's most powerful (and corrupt) family. Roark is a political kingmaker who has the influence to place his friends in family in positions of power leading all the way up to the U.S. Senate. A man thoroughly saturated with unadulterated evil, Roark not only endorses Kevin's culinary adventures in cannibalism, but apparently joins him in his repasts, in a motif that could be taken as a satirical commentary on the Catholic ritual of the Eucharist.

Roark, it turns out, had Goldie killed to shut her up. He had been one of her clients, "working" the clergy apparently having been her specialty as a hooker, which led her to learn of Roark and Kevin's gruesome hobby. Again, Roark's proclivity for hookers could be taken as a comment on the debased sexual appetites of the Catholic clergy. However, the satire of *Sin City* is not really aimed at the Catholic church or at any other particular group or institution. It is aimed at power and authority in general, the central organizing premise of its universe being that anyone in authority is bound to be corrupt, decadent, and vicious, while the more upstanding characters in the world of *Sin City* tend to be losers and outcasts, existing in only the lowliest margins of official society.

Marv gradually tracks down Kevin, despite the fact that he has a "condition" and tends to "get confused," repeatedly wondering if he is simply imagining the bizarre events he encounters along the way. He finally traces Kevin to a farm outside of town, where Kevin likes to hold women captive while he is slowly cannibalizing them. Indeed, when Marv arrives at the farm, Kevin is holding Marv's beautiful parole officer Lucille (Carla Gugino) and has recently chopped off one of her hands, eating it finger by finger, while making her watch. But Lucille, however beautiful, is a tough dame who survives this trauma far better than one might expect. Meanwhile, the stealthy, ultraquick Kevin manages to capture the formidable Marv as well, locking him up with Lucille in the room he maintains as a sort of dungeon and trophy room, the walls adorned with the heads of his victims, which is apparently the only part he doesn't eat. Marv and Lucille manage to escape, but Lucille is then machine-gunned by police who arrive at the scene (called in by Roark to take away Marv). Marv slaughters the police detachment responsible for her death (mostly with a hatchet), though first getting one of them to admit that Roark is behind Kevin's activities. Marv then resumes his quest for Kevin with renewed determination, eventually capturing him and interrogating him about Roark. In what is probably the most horrific scene even in this consistently brutal film, Marv amputates all four of Kevin's limbs in an attempt to get him to talk, applying tourniquets to the limbs to prevent him from bleeding to death. Kevin, though, stoically says nothing, refusing to talk, or even to scream in pain, even when Marv allows Kevin's pet wolf to gnaw at his master's bloody wounds. Eventually, Marv gives up and decapitates Kevin, having learned nothing from the interrogation.

He goes after Roark nonetheless, and has his continuing doubts about Roark assuaged when the priest openly admits his guilt in Goldie's death and his participation in Kevin's bizarre cannibalistic rituals. This is a man who is used to getting his way, and he seems to feel that he can talk Marv out of killing him even in the wake of these confessions. This scene that cannot fail to recall Hauer's earlier performance in the death scene of the replicant Roy Batty in the 1982 science fiction classic *Blade Runner*. Indeed, the almost legendary look of the noirish Los Angeles of *Blade Runner* is a clear cinematic predecessor to this film's Sin City, as it is in fact a predecessor to virtually all cinematic portrayals of dark urban landscapes from 1982 onward. Here, the *Blade Runner* influence even sometimes seems to lead the film away from the graphic novels. For example, in the Sin City of the film, it is always night and usually raining, just as it rains almost incessantly in the Los Angeles of *Blade Runner*, while the Sin City of the graphic novels is mostly arid. Roark portrays himself and Kevin as visionaries on a sort of spiritual quest. Marv, though, is unmoved, calmly gunning down the priest as police approach finally to bring Marv down in a hail of bullets. Given Roark's place in society, it comes as no surprise that Marv is treated brutally by the police, who provide him with the best of medical care, only so that he can recover enough from his bullet wounds to be viciously beaten and tortured by them, then eventually executed for Roark's killing—in a grisly electrocution scene in which Marv must be repeatedly jolted before he finally succumbs to death, though with the memory of Goldie alive in his brain until the last.

Marv is probably the most striking and interesting character in *Sin City*, and his story ends at about forty-seven minutes into the film, just over a third of the way through the film, which seems to be a possible structural problem. However, this situation is certainly not unprecedented in American film. One thinks, for example, of the death (and disappearance from the film) of Marion Crane, less than halfway through Hitchcock's *Psycho* (1960). In fact, Marion also vanishes at approximately the forty-seven-minute mark!

In any case, *Sin City* immediately cuts from Marv's death to the first scene of the second plot line, derived from *The Big Fat Kill*, the third graphic novel in the *Sin City* sequence. This plot line, in fact, is narrated continuously from beginning to end, without breaks or interruptions, running for approximately forty minutes—though there is a brief postscript at the end of the film that refers back to this sequence. Thus, the center third of the film serves as a sort of anchor of stability amid the fragmentation of the rest of the film; indeed, the realization that this second plot line runs continuously and chronologically begins to make it clear that *Sin City* is not actually as chaotic as it first seems—other than the fact that virtually every scene is chaotic in and of itself. On the other hand, this middle sequence, while continuous in itself, is out of sequence in relation to the rest of the film. For example, it seems to occur before the events of the first plot line in that one of its important characters is Shellie (Brittany Murphy), a waitress at Kadie's, recognizable to attentive viewers as one of the trophy heads on the wall of Kevin's dungeon.

As this central sequence of the film begins, Shellie has taken Dwight home with her after meeting him in Kadie's. While the two are in her apartment, Shellie's former boyfriend Jackie Boy Rafferty (Benicio del Toro) shows up, accompanied by a gang of his thuggish sidekicks. Actually, Jackie Boy is little more than a thug himself, though we eventually learn that he is a cop with the Sin City Police—a job that, of course, does not preclude him from being a thug. The fearless Dwight tells Shellie to let them in, after which he waits in the bathroom until Jackie Boy comes in to urinate, then overcomes the cop, issues a stern warning for him to stay away from Shellie, then tops it off by dunking Rafferty in the toilet (we get a view of his face from below, through the water), which hasn't been flushed since the urination.

Incensed, Jackie Boy stalks away with his gang in tow, then heads to Old Town to take out his frustrations with the whores there. His bad attitude leads to an altercation in which he and his gang are killed by the deadly hookers, led by little Miho (Devon Aoki), an expert with various sorts of ninja weapons, especially swords. Actually, Rafferty pretty well does himself in when his gun, the barrel plugged by Miho, backfires and explodes, driving a large chunk of the barrel into his forehead. He is left unconscious, near death, and it is up to Miho to finish him off. She does so with one deft stroke of her trusty sword, slicing his throat and cutting his head half off. "She doesn't quite chop his head off," McCarthy's voiceover, lifted verbatim from the graphic novel, tells us. "She makes a pez dispenser out of him."

This last line, however true it is to the original, is one of only a few times in the film that the hardboiled style spills over into camp, veering dangerously close to self-parody. This is not film noir, we are reminded; nor is it the hardboiled fiction of Chandler or Hammett. It is a postmodern recreation of the noir style, less serious than the originals as a potential critique of capitalist greed and corruption, more devoted than the originals to pushing the boundaries of extreme entertainment. And entertaining it is. After the killing, Dwight drives Jackie Boy out of town to dump his body in the tar pits there, where it will surely never be found, thus avoiding bringing the police down on the whores of Old Town in retribution for his death. In the scene guest-directed by Tarantino, Dwight and Jackie converse in the car on the way (presumably only in Dwight's mind); Jackie's head, loosened by Miho's sword, flaps up and down—just like a pez dispenser, his voice comically changing depending on whether his head is up, the neck wound open, or down, the neck wound closed. This shouldn't, one feels, be funny. But it is.

This whole motif is complicated by the fact that the local mob is actually trying to trigger a war between the police and the whores so that the hold of the latter on Old Town will be broken, opening the way for the mob to move in and take control. To facilitate this plan, the mob has placed a spy among the hookers in the person of young Becky (Alexis Bledel), one of their numbers whose seeming innocence is emphasized by her striking blue eyes, shining through the black-and-white matrix of the film. Soon after arriving at the tar pits, Dwight is ambushed by Irish terrorist mercenaries hired by the mob. The portrayal of the mercenaries (presumably members of the IRA) provides one of the film's few overtly political statements, even if the suggestion that the Irish, anticolonial insurgents are bloodthirsty, sadistic killers seems out of step with the antiauthority message of the rest of the film. Dwight, with the assistance of Miho, who arrives on the scene just in time, manages to dispatch the terrorists; he and the Old Town whores, themselves led by Dwight's sometime sweetheart (and fulltime dominatrix) Gail (Rosario Dawson), manage to lure the forces of the mob into a trap, then brutally gun down every last one of them, thus keeping their control of Old Town intact.

The Roark family is also central to the "third" plot line of the film (though a segment of it actually begins the film), taken from *That Yellow Bastard*, the fourth graphic novel in the *Sin City* series. Here, John Hartigan (Bruce Willis), an aging cop with a serious heart condition—but also apparently one of the last honest cops in Sin City—is nearly killed while saving an eleven-year-old Nancy Callahan (played by Makenzie Vega), who has been abducted and is about to be raped and murdered by a deranged and perverted killer (played by Nick Stahl). In the process, Hartigan blows off the right hand and blasts away the genitals of the criminal so that he can never rape again. Hartigan himself is shot both by the rapist and by his own partner, Bob (Michael Madsen).

This opening scene begins the film, and we do not return to this plot line until the other two have been completed. When we do, Hartigan awakes in a hospital, with Senator Roark (Powers Booth) looking on from the foot of his bed. Roark is the brother of the cardinal from the first plot line; he also turns out to be the father of the rapist/murderer foiled by Hartigan at the beginning of the film. The truly sinister Senator Roark asks Hartigan if it made him feel powerful to shoot his son, then delivers a statement that pretty well sums up the cynical political vision of *Sin City*: "Power don't come from a badge or a gun. Power comes from lying. Lying big, and gettin' the whole damn world to play along with you. Once you got everybody agreeing with what they know in their hearts ain't true, you've got 'em by the balls."

Roark then makes sure that Hartigan recovers from his gunshot wounds and even helps foot the bill for surgery to repair the cop's heart disease. He then proceeds to demonstrate his own power by seeing to it that Hartigan is summarily convicted of kidnapping and raping young Nancy, though Roark's minions fail in their efforts to beat a confession out of the aging cop. Hartigan insists that Nancy not come forward to clear his name, for fear that she will be killed by the Roarks, though she maintains a secret correspondence with him for the next eight years, which he serves in prison.

In the meantime, Roark, Jr., the only son of the senator, undergoes a variety of experimental treatments to try to restore his lost genitals so that he can produce a son and keep the Roark line intact. The treatments are to some extent successful, though they also have extreme side effects, turning the son into a grotesque, yellow monster, the "Yellow Bastard" of the title of the graphic novel on which this sequence is based. (The Bastard, in fact, is depicted in yellow throughout the film, as he is in the graphic novel.) Meanwhile, he keeps up his old habits of raping and murdering young girls, eventually convincing Hartigan that he has his sights set on Nancy as his next victim, though in fact he and his father do not actually know the identity of the young girl Hartigan had saved from them.

Hartigan falls for it and confesses at last to the kidnap and rape of young Nancy, thus discrediting himself once and for all, but also securing his release from prison so that he can attempt to save Nancy, now nineteen and dancing at Kadie's, from the Yellow Bastard. Unfortunately, his attempts only serve to lead the Bastard straight to young Nancy, whom he kidnaps and tortures, having presumably killed off Hartigan by hanging. The determined Hartigan manages to escape the noose, however, and to rescue Nancy, killing off the Bastard in a grisly blood-spattered scene—though the blood, of course, is yellow, rather than red.

A grateful Nancy suggests that she and Hartigan, whom she has loved since he originally saved her, could have a life together. He declines, responding that he is old enough to be her grandfather, then ultimately blows his own brains out, hoping that his death (along with that of Roark, Jr.) will close the books on his case, leaving Nancy free of the Roarks. Then, speaking of closing the books, the film ends with a brief postscript in which Hartnett returns as the hit man from the prologue, meeting up with Becky in an elevator hospital. Though it remains unspoken, it is clear that he has been hired to kill the young hooker—and that he will succeed. Mercy is in short supply in Sin City, and the rough justice of the city demands that Becky must die for her betrayal of the other Old Town whores.

The film thus ends, in a sense, as it began, which is entirely in keeping with Miller's vision of the timelessness of Sin City, a place in which dramatic events occur incessantly, but where nothing ever really changes. In another marker of its status as a quientessential postmodernist cultural artifact, *Sin City*, in both the comics and the film, takes place in a sort of land without history, recalling the argument of leading cultural critic Fredric Jameson that a loss of historical sense is central to the worldview of postmodernism. According to Jameson in his book *Postmodernism, or, The Cultural Logic of Late Capitalism* (Duke University Press, 1991), such a sense would involve the genuine "perception of the present as history," different from the past that led to it and the future that will derive from it (p. 284). However, he argues, the past in the postmodern era has been reduced to "little more than a set of dusty spectacles" (p. 18). It has become an insubstantial collection of images that can be used and manipulated in the present without any real awareness of their source in a material past that is the prehistory of the present.

Blade Runner is commonly taken as a cinematic paradigm of this effect, with its manufactured human replicants, futuristic flying cars, and building-sized television screens, all combined with costumes, hair styles, and a general atmosphere from the noir films of the 1940s. *Sin City*, with its collection of images from various decades, epitomizes this phenomenon as well. Most striking here are the cars, foregrounded by Miller in the graphic novels and crucially important in the film as well. Cars are typically used in film (especially American film) as temporal markers that roughly identify the historical setting of the action. Here, though, the cars could come from any decade from the 1940s to the early twenty-first century, as could the costumes or the skyline of the city. The implication is clear: the temporal setting doesn't matter because all times are the same in Sin City—a dangerous and politically retrograde notion that completely disarms any hope that action (by groups or individuals) can lead to change.

Then again, it is no secret that, politically, *Sin City* is pretty much a dis-aster, totally lacking in redeeming value, perhaps foreshadowing Miller's dive off the right-wing deep end in *300*. Morally, it is questionable as well—decadent, vicious, mean-spirited, and misanthropic. Aesthetically, it is pure trash (and damn proud of it). But it is formally and visually in-teresting, a glorious piece of trash that suggests sublime possibilities in the lowliest of forms. This suggestion, in turn, has potentially democratic implications, weakly reinforced by the film's vague sympathies with so-ciety's outcasts, but otherwise absolutely unsupported by the content of the film. Ultimately, *Sin City*, especially in the film version, would seem to illustrate both the best and the worst aspects of postmodernist culture as a whole. Lively, entertaining, and aesthetically groundbreaking (but in a way that is oddly derivative), it lacks historical sense, political vision, or any awareness that, as a popular work of art, it might have some sort of responsibility to the general public. One could argue, though, that the weaknesses of the film are derived directly from Miller's comics, while many of the strengths are original to the film. Perhaps, then, the formal and technological experiments of the film might have been better spent on adapting a different source. One can imagine, for example, a rousing adaptation of Garth Ennis's *The Preacher*, a comic sequence that is just as pulpy and trashy as *Sin City*, but that actually seems to have something useful to say. Then again, one could argue that the particular genius of *Sin City* as a work of graphic cinema is too dependent on the characteristics of the original comics to be transferable to a different source work. In any case, the *Sin City* film is a highly successful adaptation (or translation) of Miller's comics that points toward a bright future for graphic cinema, es-pecially if someone can produce a similarly compelling screen translation of the style and atmosphere of a comic with less objectionable tone and content.

14

A History of Violence
Released 2005; Director David Cronenberg

Unlike *Sin City*, David Cronenberg's *A History of Violence* opts for a fairly conventional cinematic style rather than attempting to reproduce the visual style of the graphic novel on which it is based. However, unlike *Road to Perdition*, the cinematic style of *A History of Violence* in no way seeks to sanitize the themes and images of the graphic novel, but simply helps the film to move in different directions from the graphic novel version. That novel, written by John Wagner and drawn by Vince Locke, is a crime thriller presented via gritty, noirish black-and-white art. Indeed, the graphic novel (more than the film) is presented very much in the style of film noir, while its subject matter—in which central character Tom McKenna (renamed Tom Stall in the film, played by Viggo Mortensen) attempts to go straight but finds it difficult to escape his violent, criminal past—would be very much at home in the world of film noir as well. One thinks, for example, of Jacques Tourneur's suggestively titled *Out of the Past* (1947), in which past criminal associates of a small-town gas-station attendant catch up with him, disrupting his new, peaceful life. The film version also draws upon film noir precedents (Cronenberg himself has identified the films of Fritz Lang as an important influence), but it also adds elements derived from other film genres, especially the Western, creating a postmodern intergeneric mix that is missing in the graphic novel. For example, whatever predecessors he might have in the world of film noir, Stall, as the former gangster attempting to go straight and live a quiet life, resembles no figure from American popular culture more than the retired gunslinger who tries to settle down peacefully, only to find that events force him to go back to his guns. Of course, Cronenberg, as I have noted in my book *Postmodern Hollywood* (Praeger, 2007), is a major postmodern director, so this aspect of the film might not be surprising: genre mixing is a common strategy of postmodern art. On the other hand, *A History of Violence* is not typical of Cronenberg's work. Known for gritty, graphic horror films that feature spectacular violence done to the human body, Cronenberg here goes for a much smoother and more expansive style in what is without a doubt his most mainstream film.

One reason, of course, for the more mainstream look and feel of *A History of Violence* is its $32 million budget, still modest by the standards of the early twenty-first century, but well beyond that of a typical Cronenberg film. For example, Cronenberg's signature film is probably *Videodrome* (1983), which had a budget of less than $6 million and grossed even less at the box office, though it went on to become a cult favorite on video. *A History of Violence*, on the other hand, grossed a respectable $60 million worldwide. It features a number of first-line Hollywood actors (if not big-time movie stars), including Mortensen, Maria Bello, Ed Harris, and William Hurt, who scored an Oscar nomination for Best Supporting Actor for his role in the film, while screenwriter Josh Olson was also nominated for Best Adapted Screenplay. In addition, though filmed largely in Cronenberg's native Canada, *A History of Violence* was produced and distributed by Time-Warner's New Line Cinema, one of the Hollywood's most important studios, especially after the success of their *Lord of the Rings* trilogy (2001–2003), which featured Mortensen in a key role. In short, *A History of Violence* provides still more evidence of the fact that in the early twenty-first century, the comics have become one of the central sources of material for mainstream Hollywood films.

A PERSONAL, POLITICAL, BIOLOGICAL, AND CINEMATIC HISTORY OF VIOLENCE

One of the most important keys to the success of *A History of Violence* is its ability to work on a number of levels at once. In detailing the story of protagonist Tom Stall and his personal history of violence, it raises numerous questions about the lives of individuals in general. Can they truly change, even in drastic and fundamental ways? Even if they do change, can they ever hope to overcome the consequences of actions undertaken before the change? Through the evocation of numerous iconic images from American culture, especially film, *A History of Violence* also poses basic questions about the significance of the history of violent images in American culture. This aspect of the film leads to the larger question of

American history as a whole and about the violent past of the United States as a nation. Finally, the film also suggests the possibility that violence is an inherent tendency in certain individuals—and perhaps in the human species as a whole, leaving it to viewers to draw their own conclusions about the implications of this suggestion.

A History of Violence begins as two men emerge into the early-morning sun from their room at a slightly rundown rural motel. The men, at this point seemingly traveling salesmen or even tourists, move slowly, languorously, as if still waking up. In an extended tracking shot that lasts approximately four minutes before the first cut (and thus emphasizes the lethargy of the two men), we see them load baggage into their convertible. The older man, Leland (Stephen McHattie), dressed all in black, saunters into the office to check out, while the younger man Billy (Greg Bryk), dressed in jeans and a tee-shirt, rolls the car slowly forward to catch up with him. Leland emerges and sends Billy back into the office to fill a plastic jug with water for the road. As he enters, the camera's point of view switches to the interior, in the film's first cut. Billy continues his slow pace, seeming sleepy and bored, as he walks though the office and past the front desk, which we now see is smeared with blood, while the clerk, also bloody, sits slumped in a chair, apparently dead, behind the counter. As Billy prepares to fill the jug from a water cooler, the camera moves to show us the floor behind the counter, where the maid lies dead in a pool of blood. Then, a little girl emerges into the office from an adjoining room, whimpering and clutching her doll, clearly traumatized by the killings of the clerk and maid, possibly her parents. Billy looks at her, then calmly pulls a gun and shoots her, just as the film cuts to another girl, Sarah Stall (Heidi Hayes), who awakes screaming from a nightmare. "There were monsters," she cries to her father, who comes to comfort her.

The father, Tom Stall (Mortensen) assures her that "there's no such thing as monsters," as fathers are wont to do. We know, however, from the opening scene that there are monsters in the world of the film. Indeed, the slow pace of that first sequence, combined with the calm, even bored demeanor of the two killers, makes it clear that these two men are indeed monsters, murderers who kill coldly, pointlessly, with no compunction and no regard whatsoever for the lives they are bringing to an end. When Sarah's older brother Jack (Ashton Holmes) and her mother Edie (Bello) come to comfort her as well, followed immediately by an idyllic scene at the family breakfast table the next morning, the stage is set for the depiction of the Stalls as an ideal, wholesome, all-American family. Their peaceful lives in the small Midwestern town of Millbrook, Indiana, stand in stark contrast to the horrifying violence of the film's opening scene.

We soon learn that Stall runs a diner in Millbrook, which gradually takes on almost mythic dimensions as the embodiment of small-town America. After breakfast, Edie drives Tom into town along a peaceful, tree-lined rural highway, while expansive, optimistic, all-American music sounds in the background. They have a fond kiss goodbye, and Tom walks down the street to his diner, greeting townsfolk on the sidewalk as he goes. In the diner, a regular customer is already at the counter having coffee, chatting with the cook, Mick (Gerry Quigley). Tom's diner is clearly a sort of public space, where many of the townspeople gather and where the regular customers, along with Tom and his staff, form a sort of community, somewhat along the lines of a small-town version of the habituées of the eponymous bar in the television series *Cheers*. The next scene, a portrayal of a youth baseball game, further establishes Millbrook as a veritable embodiment of Americana. To be precise, the game is actually a softball game being held as part of a gym class at Jack's high school, but the all-American resonance is there, nevertheless. Jack, a quiet, sensitive kid, is relegated to right field, traditional repository of kids who just can't play. To everyone's surprise, however, Jack catches a towering fly ball to end the game in a victory for his team: the good guys win, reinforcing the notion of Millbrook as the ideal American small town.

There is a slight hint of darkness in the fact that the fly ball is hit by Bobby (Kyle Schmid), the strutting school bully, who resents the catch and later confronts Jack in the locker room, trying to pick a fight. Jack, however, backs away from the conflict, weakly accepting Bobby's characterization of him as a "little faggot," though his open admission of Bobby's superior "alpha male" status appears to befuddle the bully, who seems to be trying to figure out whether the more intelligent Jack might subtly be making fun of him. Boys, of course, will be boys, and Bobby at this point seems relatively harmless (after all, Jack is able to talk his way out of the fight), doing little to contradict the vision thus far of Milltown as a quiet, peaceful town inhabited by hard-working solid citizens who all know and like each other.

The positive depiction of the life of the Stalls in Milltown is further reinforced in the next scene, in which Edie picks up Tom after his day's work in the diner, looking very seductive and bearing the news that the children are spending the night away from home, leaving the couple to themselves. She plans, she tells him, to rectify the fact that they never got to be teenagers together, having met later in life. At home, she dons her old cheerleader outfit (another piece of Americana) from Milltown High (it still fits perfectly) and they have great fun, loving sex. Tom, we must conclude from the evidence thus far, is a man who has it all, a man who has actually achieved the American dream. He himself sums it up, lying with

Edie in postcoital bliss. "I'm the luckiest son of a bitch alive," he says. "You are the best man I've ever known," she responds admiringly, unaware of the dark and violent past that he experienced before meeting her and that will soon come back to haunt him and his family.

This seemingly healthy bit of marital play might, from a feminist perspective, appear to be a disturbing example of sexism in which Edie participates in her own reification as a stereotypical object of male desire. Indeed, Edie's portrayal in the film is problematic in a number of ways. She is stipulated to be an attorney, but she seems to spend more time shopping for shoes than appearing in court. Her profession seems pretty much beside the point, leaving her to function in the film as a relatively conventional, passive, nurturing wife and mother. In general, however, the film is open to multiple interpretations on this point. On the one hand, one might argue that the film itself is sexist in its inability to imagine a stronger central female character. On the other hand, one could see the film's portrayal of Edie as a comment on the continuing secondary status of women in American society, a status that constitutes a fundamental flaw in the seeming American idyl of Millbrook, which thus becomes idyllic only for men.

Such potential problems aside, Millbrook really is in many ways the ideal enclave that it appears to be. In this, it recalls the virtuous small-town settings presented by such classic American filmmakers as Frank Capra. But we also know that this is no Capra film. At the same time, Millbrook differs from numerous more recent small towns of American film, as in the work of David Lynch, for whom the idyllic surfaces of small towns such as the Lumberton of *Blue Velvet* (1986) tend to disguise dark and even sinister cores. Then again, such dark visions of small-town middle America have numerous earlier precedents as well, including Lang's *Fury* (1936), in which the violent impulses that lie beneath the quiet surface of a small town erupt into deadly mob violence.

Given Cronenberg's general reputation as a filmmaker and his declared admiration for Lang, it should come as no surprise that Milltown isn't quite what it appears to be, either. In this case, however, the problem is not necessarily that Milltown itself harbors dark forces; the problem is that Milltown is unable to provide sanctuary from the dark forces that lurk elsewhere, either in time or space. In today's world, no town is an island, impervious to outside forces, a point that is brought home when the two killers from the film's opening sequence arrive in town (now driving a pickup truck with a camper at the back, presumably acquired from one of their victims). As they arrive, they nearly crash into Bobby, who starts to give them the finger, but backs down when he sees the murderous way Billy looks at him. Shaken, Bobby, who had been about to go after Jack again, simply drives away, now in no mood for violence. These are real bad men, not the would-be bad man that Bobby is, and we know from the opening sequence that their presence means that genuine evil has come to Milltown.

Given the size of the town, it is not surprising that the two newcomers soon come to Stall's diner, which they intend to rob. When the two demand to be served coffee and pie, even though Tom explains to them that the diner is closing, Tom agrees to serve them, just to avoid trouble. Trouble comes anyway, though, when they refuse to allow a waitress, Charlotte (Deborah Drakeford), to leave the diner when Tom tries to send her home. Leland then pulls a gun and holds it on Tom, ordering Billy to kill Charlotte to show Tom they "mean business." Tom responds by breaking the coffee pot over Leland's head. In the ensuing melee, he kills both of the thugs, reacting with a surprising gift for violence that makes the two hardened killers no match for him.

We will eventually learn that Stall's facility with violence comes from his dark past, which comes back to haunt him after the killings in the diner make him a local hero and media celebrity. Tom's family (especially Jack) seems thrilled at the attention he gets, though Tom himself seems appalled. We soon learn that the reasons for his concern go beyond any natural shyness. Modern communications being what they are, Tom's fame soon spreads beyond Millbrook, which once again proves unable to keep the outside world at bay. If this motif suggests that Millbrook cannot stand apart from other places, it also introduces the idea that the present cannot stand apart from the past. Media coverage of Tom's heroics brings attention both the outside world and from Tom's dark past (totally unknown to the rest of the Stall family) as Joey Cusack, a mobster whose brother Richie (Hurt) is now the kingpin of a Philadelphia crime syndicate, but who turns out to have some unsettled scores with the mob.

Having seen news reports of Tom's heroism in the diner, mobsters from Philadelphia come to Millbrook to fetch Stall/Cusack back to the city to settle these accounts. The mobsters, led by the disturbing Carl Fogarty (played with delicious menace by Ed Harris) are also genuine bad men, if perhaps a bit more professional than Leland and Billy. But they are violent nevertheless, and their arrival once again signals that Millbrook cannot shelter its citizens from the violence that reigns in American society as a whole. Stall at first staunchly insists that he isn't Joey and that Fogarty and his henchmen are simply mistaken, leaving the question open for audiences as well. The mobsters refuse to take no for an answer, however, even after town sheriff Sam Carney (Peter MacNeill) pressures them to leave town. Fogarty, who bears a horrible scar on his left eye apparently given him by Joey, a mobster renowned for his viciousness, follows Edie and Sarah to the mall, delivering a veiled threat that they might be in danger if Stall/Cusack doesn't cooperate. They threaten Jack as well, eventually leading to a bloody confrontation on the Stalls' front lawn in which Stall/Cusack brutally beats one mobster to death and shoots another, apparently fatally. Fogarty, however, shoots and wounds him and is about to finish him off, when suddenly the gangster is shot down by Jack with the family shotgun.

Soon afterward, Stall/Cusack receives an ominous phone call from Richie, then grimly travels to Philadelphia, where he goes to Richie's impressive mansion, hoping to make peace. Richie, played with a truly sinister flair by Hurt, who makes the mobster seems both deadly and decadent, even effeminate, responds by ordering his henchmen to kill his brother. Instead, Stall (now fully in Joey Cusack mode) kills all the gangsters, finally shooting down Richie himself, putting a bullet in his unarmed brother's forehead at point-blank range. He returns home to Millbrook having killed essentially everyone with ties to Joey Cusack and thus hoping at last to have put his past behind him once and for all. The evidence of the rest of the film, however, is that the past is not so easy to escape, so it is not at all clear that still other mobsters might not be coming for him in the future. In the meantime, he still has to try somehow to put his life as Tom Stall back together. Both Jack and Edie, shocked by the revelations about Tom's past, have reacted badly and may have had their feelings about him irrevocably changed—though one enigmatic scene (in which they have passionate sex on a stairway after he attacks her following an argument) has suggested that Edie might, despite her best efforts, find her husband's newly discovered violent tendencies sexually exciting, even she herself seems disgusted by the discovery of this fact. In a final, telling scene, Stall arrives back home just as the family is sitting down to dinner. Young Sarah, seemingly the only one unaffected by the recent events, sets a place for her father, who sits down to eat. Jack passes him the meatloaf in a gesture of reconciliation, while Edie looks at him with a tear in her eye. No one, however, speaks, and the film ends with the future of the Stall family still very much in doubt.

One question left unanswered concerns where Jack might go from here. Events of the film suggest that he seems to have inherited his father's knack for violence, despite his mild demeanor before the events of the film. Not only has he killed Fogarty in the shootout on the Stall lawn, but, shortly before that event, we had seen him, backed into a corner by Bobby and another bully, lash out and pummel them both, beating Bobby, in particular, into a bloody pulp. This surprising turn in Jack raises the question of whether or not violent tendencies might be hereditary, suggesting still another, Darwinian, dimension to the film's plot and title.

After all, Jack has received an extremely peaceful even idyllic upbringing, and yet the slightest intrusion of violence into his life has made him capable of demolishing the school bully in a brutal street fight, not to mention capable of quite accurately gunning down a seasoned killer in the heat of battle. Nature seems here to have overcome nurture. In this sense, *A History of Violence* chooses to move in precisely the opposite direction to that taken by *Road to Perdition*, which carefully excludes young Michael Sullivan from the violent proclivities of his gangster father, thus departing from the graphic novel on which it is based. The film version of *A History of Violence* departs from its source as well, but in the other direction. In the graphic novel, the son (named Buzz McKenna) does not resort to deadly violence; it is Edie McKenna who guns down (but doesn't actually kill) gangster Johnny Torrino, just as the latter is about to kill her husband.

The fact that Cronenberg specifically chose to add the motif of making Jack a natural born killer to the film would seem to lend support to a Darwinian interpretation of the film's commentary on violence. In the same way, the suggestion that Edie might find violence sexually stimulating has the Darwinian implication that violent men might have an advantage in acquiring sexual partners and thus have greater reproductive success than less violent men. In any case, if Tom Stall as an individual and the United States as a nation both have histories of violence, the same might also be said for the human species as a whole. One thinks in particular of the so-called killer ape hypothesis of human evolution, as originated by anthropologist Raymond Dart and popularized by Robert Ardrey in his widely-read *African Genesis* (1961). According to this hypothesis, the human species evolved from ancestors who gained evolutionary advantage over other primates by being more aggressive and violent than competitor species, thus becoming more successful hunters, which in turn led them to eat more meat, which made them still more aggressive and successful as hunters, and so on.

This Darwinian interpretation of the film at first seems virtually to negate any attempt to read the film politically. After all, if violence is inherent to the human species, it is hard to blame any particular person or any particular nation (such as the United States) for being violent. Similarly, the film's numerous attempts through plot, cinematography, music, and other techniques to evoke memories of the movie Western might endorse a reading of the film as suggesting that the United States, with a past drenched in blood, saturated with slavery and genocide, can hardly hope to escape its violent past. After all, the violence of the Western, so often seen as a quintessential expression of American national myths, is clear evidence of the centrality of violence to American society. In his book *Gunfighter Nation: The Myth of the Frontier in Twentieth-Century America* (University of Oklahoma Press, 1998), cultural critic Richard Slotkin details the way in which the Western as a genre has played a central role in the ongoing construction of an American national mythology. Violence, according to Slotkin, is central to that mythology, which pictures the United States as a nation defined by success in conflict. In particular, Slotkin concludes, "since the Western offers itself as a myth of American origins, it implies that its violence is an essential and necessary part of the process through which American society was established and through which its democratic values are defended and enforced" (p. 352).

Like both the Western and the film noir, the classic genres on which it centrally draws (and perhaps the two most distinctively American of all film genres), *A History of Violence* is punctuated by moments of extreme physical violence. However, except for the opening scene, most of this violence is ultimately perpetrated against villains (from a high-school bully to a mob kingpin), thus inviting the approval of audiences, who are presumably identifying with the good guys (especially central protagonist Stall/Cusack) in classic Hollywood fashion. In this case, however, the violence is presented in typical Cronenberg fashion through a graphic emphasis on the damage it does to human bodies, thus complicating the audience reaction to what might otherwise be thrilling moments in the film. In this film, we see not just blood, but actual wounds and damaged tissue, though less of it than in the typical Cronenberg film. Interestingly, however, the most abject examples of the destruction of the human body that appear in the original graphic novel do not appear at all in the film. These scenes from the novel involve the horrific, decades-long torture of Richie (in the book, not a mob kingpin but a friend of Joey who has run afoul of the mob) at the hands of the New York mob. In the novel, Richie's body has gradually been torn apart, literally destroyed, but kept alive so that he can suffer more for crossing the mob. When Joey finds the bloody, oozing stump that is all that is left of Richie's body, he accedes to Richie's request to kill him to put him out of his misery. In addition to the fact that Cronenberg omitted this entire plot line from the film, the DVD version of *A History of Violence* includes a deleted scene in which Tom Stall dreams of being confronted by Fogarty, then blasts the gangster in the chest with a shotgun, knocking him backward onto the floor with a huge, gaping hole in his chest, innards wet with blood pulsing inside. This scene, too, seems to be classic Cronenberg. Combined with his decision to forego filming what might be the most Cronenbergian motif in the entire graphic novel, the deletion of this scene would appear to suggest that the director made a conscious decision to tone down the graphic images of bodily damage, so that they would not overwhelm and dominate the rest of the film, diminishing its seriousness with a detour into the grotesque so extreme that it might verge on camp and detract from the film's implication that the violence it depicts is not an extreme and unusual event, but representative of everyday life in America.

A *History of Violence* is a serious film, indeed. Far more than a simple crime thriller, it is a complex work that interrogates numerous elements of the mythology of America. Among other things, the film's engagement with the Western and with film noir calls attention to the importance of violence as a cinematic motif in these two genres and, by extension, in American film (or even American culture) as a whole. By presenting us with so many recognizable, almost iconic, images of cinematic violence, *A History of Violence* reminds us how often we have seen such images before. However, Cronenberg seeks to defamiliarize (and thus make us think about) these images in a number of ways, as when he makes his gangsters Irish and from Philadelphia, as opposed to the more stereotypical New York Italian mobsters of the graphic novel (and so many gangster films). In addition, by giving us a better idea of what this violence does to the human body, the film asks us to interrogate our own complicity in this violence and to reconsider whether we want simply to endorse and, indeed, gleefully root for such violence, even if it is only in film.

The reminders in *A History of Violence* of how central images of violence are to the history of American cinema serve to reinforce the interpretation of the film as a commentary on the violence of American history as a whole. And, if the potential Darwinian implications of the film's plot suggest that the United States and its culture should not really be blamed for their violence, the engagement of Cronenberg's film with such central (and violent) American cinematic traditions as the film noir and the Western suggests that the violence of the United States as a society is clearly on display in these two film genres and indeed patently visible in all sorts of ways. Thus, if *A History of Violence* does not openly condemn the violence of American society, it does suggest that the obviousness of this violence makes almost laughable official American claims to be a peace-loving society willing to use violence only as a last resort and only when necessary to defend all that this society holds most dear (God, country, family). In short, the film may not condemn American violence, but perhaps it can be seen as a condemnation of American hypocrisy. Granted, any reading of the film as a comment on the history and mythology of America would seem to make Tom Stall a sort of national allegory whose individual experience stands in for that of the United States as a whole, and it is certainly true that, within the context of the film, Stall only does what he has to do to protect himself and his family. But the film also stipulates that his history of and talent for violence are extreme even by the standards of the gangster culture he seeks to escape. Further, his instinctive turn to violence when threatened suggests that his violent tendencies have not been overcome, but simply submerged.

15

V for Vendetta

Released 2006; Director James McTeigue

ALAN MOORE'S BRITISH POLITICAL FABLE COMES TO AMERICA

The single-volume graphic novel version of *V for Vendetta*, written by
Alan Moore and illustrated by David Lloyd, was published by DC Comics
in 1990. However, the sequence actually goes back to its appearance in
the British anthology comic book series *Warrior*, from 1982 to 1985, to be
finished in individual DC comic books in 1988 and 1989. *V for Vendetta*
was thus the result of several years' work. It is also the single work in
which Moore's anarchist political philosophy is expressed most clearly. It
may thus come as no surprise that Moore, with so much invested in the
work, became violently upset when the makers of the film version of *V for
Vendetta* made certain key modifications to the political implications of
the story.

As conceived by Moore, *V for Vendetta* is very much a dystopian
fiction, in the tradition of George Orwell's *Nineteen Eighty-Four* (1949).
Orwell's book had itself grown out of a rich tradition of British dystopian
fiction from the 1930s, most of which had been written in response to the
rise of fascism in Europe and the perceived threat of fascism in Britain.
V for Vendetta is directed at very much the same threat, depicting a
near-future Britain (the events of the novel are set in 1997) in which the
fascist "Norsefire" regime has risen to power in the wake of a limited
nuclear war, largely on the strength of creating fears among the general
populace by clever manipulation of the media to create a sense of crisis
and of the need for a strong, authoritarian regime to quell the threat. The

protagonist, V, is a mysterious masked anarchist, a former victim of Nazi-like medical experiments on the part of the Norsefire regime who now lives a secret underground existence, striking blows (usually through acts of terrorism) against the government wherever he can. Among other things, the Norsefire regime in the graphic novel, headed by the Big Brother-like "Leader," Adam Susan, uses religion as a tool of power, depicting its foes as immoral and its own actions as authorized by God. For this and other reasons, this dystopian regime has reminded many observers of the American Bush administration, and the makers of the film version of *V for Vendetta* have carefully adjusted the story to make it function quite clearly as an anti-Bush satire (though still set in England). Meanwhile, the anarchist V, while still a terrorist, is depicted primarily as a defender of liberal humanist values and preserver of Western bourgeois culture. Thus Moore's negative reaction to the film, including his insistence that his name be removed from the credits, which now inform us that the film is based on a graphic novel "illustrated by David Lloyd," with no mention of Moore. In an interview with the American cable television network MTV on the eve of the release of the film, Moore complained that the film adaptation was "a thwarted and frustrated and perhaps largely impotent American liberal fantasy of someone with American liberal values standing up against a state run by neo-conservatives—which is not what *V for Vendetta* was about. It was about fascism, it was about anarchy."

It is certainly the case that the eponymous anarchist protagonist of Moore's novel has been transformed essentially into an agent of bourgeois liberalism in the film, fighting for a restoration of old-style civil liberties rather than struggling against government altogether. But Moore seems to have been more upset by the shift of satirical focus from England to America than by the change in the ideology of the protagonist. In particular, he charged the filmmakers with being too timid to set their political parable in their own country, for fear of triggering too much controversy. On the other hand, one could argue that, given the American political climate at the time, the film version of *V for Vendetta*, however much it might differ from the original comics, is an extremely courageous film. After all, in the wake of the attacks of September 11, 2001, terrorists have been demonized in American culture perhaps even more vigorously than any group since communists had been vilified during the peak years of the cold war. As a result, a film whose central figure is a terrorist—and whose terrorist bombing of the British Parliament, no less, is depicted as a positive and heroic act—is already treading on dangerous ground.

The film was the brainchild of Larry and Andy Wachowski, who had earlier directed the highly successful *Matrix* trilogy of science fiction films. On this film, however, the Wachowski brothers served as producers and screenwriters, handing directorial duties over to James McTeigue, who had served as first assistant director on the *Matrix* films. To some extent, the film's depiction of V's rebellion against Norsefire is very much in the spirit of the rebellion of humans against their machine rulers in the *Matrix* trilogy. For example, Morpheus and his band of freedom fighters in the first *Matrix* film are, in essence, terrorists who find the power that rules the world so despicable in its suppression of individualism that they are willing to use any and all means at their disposal (including mass killings) to try to disrupt that power. *V for Vendetta*, however, makes its title character much more obviously a terrorist, while making its oppressive government a fairly transparent stand-in for the current government of the United States.

FILM AND THE POLITICS OF TERROR

Despite Moore's complaints, *V for Vendetta* is an unusually political film that dares to venture into territory seldom explored in the American cinema—both in the way it critiques government-sponsored terror and in its apparent endorsement of terrorism as a response to governmental oppression. Thus, even if V sometimes sounds more like Thomas Jefferson than Mikhail Bakunin, he at least has strong political convictions, which is not that common in American film. Further, despite the obvious relevance of the political satire in the film version of *V for Vendetta* to the context of Bush's Patriot Act America, the film does not abandon the "Britishness" of the graphic novel quite to the extent that Moore seems to suggest. It begins, in fact, with a pretitle sequence that reenacts the so-called Gunpowder Plot of November 5, 1605, in which Guy Fawkes and a group of Catholic coconspirators attempted to blow up Westminster Palace during the opening session of Parliament, with the goal of assassinating the Protestant King James I and key members of Parliament, thus toppling the English government and opening the way for a potential return of Catholic hegemony to England. However, the plot was detected, and Fawkes and others were arrested and executed.

This reenactment underscores the importance of Fawkes as a sort of predecessor to V (as does the graphic novel), though it also underscores the Englishness of the story, given that many American viewers probably wouldn't even know who Fawkes was without the voiceover narration that accompanies this opening sequence. As it is, Fawkes and the Gunpowder Plot are complex images. To this day, Guy Fawkes Night (also known as Bonfire Night or Fireworks Night) is celebrated annually on the night of November 5 as a sort of unofficial holiday in Britain and parts of the British

Commonwealth, but the holiday is presumably intended to commemorate the *defeat* of the Gunpowder Plot, even if some (especially Catholics) have traditionally gone against the grain and seen it as a tribute to Fawkes and his coconspirators.

There is, therefore, some precedent for V's decision to align himself with the Gunpowder conspirators by wearing a Fawkes mask and costume and by concentrating his terrorist attacks on November 5 each year, including his final climactic plot to blow up Parliament, succeeding where Fawkes failed. Given V's antiauthoritarian politics, however, this alignment is highly problematic. No matter how opposed he might have been to the official power of Protestant England, Fawkes was acting in the interest of another, possibly even more authoritarian power in his hope of bringing England back into the orbit of the Catholic Church (and back, for that matter, into the Middle Ages). On the other hand, Guy Fawkes Night has become the largest fireworks celebration in England each year, which is appropriate, given V's penchant for pyrotechnics. Safety concerns have also led to numerous official attempts to limit the Fawkes celebrations, which potentially makes V's adoption of Fawkes as his alter ego a potentially appropriate antiauthoritarian gesture.

The film version of *V for Vendetta* was originally scheduled for release on Friday, November 4, 2005, thus opening the film on the weekend of Guy Fawkes Night and suggesting a further association between Fawkes and V. Indeed, it was accompanied by the tagline "Remember, remember, the fifth of November," a line that is still featured in the film and that is derived from a well-known rhyme about the Gunpowder Plot. However, the opening was delayed until March, 2006, though the filmmakers have denied reports that this delay came about because the scheduled opening followed too closely upon the two terrorist bombing attacks that hit the London Underground in July, 2005.

The film also maintains many of the graphic novel's links to Orwell, whose famed dystopian novel is also set in Britain. These links are reinforced in the film by the casting of John Hurt (who had starred in the film version of Orwell's novel) as High Chancellor Adam Sutler, the film's version of the book's Adam Susan. Like the rulers of Orwell's Oceania, Sutler and his government make heavy use of techniques of surveillance and intimidation to further their oppressive policies, while the retro look of the film's near-future England also recalls Orwell's London, in which technology and standard of living decline over time due to the government's repressive policies. However, the film provides a number of updates to Orwell's vision. For example, the film's dystopian regime goes beyond the regime of the graphic novel in the extent to which it uses religion as a tool of power. Indeed, many have taken the self-righteous fundamentalist religiosity of the regime as a direct reference to the Bush administration, which might also be indicated in the film's Norsefire regime's declared hatred of those who do not share its moral, God-fearing agenda. In addition, Sutler's regime employs much more modern techniques for manipulation of the electronic media (including television and the "interlink") to shape public opinion in their own interest—much more in the style of Bush America than the dystopian England depicted by either Orwell or Moore. In the film's first sequence after the opening title, beautiful young Evey Hammond (Natalie Portman) dresses (on November 4) for a well-known television comedian, Gordon Dietrich (Stephen Fry), who appears on the British Television Network (BTN), for which Evey works as a lowly production assistant. Separately, V (Hugo Weaving) dons his characteristic mask (we do not see his face without it) and costume, preparing to go out on a mission of his own. Both, however, listen to a broadcast of the BTN that plays in the background as leading television personality Lewis Prothero (Roger Allam) delivers an anti-American diatribe, calling the "former" United States the "ulcered sphincter of Arserica" and speaking out against a plea from across the Atlantic for medical supplies from Britain. Sounding like an American televangelist from our own era, he declares that America has fallen from its former greatness to its current status as "the world's biggest leper colony" primarily due to "godlessness." "It wasn't the war they started," that brought down America, Prothero goes on. "It wasn't the plague they created. It was judgment." This charge, of course, might seem weird given the religiosity of America relative to Britain in our own world, yet it in fact echoes the rhetoric of the religious right in the United States, which has long railed against what it sees as the excessively secular nature of American society. In any case, thus scene quickly establishes the centrality of religious rhetoric in the dystopian Britain of the film. It also stipulates that the United States has, by this time, fallen and fragmented into chaos—to the point where it is held up by Sutler's supporters as a warning of what might happen to Britain without strong measures by the Norsefire regime. To escape the fate of the United States, Prothero declaims, Britain must continue its vigilance and willingness to do whatever is necessary to defend the country, with God's help, against "immigrants, Muslims, homosexuals, terrorists, and disease-ridden degenerates." Prothero then chants the regime's official slogan, "Strength through unity, unity through faith." Evey isn't impressed; she turns off the TV in disgust as Prothero proclaims, "I'm a God-fearing Englishman, and I'm goddamn proud of it." Indeed, citizens are often shown scoffing at the official broadcasts they view, suggesting that the Norsefire regime is unable to control public opinion nearly to the extent it would like—or to the extent that Orwell's Party is able to do. Still, this scene establishes the ubiquity of television broadcasts in this near-future society, as well as suggesting the extent to which television is used as a tool of government propaganda. Sutler, in fact, never appears in person, but only on television, including during meetings of his own cabinet, which he "attends" via a huge television screen that looms over the meeting room. Such huge screens loom over the London streets of the film as well. Indeed, though this future society has clearly gone backwards in many ways, television technology seems to have advanced, thanks to its centrality to the official program of the Norsefire regime. Appreciating this fact, V concentrates much of his activity on the media. He even conducts a daring raid on BTN headquarters, during which he momentarily seizes control of the network signal to broadcast his own antigovernment message. Having dressed in the opening scene, Evey rushes out into the night. She is, however, breaking curfew; common citizens are not allowed on the streets after 11 P.M. As a result, she is accosted by a group of "Fingermen," thug-like agents of the "Finger," the official police agency of the federal government. This confrontation makes it clear that the government's claim to righteousness is far from authentic. Rather than acting out of concern for the public safety, the Fingermen are simply agents of terror who roam the streets at night helping to create a climate in which ordinary citizens are terrified of their own government. Fear and intimidation are crucial to the success of the Norsefire government: having swept into power by creating fear of shadowy enemies, they now maintain power through creating fear of the government itself. This strategy leads to V's own central political statement in the film: "People should not fear their governments; governments should fear their people."

The Fingermen who accost Evey make sexually aggressive remarks and then make it clear that they plan to gang-rape her, thus providing an early comment on the hypocrisy of the Norsefire regime, which pays lip service to piety and morality, but in fact pursues its agenda through an obscene and vicious program of self-serving brutality. In this case, however, V suddenly appears out of the darkness and intercedes, quickly dispatching the stunned Fingermen with his flashing daggers, all the while quoting *Macbeth* and *Hamlet* and establishing himself as a defender not only of Evey but of the English cultural traditions that have been suppressed by the Norsefire regime. V then takes Evey to a nearby rooftop to observe the destruction (just after midnight, making it November 5) of the Old Bailey via a bomb he has planted there—accompanied by a spectacular fireworks display and the explosive music of Tchaikovsky's "1812 Overture," via a public speaker system he has hijacked for the purpose.

The Old Bailey (officially known as the Central Criminal Court) is a major London landmark, a central symbol of the British system of justice.

For V, however, it has become a symbol of the injustice of the Sutler regime, and he hopes that its destruction will help pave the way for a new era. Unfortunately, Sutler has the same idea, and the regime quickly responds with a classic case of spin control in which they announce that the Old Bailey was brought down by an official demolition crew because it had become a public safety hazard. They further announce plans to build a "New Bailey" that will help to move British justice into a grand new era.

Sutler also orders that the "1812 Overture" be placed on the list of proscribed works of culture, reinforcing the film's structural opposition between the government's attempts to squelch genuine culture and V's attempts to serve as a champion of culture. This opposition, incidentally, is a common one in the tradition of dystopian fiction, where the oppressive (and dehumanizing) practices of dystopian governments include the suppression of any form of culture not specifically produced to further their own agenda. Such practices are certainly pursued by the Party of *Nineteen Eighty-Four*, though Aldous Huxley's *Brave New World* (1932) is here an even more direct predecessor of *V for Vendetta*. In Huxley's book, the dystopian government's attempts to control the flow of culture extend to the banning of Shakespeare altogether because his works tend to evoke the kind of strong passions that their regime seeks to suppress through the production of mind-numbing works of popular culture. Huxley here is responding to fears that in the early 1930s, culture was being dumbed down by the new phenomenon of modern popular culture, thanks to the rise of new pulp genres aimed at readers with limited literacy and to the availability of new technologies such as radio and film. However, *V for Vendetta* acknowledges that popular culture (especially film) can have its virtues. Thus, even many works of popular culture have been banned, confiscated, and stored away in the vaults of the Sutler administration's "Ministry of Objectionable Materials." In response, V fills his subterranean hideout (which he calls the "Shadow Gallery") with such banned materials, many of them pilfered from the Ministry. Most obvious of these are the stacks of books that fill many corners of his lair, though the cultural artifacts with which V surrounds himself include examples of popular music and classic Hollywood film, as well as works conventionally regarded as "high" culture. Indeed, his favorite work of all seems to be the 1934 Hollywood film version of *The Count of Monte Cristo*, featuring British actor Robert Donat in a title performance that features a great deal of swashbuckling swordplay. V, in fact, is given to acting out the various fight scenes of the film with his own weapons as he watches the film on video, a viewing experience he later shares with Evey after taking her to his hideout for her protection when she runs afoul of the authorities by saving him as he is nearly captured during his raid on BTN headquarters.

In comparison to classic Hollywood film, the culture produced under the Sutler regime seems debased indeed. This culture seems to consist primarily of the mind-sapping fare broadcast by the BTN, apparently the only television network in this near-future Britain. Prothero's overt propaganda broadcasts are typical of the programming on the BTN, while the only entertainment programming we see is a childish (and apparently racist, from the title) superhero action show entitled *Storm Saxon* and Dietrich's comedic talk show, which features lowbrow humor, apparently modeled on that of longtime British television comedian Benny Hill. Dietrich's show, in particular, is a big hit, so much so that he feels confident enough to lampoon Sutler himself in a skit that makes fun of the administration's inability to stop V. But, in a comment on the severity of censorship in this regime, the authorities respond by raiding Dietrich's home, which contains a cache of forbidden cultural materials somewhat along the lines of V's own collection. Dietrich is viciously beaten, then taken away to custody, after which he is executed—apparently because the proscribed materials in his house include a Koran, which seems, in this society, to be the most forbidden book of all.

Meanwhile, the film stipulates that Dietrich is gay, a fact that Evey learns when she eventually flees from both V and the authorities, seeking refuge with the influential Dietrich, whom she presumes might protect her because of his sexual interest in her. That interest, it turns out, is feigned, part of an attempt to create a reputation as a womanizer and thus hide the fact of his homosexuality, something the Norsefire regime would surely never tolerate, especially in such a public figure. Dietrich does take Evey in, however, because he sympathizes with her plight as an outsider on the run from official authority. She is, in fact, there when his home is raided, and she, too, is apparently taken into official custody—only to learn later that she has in fact been incarcerated by V in a mock prison in order to put her through what he regards as the transformative experience of learning to resist the interrogation and torture she undergoes there.

The detail of Dietrich's execution for owning a forbidden copy of the Koran is added for the film and is not present in the graphic novel—in which Dietrich is murdered in prison by another inmate. In addition, Dietrich is heterosexual in the novel and becomes Evey's lover while she is staying with him. The film thus goes out of its way to place extra emphases on the Norsefire regime's antipathy toward both Muslims and homosexuals. Granted, this emphasis is not inconsistent with the portrayal of the regime in the graphic novel and could potentially be taken as an echo of the hatred of communists and Jews by the German Nazis. In point of fact, however, these key changes primarily serve to make the concerns of the Norsefire regime more in line with those of the American Bush administration.

For his part, V is not specifically defending gays or Muslims or any other group. He simply fights for liberty and justice—and seeks revenge for the wrongs that have been done to him and to England by the regime. Thus, in addition to its emphasis on swordplay, *The Count of Monte Cristo* is also appropriate as a thematic inspiration for V. One of the central themes of that film (and of the classic novel on which it is based) is revenge, as Edmond Dantès, the count of the title, systematically seeks vengeance against those who wronged him, causing him to be unjustly imprisoned for many years. V undertakes a similar program of revenge, both personal and political. Not only has the Norsefire regime destroyed British democracy with its oppressive policies, but it has done great damage to V himself, leaving him physically and psychically scarred via the gruesome medical experiments performed upon him and others at the government's top-secret Larkhill Detention Facility. In response, V strikes public blows against the regime with his terrorist bombings and his media campaign, while he seeks private revenge by systematically killing all of those he regards as responsible for the Larkhill experiments.

These programs of revenge are enabled both by V's single-minded de-termination and by the fact that the experiments done on him at Larkhill seem, as an unexpected side effect, to have given him superhuman strength and toughness. He is thus very much a superhero, albeit an unusual one, with numerous precedents in Western popular culture. His visual style and flair with daggers are particularly reminiscent of Zorro, while his dark mysteriousness and fighting skills resemble those of Batman. He also sometimes recalls such figures as the Phantom of the Opera, while Moore himself listed Robin Hood, The Shadow, legendary eighteenth-century En-glish bandit Dick Turpin, and the British comics' superhero Night Raven as being among his inspirations for the character. Perhaps less obvious as an analog (and not an influence on Moore's original conception, since V was created first) to V is the Crow, whose systematic program of vengeance against those who earlier struck him down closely resembles V's method-ical program to track down and kill everyone who had worked at the Larkhill Center while he was there. The Crow also somewhat resembles V in appearance and in the ritual nature of his killings. Thus, at the site of each killing, V leaves a rose (of a variety thought to be extinct), much in the way the Crow leaves his avian insignia. To an extent, V even resembles the Crow in making his method of killing appropriate to the crimes for which his victims are being punished, though he kills all of his victims in the same way. Though V cuts a bloody swath through various Norsefire security personnel with his handy daggers in the course of the film, he kills the vic-tims of his personal revenge program with toxic injections—apparently as a sort of echo of the injections given him and others as part of the Larkhill experiments. Actually, the film leaves open the possibility that V only kills the top officials in charge of Larkhill. It is the graphic novel that indicates that he kills everyone who worked there, period. In any case, he succeeds in killing all of the intended victims of his eponymous vendetta, though we actually see only three of the killings, out of an unspecified larger number over an unspecified length of time (indicated in the graphic novel to cover four years), though his entire program of vengeance is state as covering twenty years. Still, the list of V's victims whom we do see reads like a who's who of authority figures in this future authoritarian state. He begins, for example, with Prothero, the regime's official television face and voice, killing a sniveling Prothero in his own posh home, just after he has been viewing a broadcast of himself posing as a tough guy and blustering about how he'd like to meet V face-to-face. As usual, the BTN falsifies its official reports of the killing, claiming that Prothero died of heart failure, having worked himself to death while striving to build a better Britain. In the meantime, we learn that Prothero was a former military officer (having seen service in such places as Iraq) who had been in charge of the Larkhill facility. Next on V's list is Bishop Anthony Lilliman (John Standing), who turns out to have been a priest who was charged with overseeing the Larkhill facility to ensure that the prisoners there received humane treatment. Lilliman, however, accepted huge bribes in order to look the other way while the prisoners were subjected to drug experiments with often gruesome results. By the time of the present action of the film, the corrupt Lilliman has become a bishop, suggesting that corruption is no deterrent to success in the clerical profession. Meanwhile, Bishop Lilliman turns out to be guilty of more sins than just simony. He uses his powerful position to help him pursue his "hobby," sex with underage girls. V engages Evey to pose as one such girl to provide a diversion while he breaks into the bishop's quarters and kills him. For her part, Evey attempts to betray V, whom she thinks is deranged, but the bishop believes her warnings are part of a sexual game, then proceeds to try to rape her as she fights him off. Quoting *Richard III*, V bursts in and kills Lilliman as the bishop begs for mercy. The last victim of V's program of personal revenge is Coroner Delia Surridge (Sinèad Cusack), who (as Dr. Diana Stanton) had been a top member of the medical staff at Larkhill. Surridge has taken a new name and a new identity in an attempt to put her past behind her. She is presented sympathetically as a good person who feels genuine remorse for her participation in the Larkhill experiments. She swears, apparently truthfully, that she had hoped to achieve something good for mankind and had not known that those experiments would take the turn they did. It is from an enactment of the contents of her diary that we learn most of the details about Larkhill, including the fact that V blew up the facility (on

November 5, of course), destroying it and all records of the experiments conducted there. V himself emerged from the flames, badly burned and scarred, but still alive.

Since that time, V has built his Shadow Gallery and assumed his identity as a masked avenger, seeking retribution for the wrongs done to him at Larkhill. But V's more important program is his effort to destabilize the Norsefire government through spectacular acts of public terrorism such as blowing up the Old Bailey and the Parliament building. This program can also include individual targets, and, before his own death, V ensures that both Sutler and his sinister security chief, Peter Creedy (Tim Pigott-Smith), are killed. V himself is mortally wounded by Creedy's security men in the bloody but balletic fight scene in which those two officials die, leading to the spectacular bombing of Parliament, which becomes his sacrificial funeral pyre. Meanwhile, thousands march in the streets, wearing Guy Fawkes costumes (sent out in a mass mailing by V himself) in a sign of solidarity with V and opposition to the Norsefire government, already destabilized by the Creedy's coup against Sutler and Creedy's own subsequent death.

This final scene is a rousing cinematic moment, though in point of fact V is a difficult protagonist with which to identify. Apparently in recognition of that fact, the filmmakers have made other characters, especially Evey and Police Inspector Eric Finch (Stephen Rea), far more sympathetic than they are in the graphic novel, as if to supply viewers of the film with alternative characters with whom to identify and for whom to root. Thus, both characters are played by likeable and attractive actors, and both are ultimately complicit in the final bombing of Parliament. In addition, the film emphasizes Evey's tragic background as the only surviving member of a family otherwise wiped out by the Sutler regime. It also modifies certain of her actions to make her seem more sympathetic, while in general giving her a larger role in the film relative to the novel. Meanwhile, Finch, though pursuing V on behalf of the government, is an honest cop who is genuinely seeking the truth, even after both Creedy and Sutler warn him not to pry into certain areas. And with good reason. The Norsefire regime originally swept into power years earlier out of a perceived need for a strong response to devastating terrorist attacks with biological weapons, but Finch's investigations begin to uncover evidence that the attacks may have actually been carried out by Sutler and his supporters (on Creedy's recommendation) so that they could gain political capital from a strong response to them. In addition, several individuals seem to have gained literal capital, profiting mightily from the selling of drugs (apparently developed out of the research at Larkhill) to counteract the virus released in the terrorist attacks—but only after the fear engendered by the attacks had swept Sutler and his Norsefire party into power. All in all, while the politics of the graphic novel may be distorted in the film, it is also the case that the film represents a powerful and even daring critique of the Bush administration. For example, the film's very transformation of Moore's fascist state into a version of Bush-era America is itself a powerful statement about the affinities between fascism and the current political situation in the United States. The film version of *V for Vendetta* is particularly courageous, given the climate of Patriot Act America, in its exploration of the centrality of the war on terrorism to the agenda of the Sutler (i.e., Bush) administration. Sutler's government directly echoes the political strategies of the Bush administration in its use of the fear of terrorism as its most important tool of power. The film is also critical of America's "war on terrorism" in its suggestion (looking back from the future) that this war actually stimulated terrorism—to the point that Britain was increasingly subject to terrorist attacks, helping Sutler to rise to power. However, the film even goes so far as to suggest that the most important terrorist attack on England (the release of a deadly virus in London fourteen years before the present setting of the film) was actually engineered by the government in order to generate fear of terrorists and support for increased government power. This motif potentially suggests a conspiracy theory in which the Bush administration was actually responsible for the 9/11 bombings. However, it is probably more appropriate to read this aspect of the film merely as a comment on the way in which that administration has capitalized on those bombings to generate a climate of fear that has enabled it to pursue its own agenda essentially unimpeded by making any critics of the administration appear to be unpatriotic or even sympathetic to terrorism. The film's most controversial engagement with the issue of terrorism resides in its clear endorsement of the use of terrorist tactics by its protagonist in his attempt to bring down the Sutler government, an attempt that seems ultimately successful. When soldiers refuse to fire on the crowds of masked demonstrators who fill London's streets at the end of the film, a new day appears to be at hand. In one final flourish that signifies the death of the old regime, the demonstrators begin to take off their masks, revealing the visages of Dietrich and others who had earlier been killed by the regime among the crowd. Though physically dead, these people now live on in spirit. After all, as V tells us, "ideas are bulletproof."

Conclusion

While graphic cinema has certainly had its failures (both commercially and artistically), the films discussed at length in this volume collectively demonstrate considerable potential for the category. If one considers the original *Superman* film of 1978 as the first genuine example of graphic cinema, then this category of cinema is still less than thirty years old as of this writing. Yet the category already has a rich legacy, producing some of the most important and memorable films of the past three decades. Films such as *Superman* and *Batman* (1989) are true landmarks of American popular culture, while numerous works of graphic cinema (the three *Spider-Man* films are here the central examples) have been among the most popular and commercially successful works in the history of cinema.

Further, there are signs that graphic cinema is still gaining momentum as an important category of American film. By their very nature, the comics are a sequential form, and the most successful comics have managed to stay popular for many decades. Therefore, they are perfectly suited as source material for the kind of film franchises that Hollywood relishes. Indeed, the comics have already established a number of highly successful film franchises (*Superman, Batman, Spider-Man, X-Men*) that seem poised to continue for years to come. Graphic cinema continues to grow in other ways as well, and the first half of 2007 been one of the biggest periods in its history, with the success of such films as *300, Spider-Man 3, Ghost Rider,* and *Fantastic Four: Rise of the Silver Surfer* dominating the box office.

In addition, there is an impressive array of films based on comics that are currently in planning or production, spurred partly by continuing advances in CGI technology and partly by the huge commercial success of so many films based on comics. For example, in addition to generating huge profits for Legendary Pictures, *300* features perhaps the most effective green-screen visuals yet produced, triggering much talk of subsequent films that might be produced using the same technology. Of these, a remake of *Masters of the Universe* (originally released in 1987) has been among the most talked-about, though early rumors that this film would also be produced by Legendary Pictures are apparently not true.

In addition, Sony Pictures has already expressed an interest in producing at least three more *Spider-Man* films, and the success of the first three combined with the huge amount of Spider-Man material available from the comics, suggests that these additional films are likely to be made. Granted, some of the proposed projects, such as the film adaptation of Alan Moore's legendary graphic novel *Watchmen* (1987), have long been in planning and may never come about. A planned feature-length adaptation featuring Wonder Woman, originally to have been directed by *Buffy* creator Joss Whedon, seems troubled as well, with Whedon now off the project. However, other projected films, such as two sequels to *Sin City* and del Toro's planned sequel to *Hellboy* (2004), all scheduled for release in 2008, seem sure bets. *Iron Man* and *The Incredible Hulk*, given their backing by Marvel, seem likely to appear in 2008 as well, as does Singer's planned sequel to *Superman Returns*, and *The Dark Knight*, Nolan's planned sequel to *Batman Begins*. Marvel's *Wolverine*, an offshoot of the X-Men franchise, is also in preproduction, as is a film adaptation based on DC Comics' character the Flash. Other graphic cinema projects under development or discussion include Marvel properties such as *Ant-Man* (2008), *Luke Cage* (2008), and *Thor* (2009). Also in this category are such projected films as *Stardust* (2007, based on Neil Gaiman's fantasy comic), *Wanted* (2008, based on Mark Millar's dark action-revenge comic), and *Madman* (2009, based on Mike Allred's comic, with significant involvement by Robert Rodriguez). Thus, while sequels remain the core of the slate of films based on comics that is currently in planning or production, such films are continuing to move in new directions as well, suggesting that this category of American film will continue to grow in importance for years to come.

Films Cited

FILMS CITED (GRAPHIC CINEMA)

300. Dir. Zack Snyder, 2007.

American Splendor. Dir. Shari Springer Berman and Robert Pulcini, 2003.

Annie. Dir. John Huston, 1982.

Art School Confidential. Dir. Terry Zwigoff, 2006.

Barb Wire. Dir. David Hogan, 1996.

Batman. Dir. Tim Burton, 1989.

Batman: The Movie. Dir. Leslie H. Martinson, 1966.

Batman Begins. Dir. Christopher Nolan, 2005.

Batman Forever. Dir. Joel Schumacher, 1995.

Batman Returns. Dir. Tim Burton, 1992.

Batman & Robin. Dir. Joel Schumacher, 1997.

Blade. Dir. Stephen Norrington, 1998.

Blade II. Dir. Guillermo del Toro, 2002.

Blade: Trinity. Dir. David S. Goyer, 2004.

Bulletproof Monk. Dir. Paul Hunter, 2003.

Casper. Dir. Brad Silberling, 1995.

Catwoman. Dir. Pitof, 2004.

Constantine. Dir. Francis Lawrence, 2005.

Crouching Tiger, Hidden Dragon. Dir. Ang Lee, 2000.

The Crow. Dir. Alex Proyas, 1994.

The Crow: City of Angels. Dir. Tim Pope, 1996.

The Crow: Salvation. Dir. Bharat Nalluri, 2000.

The Crow: Wicked Prayer. Dir. Lance Mungia, 2005.

Daredevil. Dir. Mark Steven Johnson, 2003.

The Dark Knight. Dir. Christopher Nolan, 2008.

Dick Tracy. Dir. Warren Beatty, 1990.

Fantastic Four. Dir. Tim Story, 2005.

Fantastic Four: Rise of the Silver Surfer. Dir. Tim Story, 2007.

Flash Gordon. Dir. Mike Hodges, 1980.

From Hell. Dir. Albert Hughes and Allen Hughes, 2001.

Ghost Rider. Dir. Mark Steven Johnson, 2007.

Ghost World. Dir. Terry Zwigoff, 2001.

Heavy Metal. Dir. Gerald Potterton and Jimmy T. Murakami, 1981.

Hellboy. Dir. Guillermo del Toro, 2004.

Hellboy Animated: Blood and Iron. Dir. Victor Cook and Tad Stones, 2007.

Hellboy Animated: Sword of Storms. Dir. Phil Weinstein and Tad Stones, 2006.

A History of Violence. Dir. David Cronenberg, 2005.

Howard the Duck. Dir. Willard Huyck, 1986.

Hulk. Dir. Ang Lee, 2003.

The Invincible Iron Man. Dir. Patrick Archibald and Frank Paur, 2007.

Iron Man. Dir. Jon Favreau, 2008.

Josie and the Pussycats. Dir. Harry Elfont and Deborah Kaplan, 2001.

The League of Extraordinary Gentlemen. Dir. Stephen Norrington, 2003.

Lone Wolf and Cub: Baby Cart to Hades. Dir. Kenji Misumi, 1972.

Lone Wolf and Cub: Baby Cart in the Land of Demons. Dir. Kenji Misumi, 1973.

Lone Wolf and Cub: Baby Cart in Peril. Dir. Buichi Saito, 1972.

Lone Wolf and Cub: Baby Cart at the River Styx. Dir. Kenji Misumi, 1972.

Lone Wolf and Cub: Sword of Vengeance. Dir. Kenji Misumi, 1972.

Lone Wolf and Cub: White Heaven in Hell. Dir. Yoshiyuki Kuroda, 1974.

Magneto. Dir. David S. Goyer, 2009.

Man-Thing. Dir. Brett Leonard, 2005.

The Mask. Dir. Chuck Russell, 1994.

Men in Black. Dir. Barry Sonnenfeld, 1997.

Men in Black II. Dir. Barry Sonnenfeld, 2002.

Monkeybone. Dir. Henry Selick, 2001.

Mystery Men. Dir. Kinka Usher, 1999.

The Phantom. Dir. Simon Wincer, 1996.

Popeye. Dir. Robert Altman, 1980.

The Return of the Swamp Thing. Dir. Jim Wynorski, 1989.

Richie Rich. Dir. Donald Petrie, 1994.

Road to Perdition. Dir. Sam Mendes, 2002.

The Rocketeer. Dir. Joe Johnston, 1991.

Son of the Mask. Dir. Lawrence Guterman, 2005.

The Shadow. Dir. Russell Mulcahy, 1995.

Sheena. Dir. John Guillermin, 1984.

Sin City. Dir, Robert Rodriguez and Frank Miller, 2005.

Sin City II. Dir, Robert Rodriguez and Frank Miller, 2008.

Sin City III. Dir, Robert Rodriguez and Frank Miller, 2008.

Spawn. Dir. Mark A. Z. Dippé, 1997.

Supergirl. Dir. Jeannot Szwarc, 1984.

Swamp Thing. Dir. Wes Craven, 1982.

Spider-Man. Dir. Sam Raimi, 2002.

Spider-Man II. Dir. Sam Raimi, 2004.

Spider-Man III. Dir. Sam Raimi, 2007.

Superman: The Movie. Dir. Richard Donner, 1978.

Superman II. Dir. Richard Lester, 1980.

Superman III. Dir. Richard Lester, 1983.

Superman IV: The Quest for Peace. Dir. Sidney J. Furie, 1987.

Superman and the Mole-Men. Dir. Lee Sholem, 1951.

Superman Returns. Dir. Brett Ratner, 2006.

Teenage Mutant Ninja Turtles. Dir. Steve Barron, 1990.

TMNT. Dir. Kevin Munroe, 1997.

V for Vendetta. Dir. James McTeigue, 2006.

Virus. Dir. John Bruno, 1999.

X-Men. Dir. Bryan Singer, 2000.

X-Men: The Last Stand. Dir. Brett Ratner, 2006.

X2. Dir. Bryan Singer, 2003.

FILMS CITED (OTHER)

The Abyss. Dir. James Cameron, 1989.

Ace Ventura: Pet Detective. Dir. Tom Shadyac, 1994.

Addams Family Values. Dir. Barry Sonnenfeld, 1993.

Æon Flux. Dir. Karyn Kusama, 2005.

Ali. Dir. Michael Mann, 2001.

Alien. Dir Ridley Scott, 1979.

American Beauty. Dir. Sam Mendes, 1999.

American Pimp. Albert Hughes and Allen Hughes, 1999.

Apocalypse Now. Dir. Francis Ford Coppola, 1979.

Bamboozled. Dir. Spike Lee, 2000.

The Bat. Dir. Roland West, 1926.

Beetlejuice. Dir. Tim Burton, 1988.

Blade Runner. Dir. Ridley Scott, 1982.

Blue Velvet. Dir. David Lynch, 1986.

Bonnie and Clyde. Dir. Arthur Penn, 1967.

The Boys in Company C. Dir. Sidney J. Furie, 1978.

Bram Stoker's Dracula. Dir. Francis Ford Coppola, 1992.

Braveheart. Dir. Mel Gibson, 1995.

Bridge across Time. Dir. E. W. Swackhamer, 1985.

Brokeback Mountain. Dir. Ang Lee, 2005.

Buffy the Vampire Slayer. Dir. Fran Rubel Kazui, 1992.

Casablanca. Dir. Michael Curtiz, 1942.

Casino Royale. Dir. Martin Campbell, 2006.

Chasing Amy. Dir. Kevin Smith, 1997.

Close Encounters of the Third Kind. Dir. Steven Spielberg, 1977.

The Conversation. Dir. Francis Ford Coppola, 1974.

The Count of Monte Cristo. Dir. Rowland V. Lee, 1934.

Cronos. Dir. Guillermo del Toro, 1993.

Crumb. Dir. Terry Zwigoff, 1994.

The Curse of Frankenstein. Dir. Terence Fisher, 1957.

Dark City. Dir. Alex Proyas, 1998.

Darkman. Dir. Sam Raimi, 1990.

Darkman II: The Return of Durant. Dir. Bradford May, 1994.

Darkman III: Die Darkman Die. Dir. Bradford May, 1996.

The Da Vinci Code. Dir. Ron Howard, 2006.

Dead Presidents. Albert Hughes and Allen Hughes, 1995.

Death Wish. Dir. Michael Winner, 1974.

The Devil's Backbone. Dir. Guillermo del Toro, 2001.

Dr. No. Dir. Terence Young, 1962.

Double Indemnity. Dir. Billy Wilder, 1944.

Dracula. Dir. Terence Fisher, 1958.

Eat Drink Man Woman. Dir. Ang Lee, 1994.

Ed Wood. Dir. Tim Burton, 1995.

The Elephant Man. Dir. David Lynch, 1980.

Equilibrium. Dir. Kurt Wimmer, 2002.

E. T. the Extraterrestrial. Dir. Steven Spielberg, 1982.

The Evil Dead. Dir. Sam Raimi, 1981.

Frankenstein. Dir. James Whale, 1931.

Frankenweenie. Dir. Tim Burton, 1984.

Fury. Dir. Fritz Lang, 1936.

Futureworld. Dir. Richard D. Heffron, 1976.

Ghost Busters. Dir. Ivan Reitman, 1984.

The Godfather. Dir. Francis Ford Coppola, 1972.

The Graduate. Dir. Mike Nichols, 1967.

Gumnaam. Dir. Raja Nawathe, 1965.

Harry Potter and the Prisoner of Azkaban. Dir. Alfonso Cuarón, 2004.

Heroes Shed No Tears. Dir. John Woo, 1986.

Ice Storm. Dir. Ang Lee, 1997.

Independence Day. Dir. Roland Emmerich, 1996.

Indiana Jones and the Last Crusade. Dir. Steven Spielberg, 1989.

Interview with the Vampire: The Vampire Chronicles. Dir. Neil Jordan, 1994.

Invasion of the Body Snatchers. Dir. Don Siegel, 1956.

I, Robot. Dir. Alex Proyas, 2004.

Insomnia. Dir. Christopher Nolan, 2002.

Jack the Ripper. Dir. David Wickes, 1988.

Jurassic Park. Dir. Steven Spielberg, 1993.

King Solomon's Mines. Dir. J. Lee Thompson, 1985.

The Last Starfighter. Dir. Nick Castle, 1984.

Little Caesar. Dir. Mervyn LeRoy, 1931.

Lord of the Rings: The Fellowship of the Ring. Dir. Peter Jackson, 2001.

Lord of the Rings: The Return of the King. Dir. Peter Jackson, 2003.

Lord of the Rings: The Two Towers. Dir. Peter Jackson, 2002.

The Lost World: Jurassic Park. Dir. Steven Spielberg, 1997.

The Mark of Zorro. Dir. Fred Niblo, 1920.

Mars Attacks! Dir. Tim Burton, 1996.

Masters of the Universe. Dir. Gary Goddard, 1987.

The Matrix. Dir. Andy Wachowski and Larry Wachowski, 1999.

The Matrix Reloaded. Dir. Andy Wachowski and Larry Wachowski, 2003.

The Matrix Revolutions. Dir. Andy Wachowski and Larry Wachowski, 2003.

Memento. Dir. Christopher Nolan, 2000.

Menace II Society. Albert Hughes and Allen Hughes, 1993.

Mimic. Dir. Guillermo del Toro, 1997.

Murder by Decree. Dir. Bob Clark, 1979.

National Treasure. Dir. Jon Turteltaub, 2004.

Nineteen Eighty-Four. Dir. Michael Radford, 1984.

Nosferatu. Dir. F. W. Murnau, 1922.

Out of the Past. Dir. Jacques Tourneur, 1947.

The Parallax View. Dir. Alan J. Pakula, 1974.

Pan's Labyrinth. Dir. Guillermo del Toro, 2006.

The Passion of the Christ. Dir. Mel Gibson, 2004.

Pathfinder. Dir. Marcus Nispel, 2007.

Pee-wee's Big Adventure. Dir. Tim Burton, 1985.

Plan 9 from Outer Space. Dir. Ed Wood, 1959.

The Prestige. Dir. Christopher Nolan, 2006.

Psycho. Dir. Alfred Hitchcock, 1960.

Public Enemy. Dir. William A. Wellman, 1931.

Pulp Fiction. Dir. Quentin Tarantino, 1994.

Resident Evil. Dir. Paul W. S. Anderson, 2002.

Resident Evil: Apocalypse. Dir. Paul W. S. Anderson, 2004.

Robocop. Dir. Paul Verhoeven, 1987.

Robocop 2. Dir. Irvin Kershner, 1990.

Robocop 3. Dir. Fred Dekker, 1993.

Rush Hour. Dir. Brett Ratner, 1998.

Rush Hour 2. Dir. Brett Ratner, 2001.

Scarface. Dir. Howard Hawks and Richard Rosson, 1932.

Sense and Sensibility. Dir. Ang Lee, 1995.

Shine. Dir. Scott Hicks, 1996.

Sky Captain and the World of Tomorrow. Dir. Kerry Conran, 2004.

Spirits of the Air, Gremlins of the Clouds. Dir. Alex Proyas, 1989.

Starship Troopers. Dir. Paul Verhoeven, 1997.

Star Wars. Dir. George Lucas, 1977.

A Study in Terror. Dir. James Hill, 1965.

Ten Little Indians. Dir. George Pollock, 1965.

Terminator. Dir. James Cameron, 1984.

Terminator 2: Judgment Day. Dir. James Cameron, 1991.

Three Days of the Condor. Dir. Sidney Pollack, 1975.

Time after Time. Dir. Nicholas Meyer, 1979.

Titanic. Dir. James Cameron, 1997.

Tron. Dir. Steven Lisberger, 1982.

Ultraviolet. Dir. Kurt Wimmer, 2006.

Underworld. Dir. Len Wiseman, 2003.

The Usual Suspects. Dir. Bryan Singer, 1995.

Van Helsing. Dir. Stephen Sommers, 2004.

Videodrome. Dir. David Cronenberg, 1983.

Vincent. Dir. Tim Burton, 1982.

War of the Worlds. Dir. Byron Haskin, 1953.

Westworld. Dir. Michael Crichton, 1973.

Wild Wild West. Dir. Barry Sonnenfeld, 1999.

Wolverine. Dir. TBD, 2008.

Wonder Boys. Dir. Curtis Hanson, 2000.

You've Got Mail. Dir. Nora Ephron, 1998.

ZigZag. Dir. David S. Goyer, 2002.

Index

About the Author

M. KEITH BOOKER is the James E. and Ellen Wadley Roper Professor of English at the University of Arkansas. He is the author of numerous articles and books on modern literature, literary theory, television, and film, including *Monsters, Mushroom Clouds, and the Cold War* (2001), *Strange TV: Innovative Television Series from "The Twilight Zone" to "The X-Files"* (2002), *Science Fiction Television* (2004), *Alternate Americas: Science Fiction Film and American Culture* (2006), *Drawn to Television: Prime-Time Animation from The Flintstones to Family Guy* (2006), *From Box Office to Ballot Box: The American Political Film* (2007), and *Postmodern Hollywood* (2007).